Ford/Southampton Studies in North/South Security Relations
Managing editor: Dr JOHN SIMPSON
Executive editor: Dr PHIL WILLIAMS

The Central American Security System:
North–South or East–West?

Ford Foundation Research Project 'North/South Security Relations', University of Southampton

Principal researchers
  Professor P. A. R. CALVERT
    Dr J. SIMPSON
    Dr C. A. THOMAS
    Dr P. WILLIAMS
    Dr R. ALLISON

While the Ford Foundation has supported this study financially, it does not necessarily endorse the findings. Opinions expressed are the responsibility of their authors.

The Central American Security System:
North–South or East–West?

Edited by

PETER CALVERT

Professor of Comparative and International Politics
University of Southampton

The right of the
University of Cambridge
to print and sell
all manner of books
was granted by
Henry VIII in 1534.
The University has printed
and published continuously
since 1584.

CAMBRIDGE UNIVERSITY PRESS

CAMBRIDGE

NEW YORK   NEW ROCHELLE   MELBOURNE   SYDNEY

Published by the Press Syndicate of the University of Cambridge
The Pitt Building, Trumpington Street, Cambridge CB2 1RP
32 East 57th Street, New York, NY 10022, USA
10 Stamford Road, Oakleigh, Melbourne 3166, Australia

First published 1988

Printed in Great Britain at the University Press, Cambridge

British Library cataloguing in publication data

The Central American security system:
North–South or East–West? –
(Ford/Southampton studies in North/
South security relations)
1. Western world. International security
I. Calvert, Peter   II. Series
327.1'16

Library of Congress cataloguing in publication data

The Central American security system.
(Ford/Southampton studies in North/South security relations)
Includes index.
1. Central America–National security.
2. Caribbean Area–National security. I. Calvert, Peter.   II. Series.
UA606.C465   1988   355'.0330728   88–16224

ISBN 0 521 35132 4

Contents

v

Contents

Part III: Solutions

Notes on contributors

Peter Calvert is Professor of Comparative and International Politics at the University of Southampton. His most recent publications include *Guatemala, a Nation in Turmoil* (Boulder, Colo.: Westview Press, 1985) and *The Foreign Policy of New States* (Brighton, Wheatsheaf Books, 1986), and he is co-author (with Susan Milbank) of *The Ebb and Flow of Military Government in Latin America* (London: The Centre for Security and Conflict Studies, 1987, Conflict Study no. 198).

Eduardo Crawley is Editor of Latin American Newsletters, London. He is the author of *Subversión y Seguridad: La cuestión de la guerra de guerrillas en el contexto argentino* (Buenos Aires, 1970); *Dictators Never Die: A Portrait of Nicaragua and the Somozas* (London: C. Hurst, 1979 – updated as *Nicaragua in Perspective*, New York: 1984); and *Nicaragua: Key to Regional Peace* (London: 1984).

Dr Esperanza Durán is a Research Fellow at the Royal Institute of International Affairs, Chatham House, London, where she directs the Latin American programme. She has written on the politics and international relations of Mexico and other Latin American countries. She is the author of *European Interests in Latin America* (London: Routledge and Kegan Paul/RIIA, 1985) and editor of *Latin America and the World Recession* (Cambridge: Cambridge University Press, 1985).

Dr Ian Forbes is a temporary Lecturer in Political Theory in the Department of Politics, University of Southampton. He is co-editor (with Steve Smith) of *Politics and Human Nature* (London: Frances Pinter, 1983) and has published articles on 'People or Processes? Freud or Einstein on the Causes of War', *Politics*, 1985, and 'Warfare without War: the Problem of Intervention in the International System', *Arms Control*, VIII, no. 1, 1987, pp. 52–67.

Alistair Hennessy is Professor of History at the University of Warwick,

vii

where he is Director of the Centre for Caribbean Studies and Chairman of the School of Comparative American Studies. He has been teaching Cuban history since the 1960s and has written articles on aspects of Cuban politics. He is at present directing a research project on Cuban–West European relations since 1959. He is author of *The Frontier in Latin American History* (London: Edward Arnold, 1978).

Martin C. Needler is Professor of Political Science in the Department of Political Science, The University of New Mexico, Albuquerque, New Mexico. His *Latin American Politics in Perspective* (first published 1963 by D. van Nostrand) has gone into three editions.

Dr George Philip is Reader in Latin American Politics, jointly at the London School of Economics and Political Science and the Institute of Latin American Studies, University of London. His books include *The Military in South American Politics* (London: Croom Helm, 1985).

Julian Saurin has been a research student in the Department of Politics, University of Southampton, since October 1986. The working title of his thesis is 'The "Civilizing Mission", Hegemony and Counter-hegemony: the Challenge of Latin American Liberation Theology to the State and the Contemporary Political Order'.

Dr Paul Sutton is Director of the Centre of Developing Area Studies and Lecturer in Politics at the University of Hull. He is co-editor (with Anthony Payne) of *Dependency under Challenge: The Political Economy of the Commonwealth Caribbean* (Manchester: Manchester University Press, 1984) and co-author (with Anthony Payne and Tony Thorndike) of *Grenada: Revolution and Invasion* (London: Croom Helm, 1984).

Dr Caroline Thomas is Lecturer in International Relations in the Department of Politics, University of Southampton. She is author of *New States, Sovereignty and Intervention* (Aldershot: Gower, 1985) and *In Search of Security: The Third World in International Relations* (Brighton: Wheatsheaf Press, 1987).

Tony Thorndike is Professor of International Relations at the North Staffordshire Polytechnic, Stoke-on-Trent. He is author of numerous works on Caribbean Affairs, including *Grenada: Politics, Economics and Society* (1985), and co-author (with Anthony Payne and Paul Sutton) of *Grenada: Revolution and Invasion* (London: Croom Helm, 1984).

Preface

This book arises out of the work of the Study Group on Latin America organized by Professor Peter Calvert as part of the Southampton Project on North–South Security Relations, funded by the Ford Foundation. The basic focus of this section of the project is on the concept of security in Central America and the Caribbean and perceptions by states in the region of the rival claims of political independence, economic well-being, national security and regional stability. The Study Group, holding sessions which ran from September 1985 to the summer of 1986, brought together some of the leading academic specialists on the area in the United Kingdom, together with participants from the Foreign and Commonwealth Office and outside financial and research organizations.

This book contains articles specially commissioned from some of the participants on selected features of the Central American and Caribbean problem. Among so many highly qualified participants the only criterion of choice could be the subject area and its relevance to the other contributions. A United States input was additionally provided by Professor Martin C. Needler of the University of New Mexico, formerly visiting Professor in Politics at the University of Southampton.

The project, we believe, differs from earlier ventures in being tightly focused on crisis-prevention regimes and crisis-control techniques. The Central American/Caribbean region has in the early 1980s been uniquely interesting for the range of illustrations which it offers of such regimes and techniques. It has the additional advantage of having been intensively studied by scholars, though the current work will also break new ground in calling upon the services of both Central American and Caribbean experts, who hitherto have tended to work separately. A selection of topics has been made from those dealt with by the Study Group in order to cover all the major aspects as economically as possible, and it has been deliberately intended throughout to integrate theoretical and case-study approaches and not to treat them separately, as is usually the case. The contributors have all written and published, most of them extensively, in the fields of their individual contributions. Their opinions are their own, and do not necessarily reflect the views of the individual members of the Project.

We should like to take this opportunity of recording our thanks to the Ford Foundation for funding the Southampton Project on 'North–South Security Relations'; to the Institute of Latin American Studies, University of London, for providing the venue for the Study Group, and University College, London, for catering facilities; and to all who took part in and contributed to the work of the Study Group.

As editor of the volume, I personally would also like to record my thanks to all those who helped with the work of the project, and in particular to Ian Forbes, who was a great help in the preparation of this volume, to my colleagues in the Project, Roy Allison, John Simpson, Caroline Thomas, and Phil Williams, for their contribution to our discussions; and to Angela Wilkinson, Jane Tsabet and Liz Schlamm, who as secretaries to the Ford Project were responsible for organizing the study group and preparing material for circulation and for the press.

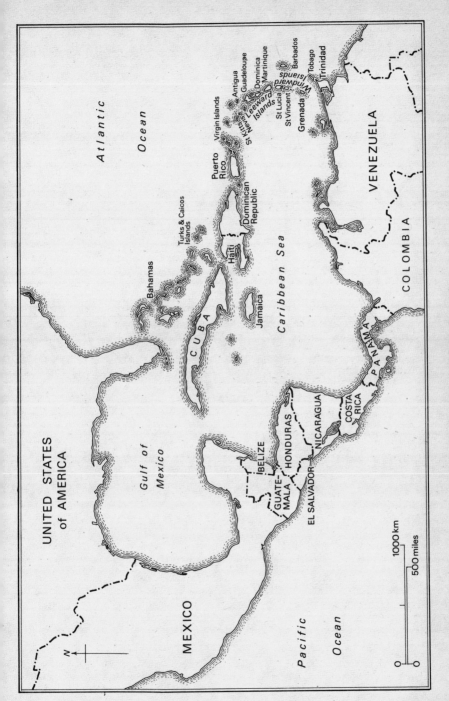

Map of the Caribbean Basin area

Part I: The problem at the interstate level

1 Security: the issues

Peter Calvert and Ian Forbes

INTRODUCTION

Since 1979 there has been a huge outpouring of works on Central America.[1] For an area previously very much neglected by English-speaking researchers, and lacking sufficient surviving indigenous tradition of scholarly research to be able to supply an adequate literature from its own resources, it has been a remarkable event and some of the books produced have been very good. From journalists, too, there has been a mass of articles and reports on the region, its constituent areas and problems, unparalleled in modern times.

This present study differs from most others in three respects. It forms part of a wider programme concerned with assessing the relations between superpowers and the Third World into the 1990s. Though it grows out of the work of a Study Group of the project, it does not simply reproduce papers from that Study Group but, rather, integrates the work of academic experts into an overview of the situation as the Reagan Administration comes to an end and we begin to discern the outlines of possible future policies within and towards the area. Thirdly, it treats the problems of Central America within the larger context of the Caribbean Basin.

There are many meanings attached to the concept of the Caribbean, and some of them totally exclude Central America. Yet the main focus of attention by policymakers in the eighties has been upon the mainland rather than the islands. What we have discussed here therefore is what we have termed 'the Central American security system'. By this is meant the geographical area of the Caribbean Basin in its widest sense, taking in the United States on the north, and Colombia, Venezuela and the Guianas to the south. The latter in turn are 'hinge states'. For most purposes they can be regarded as part of the Central American system, but for others they more naturally can be grouped with the continental states of South

America which they adjoin.[2] By using the term 'the Central American security system' the priority given in the Project to the elucidation of the concept of security is emphasized and the political system formed within the area of the Caribbean basin by the interactions which take place there can be distinguished from the geographical concepts attached to the physical form of either land or sea area.

WHAT IS SECURITY?

There are, even among specialists, several different conceptions of security, and any study which makes use of existing sources is bound to be confronted with the need to use more than one. More conceptions may arise as a result of the kinds of study undertaken, the location of research, and the methodologies that are brought to bear.

The basic meaning of the word 'security' is 'safety' (from the Latin *securitas*), for its adjectival form is 'secure', meaning safe.[3] There is, however, even in common usage a *traditional* implication of possible false confidence in one's own safety. Security is, it seems, something that we try to achieve but without real confidence that we can really do so. At the personal level 'Social Security' serves to provide the citizen with an economic 'safety net' below which he/she cannot fall, but does not serve to prevent the fall itself. So-called 'security agencies' aim to provide a service which will offer a considerable degree of protection against such possibilities as armed attack, robbery etc. But their ultimate efficacy depends on the fact that they offer not total protection, but (within certain conditions) *indemnity if their precautions prove ineffective*. And we seek 'security' through life assurance, though the one thing that is certain is that we will all die eventually.

The ambiguity is also present in the alternative legal meaning of the concrete noun 'a security' meaning a valuable consideration which is forfeit in the event of non-performance, as in Shakespeare's *Merchant of Venice*, 'security for the bond'. This usage seems to be peculiar to the Anglo-Saxon legal system, though other languages use similar terms to 'insurance' or 'to insure', such as the Spanish 'asegurar'. It is also not normally used in political, as opposed to legal, senses. Similar ambiguity exists also at the state level. It is reflected in the many modern uses to designate various sorts of organizations designed to detect or counter challenges to security of the state, e.g. 'national security', 'security risk', etc. None of these terms implies a guarantee of protection against the contingencies they are designed to meet, and hence, though the state's

4

interests may be adequately protected by them, those of the individual may well not be and are held generally to yield to that of the collectivity.

This same ambiguity is particularly marked in the *international* derivations, e.g. 'Security Council', 'collective security', etc. These, significantly, presuppose the continuing existence of the national state, but on this level the tendency is for the interest of the international community to yield to that of the state, and not the other way round.

It seems there is an inherent and inevitable conflict in the use of the term security between the security of the *state* and the security of the *individual*. Consequently we need notions of civil rights to enable the citizen to have a degree of personal security against the arbitrary actions of government. Such rights are the active subject of debate among political philosophers and have been for many centuries. Rights, however, cannot confer *absolute* security; at best they can provide for compensation and indemnity in the event of a breach, whether by deliberate order of government or the actions of subordinate officials, authorized or not. (Hence courts are established to resolve such contradictions, backed by the power to coerce and where deemed necessary punish.) It is difficult to avoid the conclusion that in general the concept of 'national security' is meaningful precisely in so far as it *overrides* the security of the individual. There is certainly no guarantee to the individual of personal protection against external attack, and indeed as a conscript he may be called upon to give his life for the national interest. Accordingly there is great danger in the growing tendency to use 'security' as a *euphemism*, e.g. 'he was shot by the security forces'.

In fact, the question of security is a *multi-level problem*, including at least the following: the international system, regional organizations, states, national governments, peoples, nationalities and individuals. At the same time, the question of security has a range of *dimensions* which may be pursued to some extent independently: these are military, economic, domestic, and psychological. A third set of variables, and variations in use, emerges when *those who use the term* are considered. These include: international agencies, regional organisations, governments, peoples and individuals. The fact is, security means very different things to different people, and little agreement exists on the nature and role of security. Perceptions of security for Central Americans themselves must depend very much on their place in the system.

Peter Calvert and Ian Forbes

CLAIMS AND SUBSTANCE ABOUT SECURITY

Developing a strategic overview of the nature of security is a major task and one which continues in parallel with other parts of our research programme. This programme is focused on states, instability and conflict in the Third World, indicating some implicit but specific normative claims about the connections between security, stability, order and change, and the future of Third World states themselves. At the least a claim is made for the validity of stability as an aim, and for the legitimacy of Third World states in general to pursue their own course without too much interference from the outside world. Thus stability is a *value* and, perhaps, a *condition* for security. Certainly it is in close association with security.

This normative element is also present in other terms which are hard to avoid (e.g., 'intervention'). This could lead one to expect that a fairly precise and agreed upon notion of security was readily available. However, this is not the case. Stability and security take on quite different meanings, and are pursued in quite different ways in balance of power arguments than in assessments of individual states. As Lars Schoultz has cogently argued, in practice United States policymakers, being unable to express in clear-cut policies their vague and indeterminate notions of what constitutes security for the United States, have settled instead for stability. Instability in Latin America has therefore been feared as a threat, not to Latin America, but to the United States.[4] But stability itself is a complex term with several competing meanings; it is not, for example, the same thing as duration, and a regime like that of the Somozas in Nicaragua may have lasted for a long time, but be on the point of collapse.[5]

This calls for a conceptual scheme that is capable of being used across the spectrum of studies that are undertaken. This presents problems of its own. For example, in his *People, States and Fear*,[6] Barry Buzan begins with an overview of the uses of the term security, and the ways in which the study of international relations is dominated by the realist and idealist perspectives. Such differences are certainly embedded within, for example, the models offered by the USSR and the USA respectively, as well as within the range of perspectives offered by various Latin American countries. Questions of the validity of opposing doctrinal positions will arise, and logically cannot be resolved by lining up the arguments one against the other. Hence Buzan, while claiming, fairly enough, that security is a concept of considerable importance in international relations theory and practice, accepts that it is an *underdeveloped* concept.[7] If this is true, then we have to take cognizance of that conceptual weakness, and be clear about the need to develop the conceptual framework of security, (a) in order to use it, (b) to reinforce the values it entails, and (c) to secure the ends that are intended or desired.

For Buzan as for the Project, security is a prime motive for behaviour at all the levels, and in the context of all the dimensions and variables listed above. In respect of realism, it is a *companion* to power, rather than derivative of power. In respect of idealism, security is a *prior condition* of peace, not its consequence. Although critical of these major perspectives in the discipline, Buzan does not rule them out, but suggests that the concept of security binds together the normative and empirical aspects of international relations subject matter. He uses Waltz's three levels of analysis[8] to show that security can provide a common framework for the examination and understanding of individuals, states and the international system. This avoids, for example, the polarization inherent in the realist and idealist tendencies to over-emphasize divisibility and indivisibility respectively. We will seek to extend this further to take account of the greater number of levels we believe is relevant.

This forging of links across methodological divides and across disparate research areas has much to recommend it. Accepting that security is a multi-layered phenomenon leads to the following representation of Waltz's three layers of analysis:

1   Territorial defence strategies, which ensure participation in national security at the level of the individual or the locality.
2   National security policy devised on self-help solutions to conspicuous vulnerabilities in the social, political or military sectors.
3   Alliance among groups of states, which has as its top layer the UN.

The model has, however, a number of crucial assumptions embedded within it. At level one, the claim about participation may look like a democratic goal of a decentralized state, but the model could well be used to examine and put in a broader setting quite particular issues such as secessionism and terrorism, and be amenable to studies with quite different foci, like human rights as opposed to social justice, developmentalist or religious perspectives. The same flexibility is apparent in level two, although this looks to be the most complex, and most likely to be severely strained in practice. Buzan stresses the need to combine levels two and three in order to grasp the national security problem generally, and the security dilemma in particular. That is, state and system cannot be disconnected from each other, and he offers the term *security complex* to

Peter Calvert and Ian Forbes

highlight the relevance of structures at the sub-system level of analysis.[9] A security complex is a group of states whose primary security interests are linked sufficiently closely together such that their national security cannot reasonably be considered apart from one another. Buzan claims that security complexes can be used either as a static or a dynamic mode of analysis, with strong connections with both policy realities and historical perspectives, while avoiding the traps of both ethnocentricism and utopianism. While this may be too much to hope for, the term 'security system' employed here is intended to express a very similar relationship.

In short, the differing conceptions of security demand one overarching conceptual approach to that which the Project examines and discovers. A revised multi-layer model appears to offer overall coherence, but allows considerable flexibility in research focus and activity. The application of the model is undertaken in the spirit of what Richard E. Feinberg terms 'neorealism': a focus at each level on the minimal vital interests of life, liberty and property.[10]

SECURITY IN LATIN AMERICA

The basic focus of the Project is on the concept of security in the South and perceptions by Southern states of the rival claims of political independence, national security and regional stability. The US and the USSR are ambiguous in their approach to crises and instability in Latin America, as elsewhere in the South. What the North sees as opportunities the South sees as dangers, and vice versa.

The Project is designed specifically to deal with seven aspects of conflict in the South:

1 The possibility of symmetrical superpower intervention.
2 The growing power of weak states; the problem of reverse influence.
3 Superpower strategic and resource rivalry in the South.
4 The possible effects of the acquisition of nuclear weapons by Southern states.
5 Developments in conventional weapon technology: impact and diffusion.
6 The activities of proxy states.
7 The adequacy or inadequacy of existing global and regional security mechanisms.

Territorial defence strategies in Latin America in general, and in Central

8

America in particular, are well established on an individual country basis. In addition they have since 1947 been co-ordinated with each other and with the hemispheric strategy of the United States, in a way that forms a distinctive security complex. Exceptions are: (a) Cuba since 1961, which relies on internal mass mobilization, its alliance with the Soviet Union, and the implicit superpower bargain of 1962; (b) Nicaragua, which relies primarily on internal mass mobilization with some aid from the Soviet Union; (c) Belize, which has a 'trip-wire' force from its former colonial power, the UK; (d) the Falklands/Malvinas, the possession of which is disputed; (e) the remaining European and US dependent territories in the Caribbean. But the general trend in recent years has been to integrate new areas in the Western Hemisphere system, with the new Commonwealth states and Suriname being admitted to the Organization of American States at or shortly after independence. Most have also been admitted to the inter-American defence system. Significant exceptions, under the Charter, are those states (such as Belize) which have had or have a boundary dispute with an existing member state.

On a country-by-country basis, by contrast, defensive strategies assume national identity, and commonly involve a selective service system for selected males. The citizen is expected to serve the state and to look to it for security within the world order. The armed services are commonly seen as serving an essential role as ultimate defenders of public order and welfare too, in the sense of providing relief in times of national disaster. On the other hand, the strength of the military institution in Latin America, relative to the slight challenges it has had to face from outside the hemisphere, has at all times been formidable, and, notably in the late 1970s, threatened individual life and liberty.

Regionalism/localism is a particularly sensitive issue in Latin America generally. Historically the balance between central power and that of the locality in Latin America has been resolved in favour of the centre, but only following the disintegration of Spanish provincial units. Perhaps significantly, external involvement has occurred where disaggregation has gone furthest, in the Caribbean area and on the periphery. In Central America it could be said that localism exists without centralism, for since the rise of the United States as a regional power the impetus to reunification in Central America has ebbed. Except in Cuba and Nicaragua, self-defence on a locality basis has not been favoured because of the danger of further fragmentation.

National security policy in Latin America has since the early 1960s and again in recent years been oriented towards countering the threat of internal subversion. The danger of attack from outside the hemisphere by any other means is not of prime concern.

A very wide range of observers of differing political persuasions concur that the indigenous roots of unrest are strong and that the major risk to the existing order in Latin America stems from widespread social inequalities and inequities. There is much less agreement on the likely scenarios and possible consequences. Broadly, more democratic governments see their stability as threatened most by their dependent position in the world economy and consequent inability to fulfil the many demands made upon them, while less democratic governments have identified the main risk as stemming from politically active individuals.

Political opposition has in any case traditionally been identified in Latin America with insurgency. Consequently boundaries between legitimate and illegitimate political expression are often blurred both in the minds of governments and in those of their citizens. Despite this, major Latin American states have since the late 1970s moved away from dictatorial rule and the obsession of the military with covert influences.[11] Such covert influences cannot be dismissed out of hand. Given the unique characteristics of Latin America, its unity of language, culture and tradition, it is hardly surprising that political links extend across national boundaries. There is extensive historical evidence of outside support for former insurgent movements; however, the question of how far the mystique of national security, by reducing all such links to threads in a global conspiracy, is actively misleading policymakers, is unresolved and remains crucial.

Latin American armed forces form a 'state within a state'. They are personally, institutionally and socially inclined to identify the security of the state with the well-being of the military institution, and have historically, in the absence of a substantial exterior threat, been central to politics. Strengthening themselves for their primary role as defenders of the state has not made them much more convincing in this role, but it has made them much more powerful as a political force. Ironically it has been their abject failure to deal with the economic problems of their countries, the target of military developmentalist policies in various states after 1964, that has done much to bring about their latest withdrawal from government.

Because of their distinctive history, maturity and unity of experience, Latin American states have a strong tradition of international law and the peaceful resolution of international disputes. They have played a major role in the creation of the UN in its present form. Until now it has not been realized how far their success in doing so has depended on their reciprocal relationship with the United States, which enabled the major South American states to retain a regional balance-of-power system relatively free of external influences. The constant undercurrent of impatience among the Reagan Administration with the United Nations has persistently threatened this relationship.

Regional institutions have been even more clearly identified with the leading role of the US. It was in the Americas that the first lasting organization of regional co-operation was created in 1889. This, the Pan-American Union, incorporated the United States and the twenty Latin American states. It was converted into a regional organization within the United Nations in 1947, taking the name of the Organization of American States (OAS), and was reorganized in 1960. Shortly afterwards Cuba was excluded from the OAS at the insistence of the United States, and despite the admission of a number of Commonwealth Caribbean states, the polarity between the United States and the Latin American states has led to it being increasingly seen as an arm of Washington and so by-passed wherever possible. The OAS continues to play a significant role in mediating disputes and furthering functional co-operation between the American states.

Though the Charter of the OAS contains security provisions resembling those of the UN, by which the United States multilateralized the principles of hemispheric isolation first adumbrated in the Monroe Doctrine (1823), the defence of the hemisphere from attack from outside (i.e. by the Soviet Union) is primarily the subject of a separate but closely related multilateral alliance, the Inter-American Treaty of Reciprocal Assistance (the Rio Pact), concluded between the then members of the Pan-American Union in 1947 at Rio de Janeiro. The Treaty has been twice invoked, by Costa Rica against Nicaragua, in 1948 and 1955. At the initiative of Mexico and other Latin American states, a regime for the denuclearization of the region was established separately by the Treaty of Tlatelolco, and accepted for most purposes by the nuclear powers.

Central America, owing to its proximity to the United States, is covered by a special regional defence organization, the Central American Defense Council (CONDECA), closely linked to US Southern Command (SOUTH-COM) in Panama, and the five states of Central America have formally established a free-trade area, the Central American Common Market (CACM), which has not worked well since 1969. A regional regime for the peaceful judicial settlement of disputes, the first such organization in the world, existed in Central America from 1907 to 1918, when it collapsed for lack of US support.

The OAS has been rendered largely ineffective since 1982; its long-term future as an effective force is even more in doubt, and it is far from clear that any alternative regional grouping – if desirable – is attainable. The Rio Pact, despite its primacy in the US alliance system, has been little used. Its military value is questionable, and, as noted above, its political effects probably counter-productive. Sub-regional groupings have been principally economic, and bilateral alliances have fallen into disuse. Latin American governments have again, as they did with the League in the inter-War period, turned towards the United Nations to help them realize their political and economic objectives, and Latin American states have been foremost both as power brokers in the international system and in calling for the establishment of a New International Economic Order (NIEO).

Projecting present trends into the mid-1990s would suggest that:
- The United States would continue to act unilaterally in support of its own perceived security interests, as in Grenada.
- It would be aided in this by the relative weakness of the Western Hemisphere security complex and its own continuing economic strength, but that towards the end of the time period, given the continued budget and trade deficits of the 1980s, its relative strength would have been substantially eroded. In 1986 the United States emerged as a bigger net debtor than Brazil and Mexico put together.
- The main threat to 'Monroeism' would come not from within the Western Hemisphere but from the breach of the reciprocal principle not to involve itself in the affairs of Europe and the Middle East; in other words, the more the United States is seen to act in other parts of the world, the more others may seek to carry the conflict back into its own sphere of influence. Connecting Soviet withdrawal from Afghanistan to US withdrawal from Nicaragua may look like an imaginative strategy but it has very considerable implications for the future.
- South America would continue to maintain itself as a relatively independent zone, off the main trade routes and largely isolated from areas of conflict outside the hemisphere. Poverty and unrest would, at the same time, in some areas (e.g. large parts of Brazil), pass beyond the point at which they are amenable to any form of outside aid, and a two-tier structure could emerge.

- Caribbean stability would continue to be amenable to relatively small quantities of aid on a fire-brigade basis. But if the US continues to try to extend its hegemony in the area and make it a 'closed sea' its capacity for intervention, already shown to be ineffective in Nicaragua, will erode further.
- Formal democracy is likely to remain in fashion for at least the next five years, during which time its restoration in Chile looks increasingly probable.

This summary, in turn, raises a number of questions:

1   Does the analytical framework described above give rise to an adequate account of security in Latin America? If not, is there anything we would wish to add or to emphasize differently?

2   What are the principal threats to security in Latin America and what is their relative weight?

3   How stable is the existing situation and what are the likely causes of conflict in the region within the next ten years?

4   How far do current policies ensure the security of (a) the individual, (b) the locality, (c) the nation, (d) the region? How far does each objective aid or impede the achievement of the others?

5   Do other powers have legitimate security interests in the region? If so, how far are those interests compatible with those of the local inhabitants? Where and how far do American states have legitimate security interests outside the Western Hemisphere?

6   What world trends have general or special relevance to Latin America up to the mid-1990s?

7   Does the Western Hemisphere need regional organization? What purposes does the existing structure serve?

8   How far is the Latin American model of world organization compatible with national security needs in the region?

9   What are the interconnections between the Latin American security complexes and other security complexes? What does the Latin American model have to offer for the understanding of other regions?

SOME RESERVATIONS

The first question is, how far do the organizing concepts of level and issue area enable us to give an adequate framework for the study of Central America and the Caribbean? The first problem comes in finding the basis for assessment, the second in the extent to which the model itself is drawn

13

from East–West thinking. Latin Americans, as specialists in the area are very aware, have read US political science and know how to talk to American policymakers in instrumental terms. The significance of the Kirkpatrick distinction between authoritarian and totalitarian regimes, for example, is that it is a rationalization of Latin American experience.[12] Similarly the Buzan model is not entirely an abstract scheme derived from first principles, but at least to some extent derives from Waltz, itself a product of sixties' thinking about 'dependent state systems' and hence a defence of the existing world order in which superpowers arrogate to themselves the right to carry out actions which Third World states find beyond their capabilities. Within the existing order the economy and psychology of Latin America are both violated. Cuba is socially and economically secure, but is not secure from military pressure from the US; Chile is the polar opposite.

It has to be admitted, however, that the model does draw attention to the primacy of different layers in different ages: in the fifties, man; in the sixties, the state; and in the seventies and eighties the international community. In some ways Latin American attitudes towards communism at present are very like those of the US in the fifties. But it is not the East–West struggle that has been salient as the Reagan Administration nears its end, but the economic crisis, and the trends this implies can be expected to deepen as we move into the 1990s.

On the question of what constitute the principal threats to security in Latin America, the answers vary according to the level of investigation. For many, if not most, Central Americans, at the individual level the state itself is the principal threat. From the point of view of governments the threats vary. In Central America the distinction between region and state is itself a matter of controversy. The 'Whig view' of Central America, embodied in the very title of Ralph Lee Woodward Jr's *Central America: A Nation Divided*,[13] is that it is one nation temporarily disaggregated and awaiting reunification. But the 'temporary' disunity of the area has now lasted since 1839, the year in which, by coincidence, Belgium received the guarantee of its right to separate existence. Rival regional states make traditional enemies and old enmities are not easily set aside, as witness the difficulty the US has confronted in trying to persuade the Honduran government to give military training to Salvadorean counter-insurgency forces. Above all, the US is not merely an observer but an actor, and for many Latin Americans it poses the main threat, incredible as this view is to Washington or New York.

From the perspective of the international system, it is perhaps understandable that the US would see socialism in Nicaragua, even under a pluralist government, as a threat and so try to force its perceptions of that government into the Cuban mould.[14] It is equally clear that the Central American states wish to invoke the international system to counter what they see as a threat to their statehood, namely US or any other hegemony in the region. Intervention they see not as a protection but as a threat to their national sovereignty and their capacity to make their own decisions in both the political and economic fields.

In short, 'security' in the Central American context cannot be interpreted in a narrow military sense. On the contrary, it can only be interpreted in the widest possible sense, in terms of the probability of satisfaction of the basic needs of the population at large. If this is done, we may come to conclude that the state policies termed 'security' policies, by diverting substantial resources into arms and armaments and exacerbating social divisions, are in fact making true security for the individual citizen much harder to attain. The relation between fundamental needs and other aspects of security is certainly complex, and many writers since Tocqueville have argued that it is not abject poverty that leads to rebellion, but the momentary prospect of improvement. Grenada can be and is cited as an example of revolt in an island where living standards were generally high and there was no land hunger; it was the institutional context of unrest that was relevant.

Some have gone further and questioned whether there is a generic problem of the Latin American state that gives it a distinctive role when it comes to mediating between internal conditions and a country's behaviour in the international arena. Threats to security may quite realistically be seen as threats to a government, as opposed to the people at large. On the other hand a government even in the most tenuously democratic state gains what legitimacy it has from assuming certain economic responsibilities and appearing to ensure the greatest good of the greatest number. The problems of inflation, public finance, debt and the balance of trade necessarily involve both external and internal considerations, and since the 1960s order and progress have been seen in the region, as elsewhere, as depending in the first instance on economic growth and the management of the economy. In this context the distinction between nation and state, systematically examined by Hugh Seton-Watson,[15] is vital; the interests of the state are not necessarily synonymous with those of the nation, the community which it exists to serve.

From this it appears that while the multi-layer framework, as employed here, has a useful role to play in elucidating possible conflicts of interest between the different levels of analysis in the region, more detailed examination of individual problem areas is essential to understand how current perceptions of them had arisen, and what alternatives, if any, might be sought to current policies. In the chapters that follow more detailed views of some of these problem areas are presented before alternative scenarios and their solutions are reviewed.

Consideration begins with the regional and international level, with studies of the Central American area and the Caribbean respectively. Next the prospects for the early 1990s are examined, before commencing the second Part containing four studies of individual states and their perceptions of their security and of the outside world. Finally, in the third Part, the principal solutions that have been advanced to the perceived problems of the region are evaluated. The United States, for its part, has seen security as being enhanced by the strengthening of regional armed forces and the elimination of foci of opposition both on the mainland and in the islands; the medium-sized regional powers have sought through the Contadora initiative to arrive through traditional processes of diplomacy at a stable regime for the mainland and so avert the spread of destabilization to their own territories.

NOTES

1. Among others consulted in the preparation of this work see in particular Centro de Estudios Internacionales, *Centroamérica en crisis* (Mexico, DF: El Colegio de México, 1980); Jenny Pearce, *Under the Eagle: U.S. Intervention in Central America* (London: Latin American Bureau, 1981); R. Daniel McMichael and John D. Paulus (eds.), *Western Hemisphere Stability – the Latin American Connection* (Pittsburgh, Pa.: World Affairs Council of Pittsburgh, 1983); Donald Castillo Rivas (ed.), *Centroamérica, más allá de la crisis* (Mexico, DF: Ediciones SIAP, 1983); Victor Millán, 'Controlling Conflict in the Caribbean Basin: National Approaches', in Michael A. Morris and Victor Millán (eds.), *Controlling Latin American Conflicts: Ten Approaches* (Boulder, Colo.: Westview Press, 1983); Stanford Central America Action Network, *Revolution in Central America* (Boulder, Colo.: Westview Press, 1983); Andrew J. Pierre, *Third World Instability: Central America as European–American Issue* (New York: Council on Foreign Relations, 1985); Giuseppe De Palma and Laurence Whitehead (eds.), *The Central American Impasse* (London: Croom Helm, in association with the Friedrich Naumann Foundation, 1986); and Jack Child (ed.), *Conflict in Central America: Approaches to Peace and Security* (London: C. Hurst for International Peace Academy, 1986).
2. South American Security issues were also discussed by the Study Group and it is hoped that the South American security system may be the subject of a later work.
3. *Oxford English Dictionary.*
4. Lars Schoultz, *National Security and United States Policy toward Latin America* (Princeton, NJ: Princeton University Press, 1987), pp. 34ff.
5. See the discussion in S. A. Calvert, 'Political Culture and Political Stability in Argentina', unpublished PhD dissertation, University of Southampton, 1987, chap. 1.
6. Barry Buzan, *People, States and Fear; The National Security Problem in International Relations* (Brighton, Sussex: Wheatsheaf, 1983).
7. Buzan, *People, States and Fear*, p. 3.

16

8. Kenneth N. Waltz, *Man, the State, and War* (New York: Columbia University Press, 1959).
9. Buzan, *People, States and Fear*, pp. 105ff.
10. Richard E. Feinberg, *The Intemperate Zone: The Third World Challenge to U.S. Foreign Policy* (New York: W. W. Norton, 1983), pp. 23ff.
11. See also Peter Calvert and Susan Milbank, *The Ebb and Flow of Military Government in Latin America* (London: The Centre for Security and Conflict Studies, Conflict Studies No. 198, 1987).
12. Jeane Kirkpatrick, 'Dictatorships and Double Standards', *Commentary*, 68, November 1979, pp. 34–45.
13. New York: Oxford University Press, 1976.
14. Robert A. Pastor, *Condemned to Repetition: The United States and Nicaragua* (Princeton, NJ: Princeton University Press, 1987), pp. 197ff.
15. Hugh Seton-Watson, *Nations and States: an Inquiry into the Origins of Nations and the Politics of Nations* (London: Methuen, 1977).

2 The Caribbean as a focus for strategic and resource rivalry

Paul Sutton

The Caribbean Sea, together with the Gulf of Mexico, has for nearly one hundred years actively exercised the minds and skills of US strategists and policymakers. During this time intervention and diplomacy in defence of interests deemed 'vital' has become a commonplace and a corresponding image of the region as first an 'American Mediterranean' and then as a 'back-yard' has become widely held throughout US society. This chapter will examine the current basis of two critical components of such a belief as they have been represented within the Reagan Administration.

The first is the Caribbean as a proximate resource of almost inestimable strategic and economic value to the US. Such a thesis has been repeatedly affirmed throughout the years, both as cause and consequence of US hegemony. Currently it finds, perhaps, its quintessential expression in the flood of testimony by US officials and interested parties before the committees of the US Congress. Here one encounters a familiar inventory of trade, investment, aid and raw materials as the bedrock of economic interest, alongside sea lanes of communication, overseas bases, military assistance and strategic minerals as the foundation of security concerns. A listing of all these dimensions is not especially meaningful since they can often be encountered in the literature and can readily be accessed in any number of directories. Instead, what will be determined are the *specific* interests encountered in the region that are of *direct* relevance to the United States, both in respect of its security and its economic development. In other words, what the region contributes that is *especially distinctive* and *absolutely crucial* in its relationship to the US.

The second is the Caribbean as a 'danger zone' requiring an adequate defence. Here a sense of history is important. Beginning with Spain, and then extending to Britain, France and the US, the Caribbean has long been regarded by outside powers as a theatre of conflict and competition where the military capabilities of Great Powers can be probed and from which appropriate conclusions as to their political resolve can be drawn. In recent memory the Cuban Missile Crisis of October 1962 has been the single most dramatic manifestation of this aspect of international rivalry, although the Reagan Administration has made much of the argument that current turmoil in the region can be directly attributed to outside interference. Certainly such a perspective is not to be discounted, although it is more appropriately understood as a matter of interpretation and re-interpretation of traditional 'spheres of influence' concepts. The current position of the Caribbean within this is a fascinating question and one which will be examined latterly and in the conclusion. Prior to this, however, and in the context of the chapter as a whole, it will be considered as a matter of *resource rivalry*, both *strategic* and *material*. That is, within the present climate of superpower competition an evaluation will be made of the extent to which the USSR directly competes with the USA for Caribbean resources or is militarily present in the Caribbean region.

Finally, there is a question of definition. The Caribbean is taken to mean the islands from the Bahamas in the north to Trinidad in the south, including the mainland enclaves of the Guianas and Belize. It does not include the Central American isthmus. Of late a number of articles, several along parallel lines to the concerns of this one, have focused on Central America.[1] Its particular problems have therefore been addressed. By contrast, the specificities of the Caribbean have remained relatively unexplored, largely subsumed within the overarching concept of a unified Caribbean basin. Yet, as Domínguez among others has argued, the two sub-regions are not similar and the United States, for one 'has clearer, more enduring, and more important objective interests in the Caribbean and in Panama than elsewhere in Central America'.[2] The extent to which these can in part be identified and continue to remain crucial to the US form the conclusion to this work.

CARIBBEAN RESOURCES

The Caribbean is generally regarded as resource-poor. That is, neither in scale nor in distribution of natural resources do the islands and enclaves offer much that is currently regarded as of significant value. This does not mean, however, that the region is without resources altogether. Two may be identified as currently possessing economic importance: people and minerals. The former are in abundance nearly everywhere; the latter in certain favoured countries.

Paul Sutton

Table 1. *The Caribbean: population indicators*

	1982 population in thousands	1980–2 % below 15 years of age	Immigrants to USA 1970–80 (in thousands)	Immigrants to USA in fiscal year 1981
Cuba	9,853	32	418.4	6,159
Dominican Rep.	6,249	41	158.4	16,690
Haiti	6,111	43	75.8	6,238
Jamaica	2,217	39	157.0	22,450
Trinidad	1,128	32	69.1	4,224
Guyana	798	39	49.3	n/a
Barbados	258	26	n/a	2,080
Bahamas	218	39	22.7	396
Belize	152	22	n/a	831
Eastern Carib.	559	(45)[a]	(75.0)[a]	n/a
Suriname	413	46	n/a	n/a

Note: [a] Estimated.

Sources: Commonwealth Secretariat, *The Commonwealth Factbook* (Commonwealth Secretariat: London, 1985); Pastor, 'Caribbean Emigration and US Immigration Policy: Cross Currents', Table 5; R. H. McBride, H. E. Jones, D. D. Gregory, 'Issues for US Policy in the Caribbean Basin in the 1980s: Migration', in James R. Greene and Brent Scowcroft (eds.), *Western Interests and US Policy Options in the Caribbean Basin* (Boston: Oelgeschlager, Gunn and Main, 1984) Table 6.2; N. A. Graham and K. L. Edwards, *The Caribbean Basin to the Year 2000* (Boulder, Colo.: Westview Press, 1984).

People

The current population of the Caribbean is approximately 33 million persons (see Table 1). Of these, some 28 million are to be found in independent states with the remainder in dependent territories of the United States (3.36 million), France (730,000), the Netherlands (260,000) and the United Kingdom (57,000). The rate of natural increase is nearly everywhere large with an expectation that the total Caribbean population by the year 2000 will be around 43 million.

The impact of such demographic growth will be felt in many sectors, but especially in the labour market. Unemployment levels throughout the region are already high (excepting Cuba) and with those under fifteen years of age presently constituting one-third or more of the population in most countries they can only increase. Recourse is therefore likely to be made to the historic 'safety-valve' of emigration, especially since prospects for economic growth within the Caribbean appear so poor. On the evidence of current trends the United States is likely to be the most favoured destination. Human resources drawn from the Caribbean are in consequence likely to be a feature of its economy, society, and to some extent its polity, for some years to come.

The quantity and quality of this contribution can to some extent be gauged from the experience of the past twenty years. In this the 1965 US Immigration Act stands out as all-important. Prior to the Act, immigration from the Caribbean had been subject to varying discriminatory provisions according to the dictates of US prejudices, manpower planning requirements and shifting priorities in US policy to Latin America. With the 1965 Act the law repealed the national origins quota system and did away with discrimination based on race or ancestry. In its place it set up an annual quota of 120,000 from the Western Hemisphere with no preference system and no country limitations. Immigration was to be controlled by a labour certificate requirement. Pastor has remarked:

The 1965 Act changed the pattern of immigration to the US fundamentally. The US opened itself to becoming a third world nation, and in particular a Caribbean Basin nation. Between 1900 and 1965, 75% of all immigrants were of European extraction, whereas 62% of the immigrants since 1968 when the Act took effect have been from Asia and Latin America, and by 1978, the percentage had increased to 82%. In the past two decades, the Caribbean Basin has become the largest source of immigrants to the US – nearly one-third of all legal immigrants.[3]

The number of immigrants from the independent Caribbean for the years 1970 to 1981 are given in Table 1. To this must be added a substantial illegal immigration from the Dominican Republic, Haiti, Jamaica and Central America.[4] The net effect has been both to diminish demographic growth in the Caribbean and to increase substantially the proportion of Caribbean population in the US. In respect of the former, for example, it has been calculated that migration to the US as a percentage of natural population increase amounted to 18.1% in Jamaica, 18.1% in Trinidad and Tobago, 33.4% in Barbados and 7.6% in Guyana for the years 1962–75.[5] The number of Jamaicans and Barbadians in the US is now equivalent to around one-quarter of the 'home' population – for the Cubans and Dominicans around one-tenth. Correspondingly, there are now substantial concentrations of Caribbean origin peoples in New York, Miami, Boston, Washington, Chicago and Los Angeles. Miami, in particular, has become an important centre for Cubans, the largest single migrant group. In a fascinating study of their impact Maingot[6] points out that Cubans now constitute more than one-half the population of the State of

Paul Sutton

Florida and that in economic terms they are doing very well – their median family income in Miami in 1978 was $13,644 (higher than non-Hispanic Whites and much higher than Blacks). He also demonstrates an increasing engagement in and impact on the political process on the part of Cubans who thus increasingly influence policy in relation to other Latin Americans. Their presence is thus expansive and dynamic, metaphorically and literally 'building Miami'. As such, the city is likely to continue to be a pole of growth and to act as a magnet to other Caribbean peoples in coming years. Maingot already notes, for example, a parallel process of arrival, adaptation and political engagement among Haitians.[7]

The quality of migrants is also an important dimension. A substantial number (around 15%) have been professional, technical and kindred workers. Between 1962 and 1976 the four main Commonwealth Caribbean countries contributed 17,649 professional and technical personnel, 16.112 clerical staff, 930 engineers, 602 doctors and dentists, 5,691 nurses and 109 pharmacists to the United States.[8] Many of these have come from Jamaica. One estimate, for example, has suggested that while only 4% of the Jamaican labour force were classified as professional and technical, 17% of all emigrants were in this category.[9] Comparable losses can be reported for Trinidad and Tobago: 4,482 professional, technical and related workers, 506 administrative, executive and managerial personnel, 5,379 clerical and sales staff, and 7,220 craftsmen and production process workers to North America between 1966 and 1970 alone.[10] The economic contribution such people make, of course, must be considerable. It is also enhanced by the fact that many are in their most productive years, i.e. the twenty- to thirty-four-year-old age group. Contrariwise, the effect this has on the development potential of the sending country is almost wholly negative.

Finally, note must be made of the small, but useful, temporary worker programme. In 1979, 9,247 persons were recruited from the Caribbean (29% of the total programme).[11] The majority of these are Jamaicans destined for agricultural work in the US that US citizens will not perform, e.g. cane-cutting in Florida or apple picking in Vermont. Their economic value is thus greater than their numbers suggest – perhaps a reason for the longevity of the scheme.

Direct resource rivalry between the USA and USSR over human 'capital' is seen only in the case of Cuba. This has taken several forms. The most obvious is the migration to the US of some 740,315 persons for the years 1959–80.[12] In so far as these migrants were, in the first wave (1959–62) and second wave (1965–72), disproportionately those with important professional, managerial and technical skills, then their economic loss to Cuba was significant, whatever political benefits may have accrued to the Cuban regime from their removal. The latest wave (1980) has been more representative, if not still fully so, of the Cuban population at large, with proportionately more factory workers, craftsmen and manual labourers than hitherto. Their skills are therefore less valuable to the US, and, correspondingly, more substitutable in Cuba than before, with the political gains reversed.[13] Also of some concern to Cuba must be the relatively youthful profile of the recent emigration comparable to previous phases – an average age of twenty-five years as compared to forty-five for earlier 'waves'. In all, then, while the trend of migration from Cuba is towards economic marginality for both it and the US, the sum effect has been towards a transfer of resources to the US of some magnitude.

Against this can be offset the activities of Cubans temporarily serving overseas. This characteristically takes two forms. One is the supply of Cubans to COMECON countries with labour deficits. Mesa-Lago has reported that some 10,000 Cubans were to be sent to cut timber in Siberia in exchange for wood; and that comparable agreements exchanging low-skilled manpower for products Cuba needs have been concluded with Czechoslovakia, Hungary and the German Democratic Republic.[14] The other, more well-known transfer, is the assignment of Cubans to work in Third World countries. Towards the end of the 1970s some 50,000 Cubans were serving in thirty-seven countries in a variety of tasks – as doctors, nurses, dentists, teachers, construction workers and soldiers. Although some of this was paid for, e.g. by Libya and Angola, much was not. In this dimension Cuba was therefore again a net contributor of resources.

In all, from wherever in the Caribbean, there has in the past twenty-five years been a net drain of human capital. It can, of course, be argued that this is beneficial, and, given the historical and geopolitical circumstances of the region, inevitable. If so, it has also been costly, not least in reinforcing dependence on the outside world, and especially the USA.

Petroleum

Since the early part of this century the availability in commercially viable quantities of strategically valuable minerals important to industrialization has made the Caribbean significant, particularly for the US. Accordingly, both US companies and the US government have shown a direct interest in their exploitation.

23

Paul Sutton

The Caribbean basin, expanded to include Mexico, Venezuela, Colombia and Guatemala, produced around 9% of total world oil production 1983–6. Exclude these countries and the region produced little over 0.3%, nearly all within Trinidad and Tobago, the sole remaining oil-exporting country.[15] The Caribbean is therefore insignificant in production, being a net importer of oil, on which a number of countries remain highly dependent. At the same time the geographic location and political status of several of the islands have made them attractive to the oil industry as refining centres and trans-shipment ports. A significant interest and investment has therefore arisen around oil products, amounting in the case of the US alone to some $1.6 billion.[16]

Refining capacity in the region is in excess of 2.5 million barrels a day (b/d). This is concentrated in the Bahamas, the Netherlands Antilles, Puerto Rico, Trinidad and Tobago and the US Virgin Islands. Trans-shipment facilities follow a similar pattern and offer a capacity of 2.8 million b/d. The companies involved include several oil majors and a number of independent and state-owned companies (see Table 2).

In recent years the refining industry worldwide has been subject to a squeeze as capacity has exceeded demand. This has particularly affected Caribbean refineries which offer only locale, i.e., they lack access to domestic crude production and to captive markets. Cut-back and closure have thus been the order of the day as have been transfers of ownership. Exxon has shut down its refinery and trans-shipment facilities in Aruba and Shell has leased its operations in Curacao to the Venezuelan state oil company for five years. Charter Oil and then Chevron have shut down operations at their Freeport refinery in the Bahamas and Texaco has sold its refinery and on-shore oil production interests to the Trinidad state oil company. Difficulties have been reported at the Burmah trans-shipment facility in the Bahamas where throughput has been reduced by over 50%. In all, capacity in the region has been severely curtailed and the risks and rewards of the oil industry have been increasingly concentrated within the producing countries.

Much of this has been in accord with US policy which has been concerned with security of supply and, in recent years, with the application of 'market solutions' to energy problems.[17] It is the latter which is most dramatically demonstrated in the Caribbean and which, in turn, directly impinges on regional states so that even the most favoured may suddenly find themselves in difficulties. Trinidad and Tobago is a case in point. Its oil production fell some 30% from 1978–84 while throughput was reduced to 25% of refinery capacity. Given the reliance of the

Table 2. *Oil in the Caribbean Basin*

Production (thousand tonnes 1986)	
Mexico	150,885
Venezuela	88,635
Trinidad	8,905
Colombia	8,900
Cuba	865
Guatemala	170
Barbados	92

Major Refining Capacity

	Capacity b/d	Principal ownership
Bahamas	500,000	Charter Oil/Chevron[a]
Aruba	480,000	Exxon[b]
Curacao	370,000	100% state[c]
Trinidad (Pointe-à-Pierre)	355,000	100% state[d]
Trinidad (Point Fortin)	100,000	100% state
US Virgin Islands	700,000	Amerada Hess.
Puerto Rico (Yubacoa)	85,000	Sun Oil
Puerto Rico (Penueles)	161,000	Apex Oil

Major Trans-shipment Facilities

	Capacity b/d	Principal ownership
Curacao	1,025,000	Shell
Aruba	444,000	Exxon
Bonaire	450,000	Northville/Pak Tank
Bahamas	100–200,000	Charter Oil/Chevron
Bahamas	400,000	Burmah
Bahamas	100–200,000	Texaco
US Virgin Islands	100–200,000	Amerada Hess

Notes: [a] Closed in 1985.
[b] Closed in 1985.
[c] Acquired from Shell by the Netherlands Antilles in 1985 and leased to the Venezuelan state oil company Petróleos de Venezuela.
[d] Acquired from Texaco in 1985.

Sources: Petroleum Economist, January 1987; T. Barry, B. Wood and D. Preusch, *The Other Side of Paradise: Foreign Control in the Caribbean,* Table 5B; *Petroleum Economist,* January 1984.

economy on oil, a period of austerity loomed large, the political costs of which were the defeat of a regime of thirty years standing at the polls in December 1986. Parallel problems can be recorded for the Netherlands

Paul Sutton

Antilles and the Bahamas. From all three countries US purchases of oil and derivatives stood at only $1.3 billion in 1986 – less than one-third what they had been in 1980.[18]

Such reliance by the US on the market, in effect an absence of policy to the Caribbean, has to some extent been countered by US concerns with security of supply. But here the Caribbean figures less as a major refiner of oil than as a transportation route for oil tankers from Venezuela, Mexico and elsewhere. It is in this sense that frequent reference is made by US officials to the fact that 'sea lanes in the Caribbean are used to transport nearly 50% of all crude oil imports, and a large percent of Alaska's North Slope crude oil transits through Panama either by Trans-Panama Pipeline or the Panama Canal'.[19] At the same time, however, the US government does not anticipate any real threat to these routes outside a situation of general war; i.e. it discounts the prospect of limited interdiction missions by Cuba or other hostile forces; and it believes that threats 'which would jeopardize the major Caribbean producer's ability to produce, refine, and export crude oil are now low'.[20] There is therefore little in the current situation to prompt the US to enter into any preferential arrangements with Caribbean producers to ensure physical security of supply. Instead, there is a trust that in times of short-run difficulty *ad hoc* arrangements can prevail, backed up by the Strategic Petroleum Reserve. This currently stands in excess of 500 million barrels of crude oil, much of it supplied by Mexico.

In the light of the above the Caribbean cannot be seen as a region of serious resource rivalry for oil. The Soviet Union is a major producer and exporter of oil in its own right. It has no need of access to Caribbean resources although, of course, it does have a Caribbean commitment in Cuba. Its requirements are currently estimated at around 200,000 b/d of which Cuba, even under the most optimistic forecasts, can supply only 20% from its own reserves by 1990. Security of supply to Cuba thus does constitute a problem, and a possibly growing one for the USSR as demand for Soviet oil increases from Eastern Europe (and as another Caribbean regional commitment is added in the shape of Nicaragua).[21] Nevertheless, the problem does not have to be an insuperable one. Since 1977 Venezuela has had an agreement with the USSR on reciprocal concession of oil quotas whereby it would ship a specified amount to Cuba (25,000 b/d in 1983) in exchange for the Soviet Union supplying Venezuelan customers in Europe.[22] Mexico was, until recently, the major supplier of oil to the Sandinista government. There is, therefore, no material reason why a regional solution could not be found for Soviet

26

commitments, although, of course, it may not be feasible politically.

For the US the prospect of uninterrupted access to all aspects of the Caribbean basin oil industry has been underscored. US crude oil imports from Mexico, Venezuela and Trinidad in 1985 were 1,155,507 b/d (33% of total oil imports) and 1,197,337 b/d (27% of total imports) in 1986.[23] This is clearly important, but it does have to be set in context. Mexican supplies do not have to transit the Caribbean. Mexico is not a member of OPEC and neither Venezuela nor Mexico gain from confrontation with the US over oil. Indeed, quite the reverse. Venezuela was thus willing to mitigate the effect of the oil embargo in 1973 and the supply shortfall in 1978-9 by increasing output and sales to the US. Both Mexico and Venezuela have every incentive to maintain or even increase supplies given current economic problems. Finally, Canada's role as a supplier (571,972 b/d in 1986) and domestic production within the US itself (equivalent of 74% of consumption in 1985) cannot be discounted. The conclusion must therefore be that while the oil industry in the Caribbean basin, broadly conceived, is important to US national security, within a narrower definition it is not. What is important here is more likely capital investment in downstream activities. And here the recent fall in demand in the US for fuel oil – in which Caribbean refineries specialize – has rendered them vulnerable, not to East–West pressures, but to those emanating from within the uncertain global market for oil and the changing patterns of demand within the US itself.

Non-fuel minerals

With respect to non-fuel mineral resources the Caribbean is a major producer of bauxite and a minor producer of nickel, cobalt, gold and silver (see Table 3). Other available resources are aragonite, salt, chromium, copper, manganese ore, lime, mercury, marble, lead and diamonds.[24] None of these, however, are at the moment of any real significance.

Bauxite mining is concentrated in Jamaica, Suriname and Guyana. Between them they accounted for 67% of total American production and 18% of world production in 1983 and 1984.[25] Jamaica is the most important producer being ranked third in world terms. Production, however, has halved since 1974 and similar levels of decline can be recorded for Guyana and Suriname. Part of this may be attributable to new competitive sources of supply, e.g., Australia, Guinea, Brazil, China, and part to successful programmes of recovery of secondary aluminium in the

Paul Sutton

Table 3. *Caribbean non-fuel mineral resources*

	Principal resource	Production[a]	Ownership structure
Cuba	Nickel (1)	38,650	100% state
	Cobalt (2)	1,745	100% state
Dominican Republic	Nickel (1)	22,250	67.5% Falconbridge
	Gold (3)	335.5[b]	100% state
	Silver (4)	1.35[b]	100% state
Guyana	Bauxite (5)	2,124	100% state
Jamaica	Bauxite (5)	8,208	Jamalcan (93% Alcan)
			Jamalco (94% Alcoa)[c]
			Kaiser Jamaica (51% state, 49% Kaiser)
			Reynolds Jamaica[d] (51% state, 49% Reynolds)
			Alpart of Jamaica[e] (36.5% Kaiser, 36.5% Reynolds, 27% Atlantic Richfield)
Suriname	Bauxite (5)	3,084	Biliton M.S. (100% Royal Dutch Shell)
			Suralco (100% Alcoa)
			Suralco (65% Alcoa, 45% Biliton)

1 = mine production (metric tons)
2 = tons of 3000 pounds
3 = thousands of troy ounces
4 = millions of troy ounces
5 = thousand metric tons

[a] Average production figures for years 1983 and 1984.
[b] Average production for 1984 and 1985
[c] Acquired by the Jamaican government in 1985.
[d] Closed in 1984.
[e] Closed in 1985.

Sources: American Metal Market, *Metal Statistics 1986*; T. Barry, B. Wood and D. Preusch, *The Other Side of Paradise: Foreign Control in the Caribbean*, Table 5C.

US and elsewhere. High energy costs associated with the production of aluminium and world recession have also had a marked downward effect. So also have resource management policies in Guyana and Jamaica. In the former, full-scale nationalization and subsequent state mismanagement have debilitated the industry to the point where external assistance for rehabilitation is now being sought. In the case of the latter the picture is somewhat more complicated and beyond the scope of the present enquiry. Suffice it to note that attempts by the Manley government from 1974 onwards to achieve improved returns from mining and to buy into the industry met with opposition from the major companies involved – Kaiser Aluminium and Chemical, Alcan, Alcoa, Revere and Reynolds Metals; and that while this was not, in the end, sufficient to frustrate the government's

28

immediate goals (a negotiated agreement on aspects of national resource exploitation was reached) the conflict was undoubtedly damaging in the medium term, both to the People's National Party government and to Manley himself.

How much the US government was involved in concerting opposition to this is difficult to determine. Manley records that immediately prior to the launch of the policy he visited Kissinger in Washington and assured him

that the action we were about to take was purely economic in its implication ... [and] that we fully recognised the importance of aluminium to US industrial and military interests. [Consequently] we would never seek to affect US access to our bauxite through the legitimate channels of its multinational corporations and wished him to pass these assurances on to the President of the United States and the members of the National Security Council.[26]

Assuming this was done, it nevertheless appears to have been insufficient to stem mounting US suspicions of Jamaican intent, although it is important as an explicit recognition by Manley of US national interest. This was understandable in terms of the magnitude of Jamaican bauxite and alumina in US imports at the time and has continued, even if production has dropped, except that the flow of concern is now the other way. In November 1981 Reagan requested the purchase of 1.6 million tons of Jamaican bauxite for the US National Defense stockpile of strategic materials, stating

While improving our own defense posture, this programme will contribute to Prime Minister Seaga's strategy for Jamaica to rely to the maximum extent possible on production and exports to fuel its own economic recovery. The stability and economic strength of Jamaica are important to our national security interests in the Caribbean.[27]

In 1983 a further request to purchase another two million tons was made.

Security of supply for bauxite from the Caribbean thus continues to exercise US decision-makers. However, it must be stressed that while this is an important concern it is by no means an overriding one. Bauxite mining operations by Reynolds Metals were closed in Haiti in 1982 and suspended in the Dominican Republic by Alcoa in the same year. The US market is currently oversupplied with aluminium as witness the spate of closures in Jamaica (Alcan now remains as the only TNC with both bauxite and alumina interests). Additionally, while around one-half of US supplies of calcined bauxite have in the past come from Guyana the virtual monopoly it held on its production until 1980 has been broken. Finally, the International Bauxite Association has scarcely been troublesome. Originally created on the initiative of the Manley government in 1974 it has been unable to unify major producers in any real defence of their interests internationally. Bauxite has thus continued to be under-valued relative to its processed form – indeed at a level lower than that of any other of the Third World's sixteen most important exports.[28]

Nickel production is concentrated in Cuba and the Dominican Republic, with the former accounting for around 5% of world mine production in 1983 and 1984 and the latter some 3%.[29] Prior to the revolution the US Department of Defense contracted to buy all Cuban nickel. Things since have clearly changed although the importance of nickel as a strategic material remains and the US is currently the world's major consumer and importer of the metal – over $1 billion in 1979.[30] Security of supply for the US is assured through access to Canadian nickel, a proportion of which is supplied by Falconbridge Ltd of Toronto. This company is the major shareholder in the sole Dominican producer, the output of which goes mainly to the US. Cuban nickel production is wholly state-owned and is currently under expansion with an expectation that refinery capacity will be doubled. The reasons for this, however, are less strategic that economic – the major purchasers of Cuban nickel are West Germany, Italy and the Netherlands and the material as a whole accounts for between 10% and 12% of hard currency earnings.[31]

Cuban production of cobalt, derived from nickel ore, was around 5% of world production in 1984 and 1985.[32] Nearly all this was sold to Eastern Europe and the USSR where, notwithstanding levels of USSR production, there has been an increasing need to import. Given its importance as a strategic material stockpiles are usually maintained by governments, e.g. in 1984 the US government purchased four million pounds of cobalt – one-third of US consumption that year.

The remaining minor minerals of limited significance are gold and silver. Both are produced in the Dominican Republic from the now wholly state-owned company Rosario Dominicana. While output is small in global terms – 0.9% of total gold production and 0.5% of silver in the same year[33] – it constitutes an important export item for the government. Gold is also prospected in small amounts in Guyana and French Guiana.

None of the non-fuel minerals produced in the Caribbean region can be considered critical to the US or the USSR. The policy of the USSR has for some time been to maintain self-sufficiency in mineral resources and while it has, in recent years, become increasingly dependent on imported bauxite, on occasion even buying Caribbean bauxite (in 1982 it signed an agreement to buy one million tons of Jamaican bauxite annually from 1984 to 1990) its major suppliers are Hungary, Yugoslavia, India, Guinea,

Greece and Italy. Nickel mined in the region is also of little concern since the USSR is the world's largest producer. There is some uncertainty surrounding cobalt as estimates of Soviet cobalt production vary considerably. However, demand is likely to grow only slowly, if steadily, suggesting that the USSR's interest in its development will be marginal. In both specific and general terms it is therefore reasonable to conclude that the Caribbean scarcely figures on the Soviet Union's inventory of need.

Similar reasoning can also be applied to the USA. The availability of supplies of bauxite is practically assured by the nature of the bauxite industry, which continues to be dominated by a number of virtually integrated transnational corporations – Alcan, Alcoa, Kaiser, Reynolds, Pechiney and Alsuisse control about 65% of alumina refinery capacity, around 60% of bauxite mining, and some 55% of aluminium production.[34] Moreover, present technologies and past experience have shown that alternative raw materials can quickly be brought into use, to which also must be added to the question of demand. While there is a reasonable expectation that this will grow, recent developments in the airframe industry threaten substitutability of graphite-epoxy and/or Kevlar for aluminium both for reasons of economy (reduced weight improves fuel efficiency) and defence (both materials are superior in radar absorption).[35] Supplies of nickel and cobalt are stockpiled and while the reliance on Canada, in the case of the former, gives a sense of security denied to the latter, attempts have been made by the US in Africa to assure this.

None of the non-fuel minerals found in quantity in the Caribbean is the object of direct competition between the USA and the USSR. There is no evidence that the USSR promotes a policy of denial of strategic non-fuel minerals in peacetime,[36] and given that the USSR aims at self-sufficiency, an equivalent policy directed at it by the USA is meaningless. US national security interests in the region in this regard are not directly at stake, although, given the structure of ownership of the bauxite industry, economic interests may count.

CARIBBEAN SECURITY

The Caribbean is littered with sunken warships and crumbling military fortifications. Its islands have long been fought over and exchanged: its sea lanes carefully guarded and patrolled. Security has been a constant preoccupation for whoever has sought to control the region and the means to secure it have been remarkably consistent over time. The characteristic form of the US military presence in the region is thus not new. As

Table 4. *US military installations in the Caribbean*

Principal bases	
Puerto Rico	Roosevelt Roads Naval Station (Fleet training and support). Fort Buchanan (logistics and administration facility). Installations of the 92nd Infantry Brigade and for the National Guard.
Cuba	Guantánamo Naval Station (port and logistic facilities).
Other installations	
Antigua	Naval facility, Air Force facility (ocean research and tracking). Expansion as a training centre for regional security forces proposed and approved in 1985.
Bahamas	Atlantic Underwater Test and Evaluation Centre. Eastern Test Range (missile-tracking and space support facilities). Naval facility, Air Force facility (ocean research and navigation).
Turks and Caicos	Ocean research, navigation and tracking and space support facilities.

Source: R. Kennedy and G. Marcella, 'US Security on the Southern Flank: Interests, Challenges, Responses', in Greene and Scowcroft (eds.), *Western Interests and US Policy Options in the Caribbean Basin.*

previously with Spain and Britain, the US seeks security through military bases; protected sea lanes; and the ability to exclude, contain or otherwise limit the challenges and depredations of hostile powers.

In recent years the permanent US military presence has been relatively modest. Excluding the US itself, and Panama, where facilities are slowly being phased out, the US has major military bases only in Puerto Rico and at Guantánamo in Cuba. The total personnel stationed in both in 1986 were estimated as 6,100, approximately one-third of those assigned to Latin American and the Caribbean.[37] Elsewhere in the region US facilities are scattered and relatively minor, employing at most several hundred personnel (see Table 4). The profile presented would thus appear to bear out the continuation of the economy-of-force approach which has marked US policy to the region since the Second World War.[38] This doctrine assigns strategic resources to other areas of greater threat or more likely conflict, reserving those in the Caribbean to perform monitoring, training and co-ordination functions and as a demonstration of political will and commitment.

To some extent, of course, this is perfectly understandable. Proximity, and the strategic disposition of the area as a whole, makes it possible for the US to concentrate overwhelming force as and when the needs arise. The means to achieve this have, over the past seven years, been demonstrated on numerous occasions. Beginning with 'Solid Shield 80' in 1980, massive military exercises have become a routine feature. In 1982 'Ocean Venture 82' was staged, involving 45,000 troops from all branches of the armed forces, 60 ships and 350 aircraft – the largest peacetime manoeuvres ever held by the US. Two years later it was repeated as 'Ocean Venture 84', this time involving 350 support ships and 30,000 personnel from all sectors of the US armed forces. In the meantime, in October 1983, and at comparatively short notice, the US had mounted a successful invasion of Grenada. The readiness, willingness and ability of the US to intervene militarily in the Caribbean – the distinguishing feature of its policy to the region – had thus once more been demonstrated, and as importantly sustained by US Congressional and public opinion.

Soviet interest in bases in the Caribbean has focused exclusively on Cuba. There is no evidence that the USSR currently seeks or is likely to gain bases elsewhere in the region.

The situation regarding Soviet forces in Cuba has been clarified in three 'accords' reached by the USA and the USSR in 1962, 1970 and 1979. The first, agreed in the wake of the Missile Crisis, established that strategic weapons would not be placed in Cuba in return for the expectation that the US would not invade the island to overthrow the government. The second, occasioned by US suspicion that a naval base at Cienfuegos was being upgraded to service Soviet submarines, specified that the Soviet navy would not use Cuban ports as a base for strategic operations. The third, following the 'discovery' of a Soviet brigade in Cuba of some 2,300–3,000 troops, underlined the understanding that the USSR would not introduce further combat troops in Cuba and accepted an assurance that other Soviet forces in place were there principally for training. Current estimates (1986–7) put Soviet forces at 8,000, to include a combat brigade of 2,800, some 3,100 military advisers and 2,100 technicians.[39] The last figure draws attention to the importance of Cuba as a base for electronic intelligence gathering, the Soviet facility at Lourdes being the largest outside the USSR. There have also been reports that Soviet pilots have flown Cuban MiGs off Cuba in a defensive role to release Cuban pilots for missions in Ethiopia.

Beyond the above, concern by the US armed forces as to Soviet intentions in Cuba is in the realm of hypothesis. Clearly Cuba could be used as a forward base to threaten the USA. TU-95 'Bear D' long-range reconnaissance aircraft regularly fly there from the USSR which opens the prospect that TU-26 'Backfire' bombers could use Cuba as a recovery and relaunch platform for strategic nuclear strikes on the USA. Similarly, improved submarine servicing facilities in Cuba could allow Soviet submarines, including ballistic-missile nuclear submarines, to extend their range and increase time on station so considerably enhancing their capabilities.[40] However, both eventualities would clearly be in breach of the 'accords' of 1962 and 1970, so inviting a strong US response. It can therefore be judged unlikely, even if not entirely to be discounted.

Confirmation of this comes from the example of Grenada. During the period of the People's Revolutionary Government, 1979–83, work began on a new Cuban financed international airport at Point Salines. The PRG claimed its purpose was purely developmental, i.e., to encourage tourism; the US thought otherwise, stating its purpose was to serve the military interests of Cuba and the USSR, both in the region and in Africa.[41] Who was right? Among the thousands of Grenadian documents captured by the US with the invasion only one makes explicit reference to the airport in a military sense – and that had the status merely of an entry in a diary of a leading revolutionary figure, Liam James. In the light of this even the most hawkish of commentators raising alarms as to Soviet designs on the region have had to acknowledge the airport as primarily a civilian venture.[42] And from the documents as a whole an interpretation of Soviet policy as cautious and uncertain, rather than rash or inflammatory, can most easily be drawn.

The US concern with sea lanes focuses on the Panama Canal, the Mona and Windward Passages, and the Florida Straits. Through them passes an estimated 50% of the peacetime maritime commerce of the US and in the event of a war through them would pass 50% or more of the planned reinforcements of men and material to the Western European Theatre and up to 40% to the Far Eastern Theatre.[43] The importance of the Caribbean for commercial and strategic reasons cannot be clearer, and although the US has for many years sought to ensure safe passage, e.g. by monitoring ship movements, both surface and submarine, it cannot guarantee it. The uncertainties arising from this admit the prospect of the interdiction of sea lanes which, in the current strategic debate allowing for conventional war in Europe, assume some importance.

Beginning in July 1969, the Soviet Union has regularly deployed naval units to the Caribbean. The number and variety of ships assigned have varied considerably as have their time on station, but it is clear that over the years the 'mix' has been such as to admit quantitative improvements to them. Whereas once the capacity of the Soviet Union to conduct

34

Table 5. *Caribbean sea lane interdiction capacity of Cuba 1986–87*

Aircraft
3 squadrons: MiG-23 BN Flogger
1 squadron: Mig-17
16 squadrons: interceptor capacity: various MiG-21 and MiG-23 Flogger E

Warships
2 Koni class frigates
3 Foxtrot class submarines
23 Fast attack craft (with Styx surface to surface missiles)
8 Fast attack craft (with torpedoes)
44 Fast attack craft (patrol)

Additional naval capacity
20 Patrol craft
15 Minesweepers.

Source: IISS, *The Military Balance 1986–1987*, p. 185.

successful interdiction missions in the region was nil it is now very much a possibility.

The same can be said of Cuba which through its own inventory of weapons now possesses sufficient capability to carry out limited interdiction missions (see Table 5). Additionally, joint Soviet–Cuban naval manoeuvres have been held yearly since 1976. The capacity of the Soviet Union and Cuba collectively to pose a credible threat to Caribbean sea lanes, especially to the 'choke' points, must therefore be acknowledged. The question of whether they would do so, however, is more uncertain.

Common sense suggests that in a situation of military conflict the protection of Caribbean sea lanes would carry a higher priority for the US than interdiction of them would for the USSR. The latter, as two US defence experts have pointed out,[44] can achieve the same effect, with greater certainty and more security, by deploying its forces in the North Atlantic. Cuba also has little incentive to conduct such a campaign since it would put its own maritime commerce at risk and would invite direct US retaliation. Finally, as Secretary of the Navy John Lehman has noted, the US could 'fight through' a Soviet–Cuban interdiction campaign in a relatively short time and with only marginal losses of supplies, aircraft and diversion of anti-submarine warfare forces. There is, therefore, little military sense in an interdiction campaign, especially when the US retains the option at the end of the day of diversifying ports of embarkation for its forces. None of this, of course, means the US military planners should not

Paul Sutton

Table 6. *Military forces and US military assistance: Caribbean*

	Regular military forces 1986–7	Number military trained by US 1980–3	US military assistance $000 1981–4
Bahamas	496	n/a	5
Belize	600	n/a	n/a
Cuba	162,000*a*	0	0
Dom Rep	21,300	496	15,607
East Carib.*	250*b*	128	10,810
Guyana	5,450	50	98
Haiti	8,000*c*	95	1,125
Jamaica	2,100	101	7,797
Suriname	2,535	14	53
Trinidad	2,130	n/a	15

* Eastern Caribbean (Antigua, Barbados, Dominica, St Lucia, St Vincent).

a Plus Reserves circa 165,000 (serve 45 days per year).
b Figures for 1980.
c Figures for 1982.

Sources: IISS, *The Military Balance, 1986–1987*; T. Barry et al., *The Other Side of Paradise*; J. Child, 'Issues for US Policy: Security' in Greene and Scowcroft (eds.) *Western Interests and US Policy Options in the Caribbean Basin.*

allow for the possibility of such a campaign, but it does reduce its probability. Caribbean sea lanes are therefore safer than President Reagan and others pleading particular causes would suggest.[45]

US MILITARY DOMINATION

The question of US military domination of the Caribbean has two aspects: conventional and unconventional. In respect of the former it recognizes the limited military capabilities of most states in the region, the influence of the US military in the provision of security assistance, and the various military agreements and regional defence arrangements to which the US is party. In respect of the latter it is the importance or otherwise of insurgency in the region.

Military force levels in the Caribbean are low (see Table 6). With the exception of Cuba, no state poses a threat in any way to the US and military forces in nearly every instance are there primarily for internal security functions. The emphasis given to enhancing capabilities in this dimension has increased considerably in recent years, especially in the

Eastern Caribbean where the US has emerged as the major supplier of security assistance. It has also been instrumental there in establishing the Regional Security System by means of which Antigua, Barbados, Dominica, Grenada, St Kitts–Nevis, St Lucia and St Vincent co-ordinate military planning and training among each other and through which they may call for direct military assistance as and when the occasion demands. Finally, within the emphasis on better equipped local forces, note must be taken of the increasing militarization of Puerto Rico. The role of the Puerto Rican National Guard has been especially emphasized. Its 12,000 personnel are regarded as 'the best trained and equipped National Guard unit of the United States'[46] and in turn provide security assistance to others. Certain provisions, particularly those relating to US Congressional limitation on overseas police training, have in this way been circumvented for Commonwealth Caribbean countries.

The thinking behind much of this, of course, relates to counter-insurgency. Yet the record of insurgency in the Caribbean, as compared to Central America, is remarkably low. With the exception of Suriname there is currently no active insurgency in the region and the record over the last ten years of successful *coup d'état* or sustained anti-regime terrorism is not such as to invite undue alarm. This is not to suggest that political violence does not occur. In Jamaica, for example, it has been widespread, and in Haiti prior to 1986 was an essential aspect of Duvalierism. Yet, in both, and throughout the region as a whole, violence is more anomic than might be thought and where it is part of an orchestrated conspiracy is as likely to be linked to organized crime as it is to political ambition *per se*. Mercenaries and the drug barons must both be guarded against but not, as the current Prime Minister of St Vincent, 'Son' Mitchell, or former Barbadian Prime Minister Errol Barrow has urged, at the cost of the needless militarization of the region.[47]

Soviet military co-operation in the Caribbean has been exclusively with Cuba and Grenada. To the former it has supplied a considerable armoury, but it has stopped short of signing a formal defence agreement such as it has concluded with a number of Middle Eastern and Sub-Saharan African countries, so arousing considerable speculation as to the real extent of its commitment to Cuba were it to be invaded. Grenada also received military assistance, although not military advisers, from 1980 to 1983. It also, it should be noted, was to receive no practical support when invaded, with even Soviet public statements being relatively low key. All this is suggestive, as Lt General Nutting has stated, of the USSR operating 'an economy-of-force strategy in Latin America'.[48] Cognizant of US interests in the

37

region the formal military presence of the USSR is thus heavily circum-scribed and its real objectives seemingly political rather than any other.

One reason why this may be so is that it can rely on Cuba as a surrogate. If this is indeed the case (and I do not find it persuasive) then it must be recognized that Cuba too has in recent years met with considerable difficulties in the Caribbean. It still has no formal diplomatic relations with Haiti, the Dominican Republic or the 'micro-states' of the Eastern Carib-bean. It has had damaging incidents with both the Bahamas and Barbados and, along with Trinidad, relations toward all three governments can best be described as distant. Finally, towards those countries with which closer feelings once prevailed – Jamaica, Guyana and Suriname – changes of government and 'fall-out' from Grenada have had a chilling effect. In such a climate it is not surprising to discover that Cuban military assistance is neither sought nor extended, or that in recent years the only real manifestation of such activity has been in Grenada. Towards the Bishop regime Cuban military assistance was indeed generous and timely, but it was also singular and arguably proportional. That is, no one yet has managed to demonstrate that in character (as opposed to volume) arms were intended other than to enhance defence capabilities. So while it is true that Grenada's army was 'a factor to be reckoned with in the West Indian environment' it is also true that 'Soviet and Cuban involvement in Grenada did not present an immediate threat to US interests. Nor is there conclusive evidence that Grenada had become a depot for large con-centrations of Soviet arms designed for future use in Latin America.'[49]

The real challenge to US military domination in the Caribbean therefore comes not from conventional but unconventional warfare. This subject is too large to be dealt with other than in summary form, but it should be noted that the Caribbean is not propitious territory for such activities. The record of the 1960s and 1970s points everywhere to the failure of guerrilla groups and in the 1980s political circumstances have been such as to not give them many grounds for hope. Communist parties in the Caribbean are scattered and fragmented, committed mainly to party-building, trade union activity and electoral campaigns. Other groups are virtually non-existent and all are small in number (see Table 7). They are also, official communist parties aside, not given to longevity. The influence of revol-utionary groups, accordingly, is minimal, and even where communist parties do enjoy fraternal relations with the Soviet Union or Cuba they are unlikely to be counted for much. The Caribbean is as secure from such warfare as can reasonably be expected with the turmoil in Central America providing no noticeable demonstration effect. Indeed, the environment of

Table 7. *Non-ruling communist parties and revolutionary groups in the Caribbean*

	Name of official communist party	Membership – claim or estimate	Status	Number of other revolutionary groups or factions
Dominican Republic	Partido Comunista Dominicano	500–1,000	Legal	7
Grenada	New Jewel Movement	n/a	Legal	–
	Maurice Bishop Patriotic Movement	n/a	Legal	–
Guadeloupe	Parti Communiste Guadeloupéen	3,000	Legal	2
Guyana	People's Progressive Party	100–300	Legal	1
Haiti	Partie Unifié Communiste Haitien	350	Legal (from 1986)	n/a
Jamaica	Workers' Party of Jamaica	50	Legal	2
Martinique	Parti Communiste Martiniquais	1,000	Legal	n/a
Puerto Rico	Partido Comunista Puertorriqueño	125	Legal	1
Suriname	Revolutionaire Volkspartij	100	Legal (from 1985)	2

Source: Richard F. Staar (ed.), *Yearbook on International Communist Affairs, 1986* (Stanford, Cal.: Hoover Institution Press, 1986).

the region itself provides substance to Castro's assertion 'that we cannot export revolution and the US cannot prevent it',[50] i.e. that indigenous circumstances are always paramount in determining the revolutionary calculus. Among the better informed of the policymaking and academic community in the US it is difficult to believe that this is not other than well known and understood.

THE CARIBBEAN AS A 'SPHERE OF INFLUENCE'

At the outbreak of the Second World War, J. Fred Rippy wrote:

The Caribbean policy of the United States accords with a maxim almost as unchanging as a law of mathematics or physics. That maxim is the domination of the area at least to the extent necessary to prevent its domination by any other strong power. If the control exercised in the region has occasionally been less than required by the maxim, this has been due to the temporary imprudence of enforcing it. If the domination has ever been greater than the maxim demanded, this has been caused by the hasty action of nervous statesmen, by zeal to assist the Caribbean nations in their efforts toward improvement, or by the pressure of economic forces. No diplomat has ever baldly formulated the maxim. Perhaps that would have been unwise. But it may be asserted with confidence that the policy the maxim describes began to take form between 1800 and 1850 and became full grown shortly after 1900.[51]

Nothing in the last fifty years suggests these conclusions need in any way be revised. US policy to the Caribbean has been remarkably consistent and contemporary manifestations of Rippy's concerns can easily be cited. Indeed, they may be elaborated and compounded by reference to a work published even earlier which delineated the features of dollar diplomacy in the region:

Determination of boundaries; prevention of or assistance to filibustering in line with American financial interests; administration of customs houses; annexation of Porto Rico and the purchase of the Virgin Islands; establishment of financial protectorates; armed intervention to further economic interests; destruction of independent government; fomenting of revolution; building of the Panama Canal; promoting a canal route in Nicaragua; interference with elections; controlled use of recognition policy; acquisition of naval bases; establishment of local constabularies under American influence; economic interpretation of the Monroe Doctrine to exclude European investors; solicitation of loan business for US banks; campaigning on behalf of oil interests against nationalization of Mexican natural resources.[52]

Very few, if any, of the above have lost their force or do not find echoes in current US policy. And they continue to inform and incite both liberal and left-wing critiques of US policy to the region, anticipating both the structural form and substance of such works.[53]

If US policy has had such consistency and force over time it follows that

US understanding and practice towards the region is internalized and entrenched. It admits to the Caribbean as a 'sphere of influence' and allows within the concept for re-interpretation of policy, but not for any re-definition of parameters. Innovation, such as there is, is always less than it seems at the time, essentially a matter of re-adjustment and muddling through. Reagan's 'new' policies to the region very much partake of this heritage.

The distinguishing feature of his Caribbean basin policy is to reassert the long-established position of the Caribbean in world affairs. This ascribes to it a subordinate position and defines its utility solely in relation to the needs of the hegemonic power. So that where once John Stuart Mill could refer to the West Indies as a place convenient for Britain to grow sugar, so now President Reagan finds it a place convenient from which to proclaim US power. Or more precisely, the region assumes the status of symbol in the exercise of that power. As President Reagan so neatly summarized it in his speech of 1983 on Central America (which subsumed the Caribbean within it),

I say to you that tonight there can be no question: The national security of all the Americas is at stake in Central America. If we cannot defend ourselves there, we cannot expect to prevail elsewhere.[54]

Exactly so. The value of the region is not primarily economic (although it plays a part), nor even overwhelmingly strategic (although this is under-standably important). It is political – as proof of American power. And since this may, by definition, take on board a host of factors, subjective and objective, in its determination, then so policy towards the region is as universal as it is particular, and addressed as much to matters outside the region as to those pertaining only to it.[55] No wonder, at the end of the day, that an effective Caribbean policy addressing the real and more especially *sui generis* issues of the region is so elusive for US presidents and US public alike.

CONCLUSION

The real interests of the US in the Caribbean are geopolitical. Within this perspective the Caribbean matters, not for the resources it commands, nor for the strategic flexibility it permits, but because of what it represents to the people of the US and to the outside world. This is a belief that if the US cannot deal effectively with events in its own sphere of influence it will not deal effectively with events elsewhere. The US role as a global power is thus intimately tied to its policies to the Caribbean, and while in practice the

41

Paul Sutton

latter can be identified with some certainty, the philosophy governing them cannot since it is no less than part of the US national interest itself.

There is very little evidence that the Soviet Union seeks to challenge this in any fundamental way. Cuba excepted, it has little interest in Caribbean resources and remains strategically vulnerable to US military superiority in the region. Such competition as it engages in is therefore overwhelmingly political: dialogue with governments to expand diplomatic and consular representation; promotion of the ideology of Marxism–Leninism as a blueprint for political and social change; and with considerable variation according to circumstance and opportunity, practical support (overt and covert) for fraternal communist parties and select anti-imperialist, pro-revolutionary groups throughout the region. Nearly all of this is conducted in a very low key, suggesting that the USSR recognizes 'limits' that cannot be transgressed. It also confirms that the region itself is accorded a low priority in Moscow and that its interests and its influence there is weak.

Which, finally, leaves Cuba. Without US–Cuban hostility it is difficult to see that there would be any serious resource or strategic rivalry in the Caribbean. It is also difficult to believe that there would be any credible challenge to its status as a sphere of influence. US–Cuban relations are thus central to the future of the Caribbean and by extension to the economic development and security of the US itself. If there is an overwhelming objective interest in the region today it is that there should be progress on US–Cuban relations. No one expects this to be easy, but strategies can be devised which make it both possible and credible.[56] Opportunities earlier foreclosed by the Reagan Administration but now reopened should be taken, if only because the alternatives available to either side are too debilitating and uncertain of long-term success than realistically to do otherwise.

NOTES

1. See, in particular, R. H. Girling and L. Goldring, 'US Strategic Interests in Central America: The Economics and Geopolitics of Empire', in Stanford Central American Action Network, Revolution in Central America (Boulder, Colo.: Westview Press, 1983), pp. 186–205.
2. Jorge I. Domínguez, US Interests and Policies in the Caribbean and Central America (Washington DC and London: American Enterprise Institute for Public Policy Research, 1982), p. 1.
3. Robert A. Pastor, Caribbean Emigration and US Immigration Policy: Cross Currents (Working Paper, no. 4, Caribbean Institute and Study Center for Latin America, Inter American University of Puerto Rico, San Germán, Puerto Rico), p. 22.
4. This has been estimated as yielding an illegal Caribbean population of around 760,000.

42

Testimony by Virginia Domínguez before the US House of Representatives, 1978, cited in Pastor, *Caribbean Emigration and US Immigration Policy*, p. 30.
5. Ransford Palmer, 'A Decade of West Indian Migration to the United States 1962–1972: An Economic Analysis', *Social and Economic Studies*, vol. XXIII, no. 4, 1974, pp. 155–8.
6. Anthony Maingot, *The State of Florida and the Caribbean* (Working Paper no. 2, Caribbean Institute and Study Center for Latin America, Inter American University of Puerto Rico, San Germán, Puerto Rico).
7. *Ibid.*, pp. 15–23.
8. Figures cited by Dr Eric Williams, *Forged from the Love of Liberty: Selected Speeches of Dr Eric Williams* (Port-of-Spain: Longman Caribbean, 1981), p. 442.
9. Pastor, *Caribbean Emigration and US Immigration Policy*, p. 32.
10. International Bank for Reconstruction and Development, International Development Association, *Report of Employment in Trinidad and Tobago*, Report no. 53A – Tr, March 1973, Table 1.10.
11. Pastor, *Caribbean Emigration and US Immigration Policy*, Table 7.
12. Calculated from Alejandro Portes and Rafael Mozo, 'The Political Adaptation Process of Cubans and Other Ethnic Minorities in the US: A Preliminary Analysis', *International Migration Review*, vol. XIX, no. 1, 1985.
13. See, in particular, Gastón A. Fernández, 'The Freedom Flotilla: A Legitimacy Crisis of Cuban Socialism?', *Journal of Inter-American Studies and World Affairs*, vol. XXIV, no. 2, 1982.
14. Carmelo Mesa-Lago, 'The Economy: Caution, Frugality and Resilient Ideology', in Jorge I. Domínguez (ed.), *Cuba: Internal and International Affairs* (Beverley Hills: Sage Publications, 1982), pp. 137–8.
15. Figures calculated from *Petroleum Economist*, January 1985; *Petroleum Economist*, January 1987.
16. Tom Barry, Beth Wood and Deb Preusch, *The Other Side of Paradise: Foreign Control in the Caribbean* (New York: Grove Press, Inc., 1984), Table 1.C.
17. See, in particular, Edward F. Wonder and J. Mark Elliot, 'Caribbean Energy Issues and US Policy in the Caribbean Basin', in James R. Greene and Brent Scowcroft (eds.), *Western Interests and US Policy Options in the Caribbean Basin* (Report of The Atlantic Council's Working Group on the Caribbean Basin) (Boston: Oelgeschlager, Gunn and Main, 1984), pp. 269–304.
18. Figures from *Latin American Regional Reports: Caribbean*, 18 June 1987, RC-87-05.
19. 'Availability of US Oil Supplies from the Caribbean', *Inter-American Economic Affairs*, vol. XXXIX, no. 3, 1985, p. 92 (paraphrasing a report by the US General Accounting Office to Congress on 13 September 1985).
20. *Ibid.*, p. 90.
21. The Soviet Union became the main oil supplier in 1985 providing for three-quarters of Nicaragua's imports of 12,500 b/d. See *Petroleum Economist*, July 1985.
22. For details see *Petroleum Economist*, February 1985.
23. Figures calculated from *Petroleum Economist*, March 1987.
24. Derived from N. A. Graham and K. L. Edwards, *The Caribbean Basin to the Year 2000: Demographic, Economic and Resource-Use Trends in Seventeen Countries* (Boulder, Colo.: Westview Press, 1984), Table 1.6.
25. Calculated from American Metal Market, *Metal Statistics, 1986* (New York: Fairchild Publications, 1986), p. 19.
26. Michael Manley, *Jamaica: Struggle in the Periphery* (London: Third World Media Limited, n.d.), p. 100.
27. Barry *et al.*, *The Other Side of Paradise*, p. 104.
28. *Ibid.*, p. 102. Some 4 to 6 tonnes of bauxite and about 16,000 kilowatt hours of electricity are needed to produce one tonne of aluminium.
29. Calculated from *Metal Statistics, 1986*, p. 116.
30. See Michael Calingaert, 'Minerals and Foreign Policy', *Materials and Society*, vol. IV, no. 3, 1980, pp. 247–52.
31. Graham and Edwards, *The Caribbean Basin to the Year 2000*, pp. 43–7.
32. Calculated from *Metal Statistics, 1986*, p. 49.
33. *Ibid.*, p. 84; p. 135.

34. Figures given in Hans W. Maull, *Raw Materials, Energy and Western Security* (London: Macmillan for the International Institute for Strategic Studies, 1984), p. 269.
35. Graham and Edwards, *The Caribbean Basin to the Year 2000*, p. 86.
36. See, in particular, Robert Levgold, 'The Strategic Implications of the Soviet Union's Non-Fuel Mineral Resources Policy', *Journal of Resource Management and Technology*, no. 12, January 1983.
37. Individual totals are: Puerto Rico 3,600; Guantánamo Bay 2,500; Panama 9,300; other regional Latin America/Caribbean 3,900. Figures from International Institute for Strategic Studies, *The Military Balance, 1986–1987* (London: IISS, 1986), p. 30.
38. See Jack Child, 'Issues for US Policy in the Caribbean Basin in the 1980s: Security', in Greene and Scowcroft (eds.) *Western Interests and US Policy Options in the Caribbean Basin*, pp. 139–85.
39. Figures from IISS, *The Military Balance 1986–1987*, p. 46.
40. These matters are considered in detail by Bruce M. Watson, 'Soviet Involvement in the Caribbean Basin', in P. M. Dunn and B. W. Watson (eds.), *American Intervention in Grenada: The Implications of Operation 'Urgent Fury'* (Boulder, Colo. and London: Westview Press, 1985), pp. 35–44.
41. The US case was set out in detail before the Sub-Committee on Inter-American Affairs, Committee on Foreign Affairs, House of Representatives, 97th Congress, Second Session, 15 June 1982 (Washington DC: US Government Printing Office, 1982).
42. See Jiri Valenta and Virginia Valenta, 'Leninism in Grenada', *Problems of Communism*, vol. xxxiii, July–August 1984, p. 13.
43. Figures from a speech delivered by General Gorman, Chief of United States Southern Command, to the Council of the Americas, 8 May 1984, reproduced in *Vital Speeches of the Day*, vol. l, no. 18, 1984.
44. Joseph Cirincione and Leslie C. Hunter, 'Military Threats, Actual and Potential', in R. S. Leiken (ed.) *Central America: Anatomy of Conflict* (New York: Pergamon Press, 1984), pp. 173–92. Material in this paragraph summarizes their excellent arguments on pp. 184–8.
45. The image of a threat to sea lanes is frequently invoked. Reagan used it to good effect in his celebrated address to the Joint Session of Congress in April 1983 when he stated: 'It is well to remember that in early 1942 a handful of Hitler's submarines sank more tonnage [in the Caribbean] than in all of the Atlantic Ocean. And they did this without a single naval base anywhere in the area', *Vital Speeches of the Day*, vol. xlix, no. 15, 1983.
46. Barry *et al.*, *The Other Side of Paradise*, p. 202.
47. See *Latin American Regional Report: Caribbean*, RC-86-08, October 1986.
48. Lt General Wallace Nutting, Commander-in-Chief, US Southern Command, before the House Appropriations Subcommittee on Supplemental Appropriations, 1982, in 'Can the Panama Canal Be Defended?' *Inter-American Economic Affairs*, vol. xxxvii, no. 2, 1983, p. 92.
49. Valenta and Valenta, 'Leninism in Grenada', p. 23.
50. Fidel Castro, 'Cuba, Grenada and Central America' (interview with *Newsweek* correspondent, December 1983), in M. Taber (ed.), *Fidel Castro Speeches 1984–85: War and Crisis in the Americas* (New York: Pathfinder Press, 1985), p. 5.
51. J. Fred Rippy, *The Caribbean Danger Zone* (New York: G. P. Putnam's Sons, 1940), p. 14.
52. Scott Nearing and Joseph Freeman, *Dollar Diplomacy: A Study in American Imperialism* (New York: Monthly Review Press, reprinted 1966), pp. 279–80.
53. See Barry *et al.*, *The Other Side of Paradise*; Jenny Pearce, *Under the Eagle: US Intervention in Central America and the Caribbean* (London: Latin America Bureau, 1981).
54. Address to the Joint Session of Congress, *Vital Speeches of the Day*, vol. xlix, no. 15, 1983.
55. The point is fully developed in Harold Molineu, 'The Concept of the Caribbean in the Latin American Policy of the United States', *Journal of Inter-American Studies and World Affairs*, vol. xv, no. 3, 1973.
56. See, in particular, Jorge Domínguez, 'US–Cuban Relations in the 1980s: Issues and Policies', *Journal of Inter-American Studies and World Affairs*, vol. xxvii, no. 1, 1985.

3 Challenges to security in Central America and the Caribbean

Peter Calvert

In May 1987 there were 50,000 US troops in Honduras. As in each of the previous three years they were nominally there on an 'exercise'. But these 'exercises' have in fact run end to end since 1983 so that the United States presence in Honduras has become continuous. What is striking about these forces is their number. They were over three times the total size of the Honduran army, and together with it the combined strength mobilized was for the first time roughly equivalent to that of the armed forces of neighbouring Nicaragua. During the same period the United States has also raised, armed and equipped an insurgent force (the 'contras') in Nicaragua and established a formidable naval presence off its coast. The Reagan Administration has claimed that Nicaragua poses a strategic threat to the United States and has made no secret of its desire to overthrow its government. The Nicaraguans, pointing out that the United States is a world superpower, say that they have built up their forces because they fear that it will invade them. Each, therefore, sees the other as the prime challenge to its national security.

So why is Central America seen as a crucial area of instability threatening the security of the United States? Why is the United States in Central America? What is so special about Nicaragua that it can pose a threat to the United States? Can it do so? Or does not the United States, rather, pose a threat to Nicaragua? In trying to give a balanced account, Europeans have both advantages and disadvantages.[1] Like most problems in world politics, the current tension in Central America has deep historic causes, and Europe has played its part in creating them.

The story begins (of all places) in a Portuguese monastery where Christopher Columbus first conceived the idea of reaching India and Cathay by sailing West. Despite his initial success in 'discovering' Cuba and Santo Domingo, on his later voyages he found his way blocked by the

45

coasts of Nicaragua and Honduras and the isthmus of Panama. Only when Balboa (*not* 'Cortez', stout or slender!) crossed the hills of Darien and sighted the Pacific did the Spaniards realize how far they had still to go, and not till they sailed that sea did they come to see the true importance of Panama, the shortest crossing. For three hundred years it remained a vital link in the chain of communication by which Spain ruled its Empire in the Indies, and the treasures of Peru and Bolivia carried on muleback across its winding trails to the fleet that waited to take them first to Havana and then on to Seville.

Scarcely was the Spanish Empire in the Americas consolidated when other European powers began to push into the Caribbean. The British, looking for any opening they could find, settled in the remote island of St Kitts in 1628, only eight years after the Pilgrim Fathers sailed from Southampton for Massachusetts Bay. In the 1640s the British were disputing the Bay Islands off Honduras; in 1655 they took Jamaica and kept it. A century later, in the American War of Independence (1780), Horatio Nelson nearly lost his life on the San Juan River, seeking an alternative crossing of the Isthmus in what is now Nicaragua. The collapse of Spain before Napoleon, however, found Britain too busy to see the Caribbean as an urgent priority. The Central American provinces proclaimed their independence in 1821, and after a brief unity went their separate ways as the states of Guatemala, El Salvador, Honduras, Nicaragua and Costa Rica. Panama remained part of the large South American state of Colombia.[2]

Disunity seemed to be temporary and for some thirty years the separate states enjoyed the luxury of fighting among themselves without any real interference from outside. As Canning had realized, Britain had much to gain from Latin American independence, but it had little interest in the smaller states. (Smallness is relative – Panama is slightly larger than Scotland; Nicaragua noticeably larger than England!) The Royal Navy protected them from the possibility of reconquest from Europe, and Britain's interest was mainly to prevent them falling into other hands. Britain was by far the most important naval power in the region, and in 1850 safeguarded its dominant position by an agreement with the United States (the Clayton–Bulwer Treaty) which prohibited either party from building an inter-oceanic canal. This aroused great interest in the United States in the region of the Isthmus, and amid great hostility Britain relinquished its ambitions in the Bay Islands and the Mosquito (i.e. Miskito) Coast of Nicaragua in the 1860s.[3]

THE ENTRY OF THE US

Thomas Jefferson, by the Louisiana Purchase, was the first American president to make his country a Caribbean power, and in 1823, President Monroe – speaking with the voice of John Quincy Adams – enunciated what was to become the Monroe Doctrine: the US would not interfere with Europe or with existing European colonies in the Americas, but would oppose further colonization or the transfer of colonies between European powers.[4] The expansion of the United States itself went on. Florida was captured in 1816. American settlement in Texas began in 1824, and Texas was annexed in 1845. But the southward expansion of the United States was checked by the growing conflict between North and South, and while ambitions ('Manifest Destiny') were voiced for a giant Republic stretching from the Arctic Ocean to Panama – or, in some of the wilder versions, Cape Horn – expansion turned instead towards the West.

This had immediate and significant consequences for Central America. With the acquisition of California in 1849 and the discovery of gold there a few weeks later Americans flocked to the isthmus as the quickest and safest transit route to the West Coast. Yet neither Commodore Vanderbilt nor the early 'filibusters' (soldiers of fortune) in Nicaragua in the 1850s could rely on US government backing. It was not until after the Civil War that the Grant Administration, wishing to safeguard the sea route to California, actually surveyed both Panama and Nicaragua for the route of a canal, and only after the Spanish–American War (1898), when the United States fought simultaneously in Cuba and the Philippines, that the long-awaited canal came to be seen in Washington as an urgent strategic necessity. Theodore Roosevelt acted, where his predecessors had waited. United States ships stood off Panama to protect a revolution for independence, and the newly independent government of Panama signed away rights over the canal route in exchange for recognition (in 1903).

The acquisition of the Canal Zone, with its American garrison, now became the keystone of American hegemony in the Caribbean region. Britain, which had bowed to the inevitable and agreed to waive its rights, withdrew most of its naval forces almost at once. The United States had annexed Puerto Rico and established a naval base in Cuba, at Guantánamo Bay. To protect these new commitments from the rising powers of Germany and Japan, successive American presidents tried to maintain some semblance of stability among the warring states. The United States landed forces in Cuba in 1906, Nicaragua in 1912, Mexico and the Dominican Republic in 1914, and Haiti in 1915. With this came control over the possibility of a rival Nicaraguan Canal and the lease from Nicaragua of the Corn Islands. All these moves were made with one eye on the First World War and the consequent sudden debility of Europe which led to the consolidation by 1920 of American hegemony in the Caribbean region.

Theodore Roosevelt, the 'realist', justified his intervention on the grounds that, since under the Monroe Doctrine European powers could not be permitted to intervene in the region, the United States must do so instead (the 'Roosevelt Corollary', 1904). Woodrow Wilson, the 'idealist', went further – and is remembered, somewhat unfairly, for his aphorism that the United States had a moral duty to teach the Latin Americans 'to elect good men' (sometimes called 'the Wilson Doctrine', 1914).[5] These two strands of American policy have continued down to our own time, and in recent years the Carter Administration has typified the Wilsonian tradition and the Reagan Administration the Rooseveltian one. Both, however, accept the same notion of US primacy of interest which goes back to the Monroe Doctrine itself. To be fair to Monroe, his intention was only to try to keep the Europeans out of the Americas, and as Latin American resistance to intervention grew in the 1920s the political price of intervention was realized, even by the ruling Republicans. In 1933 the Democrat Franklin D. Roosevelt, despite his past service under Wilson, at once accepted the principle of non-intervention and proclaimed what he called his 'Good Neighbor policy'. US troops were withdrawn from Cuba and Nicaragua. The results were far from happy. Left to their own devices they and the other Central American states were quickly taken over by indigenous military dictators – Jorge Ubico in Guatemala,[6] Maximiliano Hernández Martínez in El Salvador, Fulgencio Batista in Cuba,[7] Rafael Leonidas Trujillo in the Dominican Republic, and Anastasio Somoza Garcia in Nicaragua.[8] In 1936 at Buenos Aires the United States formally gave up any right it had previously claimed to unilateral military intervention in the Americas.

So between 1934 and 1961 the independent countries of the region came to be dominated by their own military forces. After Pearl Harbor, however, those forces were in turn hastily integrated into a system of hemispheric defence. US troops still controlled key points in Cuba, Puerto Rico and the Canal Zone, while in 1940 as a result of the destroyers/bases deal with Britain the United States acquired for the first time an outer ring of defences in the Eastern Caribbean and a foothold in the British colonial possessions.

The creation in 1947 of the Organization of American States (OAS) as a regional organization of the United Nations was intended to leave this system undisturbed, and it did so.[9] The Monroe Doctrine was multi-lateralized by the Havana Declaration of 1940 which, while maintaining that unilateral intervention was wrong, asserted the right of collective intervention, and both points were reaffirmed in the Charter of the OAS. The American states became vigorous and active members of the United Nations, but the United Nations left inter-American affairs to the OAS. This body failed to act when the American government of the day, fearful of communist influence in the region, sponsored a clandestine intervention in Guatemala[10] in 1954 and in Cuba[11] in 1961. It actively backed sanctions against Cuba[12] and the US intervention in the Dominican Republic in 1965, thus retroactively 'legitimating' what had begun as a unilateral intervention.[13] In addition the countries of the Western Hemisphere (excluding Canada) were linked into the American security system through the conclusion of the Inter-American Treaty of Reciprocal Assistance (the Rio Pact).[14] In this way the United States retained, and retains, a dual interest in the region, both military and political. Economically the region is not of major interest.[15] Investments there, though large by local standards, are tiny in comparison with the massive US investment at home or in Europe. Tropical products such as coffee and bananas are grown in many different countries, and until the 1980s no oil had been found in the area between Mexico and Colombia, though in the past few years Guatemala has emerged as a potentially significant producer.

NICARAGUA

In Nicaragua, where the first Somoza was gunned down in 1956, his two sons succeeded him in power, and in 1979 the second of them, Anastasio Somoza Debayle, was overthrown in a massive popular uprising, touched off when his leading political critic, the Conservative newspaper editor, Pedro Joaquín Chamorro, was shot in the street after a particularly sharp criticism of the regime. There was, in truth, plenty to criticize. At their fall the Somoza dynasty owned some 43% of the country's land and held a stranglehold on the economy. The dictator had even embezzled the money raised abroad for the relief of the great Managua earthquake of 1973, and stopped the city from being rebuilt until he and his cronies had bought up the land on which rebuilding was to proceed – hence the work was not done.[16] He kept himself in power with the backing of the National Guard.[17] As the revolutionaries fought their way street by street into Managua in July 1979, the Guard bombed the capital indiscriminately in a last

49

desperate attempt to preserve the regime from which they had benefited so much.[18] Somoza himself could not take refuge in any of the five homes he had provided for himself in the United States alone. In 1980 in the streets of Asunción, Paraguay, his career came to an end when an Argentine revolutionary group blew his armour-plated car open with a bazooka and sprayed its interior with machinegun fire, killing all its occupants.[19]

Nicaragua, occupied from 1912 to 1926 and from 1926 to 1933, has remained of particular interest to the United States since it contains the best potential rival route to Panama – using the waters of the San Juan River and Lake Nicaragua, where the only freshwater sharks in the world still bear witness to its recent maritime origins. In 1913 the Wilson Administration obtained exclusive rights to a Nicaraguan Canal by the Bryan–Chamorro Treaty, but these rights were not used. The younger Somoza was the last to revive the idea when, as the supertankers and warships became too big for the locks of the Panama Canal, he offered to let the United States construct a new canal at sea level in Nicaragua which could take the largest ships going. He was even prepared to let them use nuclear explosives – something which brought a speedy protest from neighbouring Costa Rica.

The Somozas had always expressed an embarrassingly warm friendship for the United States, whether or not it was reciprocated – and all too often it was. Among his other qualifications for the job of President the elder Somoza had worked as a filling-station attendant in the United States and was popular with US military advisers for his ability to swear in idiomatic American. It was they who made him first Commander of the National Guard. Even now the fact that Nicaraguans play baseball and watch American movies testifies to the strength of American cultural penetration. But there was also some armed nationalist resistance to the American occupation, led by General Augusto Sandino. Thirteen months after the Americans left, on 21 January 1934, Sandino was invited to dinner at the Presidential Palace. On his way out he was seized by National Guardsmen, shot, and his body buried under the runway at Managua airport, leaving the way clear for Somoza to take power. Hence though Sandino himself was not a socialist, he became a hero of the left and of the increasingly left-wing anti-Somoza opposition, and it was the Sandinista National Liberation Front (FSLN) who became the dominant force both in the Revolution of 1979 and in the provisional government that followed.[20]

Had the opposition been exclusively left-wing it is very unlikely they could have succeeded. The Somozas had done a very rare thing: they had united all possible opposition groups against them – the Sandinistas, the business community, the Church and the Conservative Party. Panama and Costa Rica gave as much support to the revolution as Cuba. Even then it had been a hard fight and many had died in it. An attempt in the following year to promote a revolution in neighbouring El Salvador failed as much because it lacked the same kind of indigenous support as because the United States, under Ronald Reagan, came to the aid of its government. To explain why and how the United States did so, we have to consider the role of ideology as well as of strategy in the Central America of today.

A SEA OF SPLASHING DOMINOES

The Cuban Revolution, too, had been an indigenous revolt against an outdated dictatorship, but there were few other similarities between Cuba and Nicaragua. American public opinion had been largely with the guerrillas of the Sierra Maestra. Only when they had come to power did a combination of their innate anti-Americanism and the threats and clumsy invasion launched by the Kennedy Administration drive them into the arms of the Soviet Union. By 1979 it was costing the Soviet Union some $8 million a day to prop up the Cuban economy. One Cuba was a valuable diplomatic asset; two would have been an impossible burden. When a socialist government seized power in the tiny island of Grenada the Russians ignored it almost completely.

The Carter Administration had tried to the last to block the Sandinistas' path to power. Once in power, however, it treated them cautiously and with reasonable friendliness, given the great distrust of their intentions. It did not help Carter win the presidential election of 1980. In that campaign Ronald Reagan's warm, friendly smile and evident good humour went far to eradicate the 'mad bomber' image and ease acceptance of the plain sense of his actual words, which were that the United States could 'walk tall', negotiate from strength and 'roll back the frontiers' of Communism.[21] It was and is his belief that 'the Soviet Union underlies all the unrest that is going on'. As he once told the *Wall Street Journal*, he believes that 'If they weren't engaged in this game of dominoes there wouldn't be any hot spots in the world.'[22]

Such ideas do fit with the traditional planks of American foreign policy. The role of leadership within the Hemisphere and wherever it is needed is consistent with Manifest Destiny. Cuba, like the other Western Hemisphere countries, is clearly seen as lying within an American sphere of influence.

Hence Cuba's association with the Soviet Union is an intrusion from outside. Active opposition to such an intrusion is in the tradition of both Monroe itself, as a breach both of the reciprocal non-interference and unilateral no-transfer principles of the Doctrine, and even more in the tradition of the first Roosevelt, since Reagan proposes to use a kind of 'international police power', unilaterally if necessary, to safeguard the 'true' interests of the countries concerned. Foreign 'intrusion', moreover, in turn 'authorizes' the United States to act in other parts of the world (Afghanistan, Libya, the Gulf) to redress the balance.

Hence the newly formed Reagan Administration immediately announced a substantial increase in military aid to the government of El Salvador. What the Administration was seeking to do there was to present the image of 'standing up to' Moscow. It chose El Salvador, which a spokesman termed a 'textbook case' of communist subversion, to do it in, not necessarily because it was of key importance, but because it was already on the agenda and the insurgents were apparently already on the retreat.[23] Hence the risk that the United States might get actively involved was minimal – an important consideration when it was remembered how strongly popular and Congressional feeling had been against any further overseas involvement in 1975–6.[24] Then, reasoning that the arms for the rebels must be coming from somewhere, in the summer of 1981 the Administration turned its attention to Nicaragua.

In Nicaragua, after the devastation of the civil war, the provisional government had from the beginning proclaimed itself a revolutionary government. Its spokesmen were equally clear that the revolution was the Nicaraguan Revolution, not the Russian nor the Cuban. They took over the vast holdings of the Somozas, but kept a mixed economy otherwise. Education was a major priority, but though Cuban volunteers did come to serve with literacy teams the programme itself was devised by Nicaraguans themselves with the advice of experts from Colombia.[25] Radical churchmen, though not the hierarchy, gave it much support, and three priests serving in the government were suspended by the Pope rather than leave it. Somoza had not inspired much respect for elections and so elections were not held, and this was later to prove a mistake. For the United States the broad composition of Nicaragua's provisional government and its clear willingness to talk were at first an impediment to dealing with it publicly as an enemy, and an early election could have given it a constitutional legitimacy. Instead, as was only to emerge much later, the decision was taken in Washington to set up, through the CIA, a force of alleged exiles, to operate from Honduras across the border into Nicaragua itself, and this decision became effective with President Reagan's signature of National Security Decision Directive (NSDD) 17 on 23 November 1981.[26] In Nicaragua they were described as 'counter-revolutionaries' (contras) and the name stuck, though the anodyne name chosen for them was 'the Nicaraguan Democratic Force' (FDN). Publicly, however, US spokesmen said they had nothing to do with them. The United States wanted only to stop Nicaraguan aid to the insurgents in El Salvador. (Even this was based on a misunderstanding, in that the revolution in El Salvador stemmed from indigenous roots,[27] and European reporters repeatedly confirmed that the bulk of their arms were captured, or even bought, from the government's own forces.)

In 1983, frustrated by the stalemate in El Salvador, the Administration seized the opportunity presented by the fall and death of the Grenadan leader, Maurice Bishop, in an internal conflict to demonstrate their resolve by occupying that small Commonwealth country. Yet by the beginning of 1984 the glow of success in Grenada was wearing off, while the contras had still to take control of a single Nicaraguan town. At this point the campaign was stepped up. Co-ordinated from a US warship, naval forces struck on 3 January at the oil facilities at Puerto Sandino. Similar attacks followed on 25 February on the Atlantic port of El Bluff and the Pacific port of Corinto, and mines were laid which damaged four freighters, one of them of Soviet registration. On 5 April the US vetoed a Security Council resolution condemning the mining of the ports, after the President had told a press conference that he would take no steps to stop it. At a press conference he said that the Nicaraguans were 'exporting revolution'. 'We are going to try and inconvenience the government of Nicaragua until they quit that kind of action', he promised.[28]

It was only after the growing US involvement had become plain (26 July) that, under the Boland Amendment, Congress voted to cut off all funding and to declare it illegal, which it remained until late 1986. They were aided by the diplomatic moves of the Sandinistas, who had, rather belatedly, realized the value to their case of holding free elections. The elections were denounced by the White House as 'a sham' before they could even take place. Mediation by the so-called Contadora group of states – so called because the states, Mexico, Panama, Colombia and Venezuela first met to discuss the initiative on the Panamanian island of Contadora – resulted in a draft treaty which was accepted by Nicaragua and three of the other Central American states, who subsequently, under US pressure, decided that it did not go far enough.[29] Meanwhile US officials had publicly proclaimed that they would 'not allow' Nicaragua to acquire 'advanced performance' jet interceptors; threatening to use force to destroy them if they arrived.[30] When the Nicaraguan elections took place in November the US encouraged opposition parties to boycott them, refused to send observers and continued to denounce the elections as false. European reporters, however, confirmed that by Central American standards they had been free and fair, and at least as much so as those conducted the same year under American auspices in El Salvador.

The re-election of Reagan in 1984 brought a major change of personnel in the White House with the appointment of the abrasive Donald Regan as the White House Chief of Staff. The most immediate effect of the change of style in foreign affairs was felt directly through the decision to confront Congress publicly to demand funding for an open US campaign against the government of Nicaragua. The illusion that the contras were Nicaraguan 'freedom fighters' was dropped in favour of a frank admission of US desire to put pressure on the Nicaraguan government.[31]. The presentation of policy, too, was sharpened by the appointment, at Regan's suggestion, of Patrick Buchanan as White House Director of Communications. This gave the President's public statements a revived belligerence, while Presidential spokesman Larry Speakes, well before his departure from the White House in January 1987, succumbed to the fate that has befallen so many of his predecessors – to find himself mouthing words that were self-evidently untrue.

Speakes presented an absurdly over-optimistic picture of the President's erratic health and visibly declining capacity to conduct business ('He's fast returning to championship form'), while behind the scenes in the National Security Council offices strenuous efforts were being made to raise funds for the contras. In the end they hit on the ingenious ruse of channelling the funds from the sales of arms to Iran through a Swiss bank account to certain contra leaders, one of whom, Alfonso Robelo, has latterly stated in public that he received funds from the NSC staffer Colonel Oliver North. The President has admitted that he is totally unable to recall being briefed on the sale of arms to Iran, even though he repeatedly denounced Carter for the same thing and said he would never do it. No doubt the same amnesia prevents him recalling any briefing he may or may not have received with regard to the ultimate destination of the fund. The question remains: does he still remember why the United States is in Central America?

THE REASONS WHY

All countries claim to have 'legitimate security interests' in whatever region they inhabit. The United States is a Caribbean state, and, given its two-ocean seaboard, has historically feared interruption of its sea communications. Today, however, this is of declining importance, and, though missiles from Nicaragua could undoubtedly complicate the task of defending the United States, no one has ever suggested that the Nicaraguans have potentially dangerous missiles or, indeed, that they want them. Similarly the army of Nicaragua is a militia army, effective enough in civil defence (as the defeat of the contras has shown) but of no danger to the United States. This said, there is no doubt that it has been very useful to the military establishment in Washington to play up the 'communist threat'. Reality hardly seems to matter – of all places, tiny Grenada was used by Reagan himself in his 'Star Wars' speech to justify a vastly overinflated military budget.[32]

The more ideological Reaganites in Washington are probably more concerned about the 'danger' Nicaragua presents as an example for others. They genuinely believe that Nicaragua may 'go communist', and topple dominoes from San Salvador to the Rio Grande. They are quite certainly wrong. Historically Central America has been a political layer cake: each country in the stack tending towards the political opposite of its neighbours. For all his bad public image, Carter realized this, and his decision to settle the Canal Zone question with the Panamanians in 1977 (it reverts to Panama finally in the year 2000) was a major diplomatic success, even if it, too, helped lose him re-election.

The Nicaraguans have every reason to fear the invasion against which they have armed these past six years. American policy has been so unpredictable that the Nicaraguans have become jumpy and made mistakes which their long familiarity with the United States might have warned them to avoid. They have lost precious lives and their economy has been blasted by the American blockade and contra attacks on what are euphemistically termed by the Reagan Administration 'economic' (i.e. civilian) targets. Ironically an actual attack by Washington, which would be fiercely resisted, would have the reverse effect to that which its advocates claim. By tying up American troops in a no-win situation in Central America, it would divert at least some of their attention from Europe, Libya, the Gulf and Afghanistan, and the ultimate consequences of that are quite unpredictable.

CRISIS MANAGEMENT OR CRISIS PREVENTION?

Americans generally have come to regard the present problem as one they have to live with in some form, and the existing structure of hemispheric security, a 'free competition but crisis controlled zone', put together in haste in 1945–7, as the only possible security framework for the region. If so, a necessary corollary of it, as far as Central America is concerned, is the maintenance of an armed US presence in the region and arms limitation – until 1969 jet aircraft were totally excluded under a self-denying ordinance of successive US administrations. Both conditions have become increasingly difficult to provide, while the emphasis on crisis management is increasingly being seen as unnecessarily risky for the United States as for the many others affected.

Later a case will be put forward for the United States voluntarily agreeing to a new crisis prevention regime for the region. At this stage it is only necessary to point out that historically there have been several other regimes in the region: a 'competition free zone', as in the 'closed sea' of the Habsburg and (partially) 'open sea' of the Bourbon Empire; a unified independent confederation between 1821 and 1838; and, for the rest of the nineteenth century, a period of 'warring states' not substantially affected by outside intervention (for the expedition of William Walker, however romantic – and it does not seem to have been very pleasant for those most affected – was a failure[33]). Least known (though in this context perhaps of most interest) is the brief period after 1907 when the United States collaborated in establishing the Central American Court, the purpose of which was to create a self-regulating regime capable of settling the warring states' disputes without drawing in outside powers; what we will term here a self-regulating no-go zone.[34] These historical examples are in themselves sufficient to illustrate the range of possibilities available as alternatives to the present situation.

The present situation is predicated on the assumption that the main threat to national security in the region comes from outside the Hemisphere. In strategic terms, it assumes the military challenge will come in the form of an armed invasion. The inter-American system has undoubtedly at times been seen as a true alliance designed to afford mutual protection to the American states against physical attack in the form of a foreign invasion. Before the First World War periodic waves of alarm swept the United States at the prospect of attack by Japan ('the Yellow Peril') or by Germany – the Germans had established a substantial presence in Colombia and Guatemala, and a German sea-captain even landed on the coast of Brazil and proclaimed its annexation – he was speedily disowned by his government. In the late 1930s the 'Rainbow Plans' were drawn up to provide for the various contingencies associated with the prospect of invasion by Nazi Germany.

Since the Second World War, however, the world dominance of the United States has made the prospect of invasion so unlikely as to be hardly worthy of consideration. But it had heightened the sensitivity of governments, both in the United States and in the Latin American states allied to it, to the possibility of internal subversion long before the Cuban Revolution. On the positive side, Castro's switch of alliances established Cuba as the only country that had tried to pursue a policy independently of the United States and had been able to get away with it, thanks to the friendly aid and support of the Soviet Union.

There are today many Latin Americans who know little of the Soviet Union. But they live in countries which fought long and hard to gain their independence both from Spain and from one another. They fear the strength of the United States and they do not see it as the benign force for good in the world that Americans believe is axiomatic. Anti-Americanism is a convenient bogey for both left and right. What began as internal Cuban politics became, in 1962, the occasion for a major confrontation between nuclear superpowers. It is obviously of the highest importance that a situation of this kind does not arise again in an area which one major superpower regards as vital to its continued national security. The resolution of the Central American crisis, therefore, is a very sensitive matter with profound long-term implications for the rest of the world. Much depends on the way in which all parties act to seek an honourable solution to what they perceive as the challenges of others. Hence, before a crisis prevention regime can be agreed, some way has to be found to manage the present crisis of Central America. And that in turn depends on the painstaking rebuilding of mutual confidence through confidence-building measures and the continued desire to seek an outcome through the processes of traditional diplomacy rather than the use of force. The first attempt to do this, the Contadora negotiations, foundered in part because of the sheer complexity of the task.[35] The second, the Arias Plan, the creation of the Central American states themselves, would however have been impossible but for all the work that had gone before.[36]

NOTES

1. Though inevitably dated, the best general historical introduction to Central America remains Franklin D. Parker, *The Central American Republics* (London: OUP for RIIA, 1965).

2. Ralph Lee Woodward, Jr, *Central America: A Nation Divided* (New York: Oxford University Press, 1976).
3. M. W. Williams, *Anglo-American Isthmian Diplomacy, 1815–1915* (Washington, DC: American Historical Association, 1916).
4. Dexter Perkins, *A History of the Monroe Doctrine* (London: Longmans, 1960).
5. Peter Calvert, *The Mexican Revolution, 1910–1914; the diplomacy of Anglo-American Conflict* (Cambridge: Cambridge University Press, 1968), p. 271.
6. Kenneth J. Grieb, *Guatemalan Caudillo: the Regime of Jorge Ubico, Guatemala 1933 to 1944* (Athens, Ohio: Ohio University Press, 1979).
7. Irwin F. Gellman, *Roosevelt and Batista: Good Neighbor Diplomacy in Cuba, 1933–1945* (Albuquerque, NM: University of New Mexico Press, 1973).
8. See *inter alia* Eduardo Crawley, *Dictators Never Die: A Portrait of Nicaragua and the Somoza Dynasty* (London: C. Hurst, 1979).
9. Gordon Connell-Smith, *The Inter-American System* (London: Oxford University Press, for RIIA, 1965); see also Tom J. Farer, *The Future of the Inter-American System* (New York: Praeger, 1979).
10. For a brief account, see Peter Calvert, *Guatemala, a Nation in Turmoil* (Boulder, Colo.: Westview Press, 1985), pp. 79–80. The most comprehensive revisionist study, making extensive use of declassified material, is Stephen Schlesinger and Stephen Kinzer, *Bitter Fruit: The Untold Story of the American Coup in Guatemala* (London: Sinclair Browne, 1982).
11. Haynes Johnson, *The Bay of Pigs: the Invasion of Cuba by Brigade 2506* (London: Hutchinson, 1965).
12. As a first-hand account of the diplomacy involved De Lesseps S. Morrison (ed. and intro. Gerold Frank), *Latin American Mission, An Adventure in Hemisphere Diplomacy* (New York: Simon and Schuster, 1965) is still enlightening.
13. Piero Gleijeses, *The Dominican Crisis: the 1965 Constitutional Revolt and American Intervention* (Baltimore, Md.: Johns Hopkins University Press, 1979).
14. Fred Parkinson, *Latin America, the Cold War and the World powers 1945–73* (Beverly Hills, Cal.: Sage, 1974).
15. But see also *inter alia* Richard R. Fagen (ed.), *Capitalism and the State in U.S.–Latin American Relations* (Stanford, Cal.: Stanford University Press, 1979); and Ransford W. Palmer, *Caribbean dependence on the United States economy* (New York: Praeger, 1979).
16. See Crawley, *Dictators Never Die*.
17. For the earlier history of the National Guard see Richard Millett, *Guardians of the Dynasty; A History of the U.S. Created Guardia Nacional de Nicaragua and the Somoza Family* (New York: Orbis Books, 1977).
18. Bernard Diedrich, *Somoza and the Legacy of U.S. Involvement in Central America* (London: Junction Books, 1982), pp. 284–5; see also pp. 291, 298 for attacks on Masaya.
19. *Ibid.*, pp. 329ff.
20. On the relations between Sandinismo and its precursor see *inter alia* George Black, *Triumph of the People: The Sandinista Revolution in Nicaragua* (London: Zed Press, 1981), pp. 15–27; but cf. Pierre Vayssière *et al.*, *Nicaragua: Les Contradictions du Sandinisme*.
21. Cf. E. Bradford Burns, *At War in Nicaragua: The Reagan Doctrine and the Politics of Nostalgia* (New York: Harper and Row, 1987), p. 23.
22. Robert Dallek, *Ronald Reagan: the Politics of Symbolism* (Cambridge, Mass.: Harvard University Press, 1984) p. 141.
23. Adam M. Garfinkle, 'Salvadorians, Sandinistas and Superpowers', *Orbis*, vol. xv (1981), pp. 11–12.
24. *Ibid.*, pp. 5–6; see also Richard E. Feinberg, *The Intemperate Zone: The Third World Challenge to US Foreign Policy* (New York: W. W. Norton, 1983), pp. 186–7.
25. Valerie Miller, *Between Struggle and Hope: The Nicaraguan Literacy Crusade* (Boulder, Colo.: Westview, 1985).
26. Peter Kornbluh, *Nicaragua: the Price of Intervention* (Washington, DC: Institute for Policy Studies, 1987).
27. See David Browning, *El Salvador – Landscape and Society* (Oxford: Clarendon Press, 1971); Alistair White, *El Salvador* (London: Ernest Benn, 1973); Stephen Webre, *José Napoleón Duarte and the Christian Democratic Party in Salvadoran Politics, 1960–1972* (Baton

58

Rouge, La.: Louisiana State University Press, 1979); James Dunkerley, *The Long War: Dictatorship and Revolution in El Salvador* (London: Verso, 2nd edn, 1985).

28. *The Guardian*, 6 April 1984.
29. For a Latin American view on the problems of a negotiated settlement, see Adolfo Aguilar Zinsser, 'Obstacles to Dialogue and a Negotiated Solution in Latin America' in Jack Child (ed.), *Conflict in Central America: Approaches to Peace and Security* (London: C. Hurst for International Peace Academy, 1986), pp. 55–68.
30. *The Guardian*, 20 August 1984.
31. *The Guardian*, 26 February 1986. Reagan had already publicly stated his approval of US 'volunteers' fighting in Nicaragua; see *The Sunday Times*, 28 October 1984.
32. Text of speech and photograph in *Congressional Quarterly Weekly Report*, 41, no. 12, 16 March 1983, p. 621; *The Guardian*, 24 March 1983, see also 29 March 1983. David Stockman, *The Triumph of Politics*, discusses the effect of 'Star Wars' on the US budget.
33. Contemporary sources for the expedition include Walker's own memoir, *The War in Nicaragua* (Mobile, Ala.: 1960), and W. V. Wells, *Walker's Expedition to Nicaragua; a history of the Central American war* (New York: 1956). See also W. O. Scroggs, *Filibusters and Financiers; the story of William Walker and his associates* (New York: Macmillan, 1916).
34. Dana Gardner Munro, *Intervention and Dollar Diplomacy in the Caribbean 1900–1921* (Princeton, NJ: Princeton University Press, 1964). See also M. O. Hudson, 'The Central American Court of Justice', *American Journal of International Law*, vol. xxvi (1932), pp. 759–86.
35. Jack Child, 'A Confidence-Building Approach to Resolving Central American Conflicts', in Child (ed.), *Conflict in Central America*, pp. 113–31; see also Victor Millán, 'Controlling Conflict in the Caribbean Basin: National Approaches', in Michael A. Morris and Victor Millán (eds.), *Controlling Latin American Conflicts: Ten Approaches* (Boulder, Colo.: Westview Press, 1983).
36. The text of the Arias Plan, with a brief background explanation, can be found in *International Legal Materials*, vol. xxvi, no. 5, September 1987, pp. 1164–74.

4   The 1990s: politics, drugs and migrants

George Philip

If we turn to future developments, in the very long term, the most significant development within the Caribbean and Central America is the relative decline of US power, not only in the Caribbean and Central America, but globally. The main security threats, therefore, are of two kinds. The first is of groups or forces, some or all of whose objectives are in conflict with US policy, resorting to aggression in order to change the status quo. The second is of an exaggerated and disproportionate US reaction to these forces resulting, not simply from the local reality, but from deeper insecurities which stem from difficulties in the United States' international position. These threats could perhaps be resolved by some form of regional consensus based on a realistic view of US power capabilities and US (and other) interests but a more likely outcome is a frustrated (and frustrating) extension of US involvement without a corresponding increase in its ability to control events.

There can be little doubt that, at a global level, US power has declined from the peak it reached just after the Second World War. Such a decline has not been drastic; indeed it has often been exaggerated. However even a modest loss of international prestige and influence from so high a level is hard to take. Public opinion in the United States (as once in Britain) tends naturally to regard the period of its previous ascendancy as normal and any subsequent decline as an unexpected and sinister deviation. Moreover the unquestionably democratic nature of political debate and policy-making in the United States tends to make it more difficult still for policymakers to adapt intelligently to new realities.

Yet new realities obviously have emerged in the region in the past fifteen years. Events such as the Cuban Revolution and the Vietnam War still shape US responses to Central America, and also influence events within the region itself. Even so it is helpful to reconsider just how far and how fast the region has changed in the past fifteen years and how unlikely it is that the next decade will be free of similar shocks and upheavals.

In 1972 most observers of the Central American and Caribbean region would have focused attention on two points. On the one hand, there was the long-term danger apparently posed by the continued prevalence of unpleasant dictatorships or semi-dictatorships and oligarchic and unjust social systems in the Spanish- and French-speaking countries of the region (with the significant exceptions of Costa Rica and Panama). On the other, especially in the English-speaking Caribbean, there were fears that, at least in some countries, the precipitate granting of independence might permit unstable or undesirable forms of government to emerge.

By 1977 the same observers would have had some reason to change their emphasis. Social and political conditions in the Spanish- and French-speaking countries were not significantly improving. New political factors were, however, emerging. President Carter's Washington was making a determined attempt to persuade the worst Central American despotisms to improve their human rights' records and to permit a greater degree of democratization. More ominously, insurgent movements – though still some way from success – were having an increasing impact in Nicaragua, Guatemala and El Salvador.

An additional problem, affecting the whole region, was the onset of slower world growth in the wake of the first oil shock. The damaging effects of this were partially offset by (temporarily) high coffee prices which helped several Central American countries, and by Jamaica's ability to extract significantly better terms from the big aluminium companies. An optimist would have felt confident that the whole region would eventually benefit from the much-promoted New International Economic Order of which Michael Manley, Prime Minister of Jamaica, was an articulate and vigorous advocate. Another positive point was the apparent willingness of oil-rich Venezuela (to be joined later by Mexico) to take an active part in financing economic development and supporting social reform in the region. Some form of alliance seemed in prospect between US liberals in government and the aspirations of at any rate the more reasonable Third World countries. Less optimistically, the observers might have noted the beginnings – in the late 1970s – of a serious international narcotics trade to the US from the Caribbean area.

By 1982 the situation appeared quite different and much more difficult. Right-wing despotisms no longer ruled in Nicaragua or the Dominican Republic, and the situations had also changed – though in a more complicated way – in El Salvador and Guatemala. Different, however, did not mean better. In Central America, the brief moment of hope which followed the Sandinista victory in Nicaragua and the movement of reformist military officers in El Salvador had long since passed. The Sandinista victory had initially been reluctantly accepted in Washington, but relations had deteriorated to near-breaking point as much because of developments in other parts of Central America as of the right-ward shift in US foreign policy. There was a strong rebel military challenge in El Salvador which triggered off right-wing counter-massacres; Washington was trying desperately to rescue the situation by stepping up military aid and seeking to encourage the Salvadorean military to set up democratic institutions. Meanwhile the Guatemalan military was having more success in fighting off its own insurgents and the contra movement was being set up in semi-secrecy in Honduras. The 'Marxist threat', in Washington's definition, appeared to be spreading into the English-speaking Caribbean in the shape of Maurice Bishop's left-wing government in Grenada. To put the matter briefly, Central American politics had polarized, new and threatening political forces had emerged in the region as a whole and the prospect of an alliance between US liberals and Third World moderates had effectively died. There were still those in Washington however, and these included Ronald Reagan, who were confident that a strong and persistent application of American power would 'roll back' communist influence in the region and permit the restoration of an uncomplicated US hegemony. This, the State Department moderates would add, would be a prelude to the socio-economic reforms and political modernization which the area evidently needed.

Meanwhile if the first oil shock had been damaging to the region, the second oil shock and subsequent world recession were incomparably worse. In the short term this deprived the most ambitious Third World leaders of the means to challenge the existing world order. Michael Manley was defeated electorally, the 'oil weapon' was no more and the Mexican authorities, desperate for Washington's support because of their debt crisis, could no longer hope seriously to challenge Washington's aspirations in the region. In 1982 the United States could still hope that aggressive Reaganite policies – pursued by governments such as Seaga's in Jamaica – would eventually restore economic health in the countries which followed them, and would show up Third World socialism as a sham. However the immediate economic reality was bleak. US foreign aid to the region was increasing, but not by enough to compensate for the general economic decline.

Towards the end of 1987 it appears that the Reagan Administration may have lost control over US policy without having achieved its main objectives in Central America. Its one clear-cut victory was its invasion of Grenada (made feasible only because of Hudson Austin's brutal *coup* from within the left shortly beforehand) and it is true that the English-speaking Caribbean does not seem any longer to present an ideological threat to Washington. However the Sandinistas remain in Nicaragua and the contras have so far been an expensive failure. The Salvadorean left remains armed and sporadically effective, although the state in that country is under no immediate threat. The armed left has been seriously set back in Guatemala, and a form of democratic government introduced, but there has not been a sufficient improvement in social conditions to suggest that we have seen the last of large-scale political violence. Finally, and perhaps most important of all, some concerns are now being expressed (which they were not five years ago) about the long-term stability of the Mexican political system. It is important that these are not exaggerated, but neither can they safely be ignored; the problems posed to regional security by Mexico's combination of economic vulnerability, population growth and social modernization may not be as great as the pessimists fear, but they will still be significant.

All of these developments have been overlaid, for the time being at least, by the 'peace process' which has already won a Nobel Prize for President Arias of Costa Rica and has temporarily removed the Reagan Administration from the centre of the diplomatic process in the region. If the peace process works in full, the effects will be far-reaching and, as this brief review of the past fifteen years might indicate, to some extent unpredictable. The most important effect will probably be to ensure that the Sandinistas remain in power in Nicaragua, with the larger Latin American republics replacing the Soviet bloc as that country's main foreign allies. (There should also be a degree of internal liberalization, but the Sandinistas were never totalitarian and they should find it possible to retain control in a moderately free society.)[1] The question of peace negotiations in El Salvador will be more difficult to answer. However, even if these can be resolved satisfactorily, we shall not know for some time what effect the consolidation of Sandinista rule in Nicaragua under more peaceful conditions will have upon the region as a whole. One does not need to be a slavish adherent of the domino theory to suggest that this may be considerable.

One sign that Washington has learned something from previous errors has been its connivance at the expulsion of the Duvalier family from Haiti and its support for the partial opening up of that country's political system. It is too early to say whether Haiti will evolve benignly towards some form of democracy, or, as with events in the Dominican Republic from 1961 to 1965, the creation of a political vacuum will lead to instability, civil war and US invasion.

FUTURE SHOCK: MARXISM

Nothing has so much emphasized the relative decline in US power in the region as the survival of the Castro government in Cuba and the Sandinistas in Nicaragua. As already mentioned, the problem here is not so much that the United States *is* threatened but that it *feels* threatened, as only a relatively declining power challenged in its field of influence can.[2] There are, however, some grounds for hope that US concern about the spread of communism in Central America will be less in the early 1990s than it was in the early 1980s, and that this general reduction of tension will rebound to the benefit of the people in the region. Even so, difficulties are likely to remain and the outlook, even if the Arias plan works in some form, is far from completely benign; if the Arias plan fails, it is still likely that some of the Cold War tensions will be taken out of the situation by the end of the decade.

This conclusion emerges if one asks what factors have contributed to the strengthening of armed Marxism–Leninism in the region, and whether the next few years are likely to see a strengthening or a weakening of them. Obviously the factors involved are complex but the evidence appears to suggest that relatively narrowly defined political factors have, until the late 1980s, carried greater weight than broader socio-economic ones (though these should certainly not be ignored).[3] If land-hunger, objective poverty and ethnic resentment at racial discrimination were the key factors – as some social anthropologists have suggested – then one would expect the greatest radical threat to have come in Guatemala and Southern Mexico (as it indeed has in the Southern Sierra of Peru). In fact the 26 July Movement in Cuba and the Sandinistas both had significantly middle-class support and were by no means peasant upheavals. It would be dangerous to suggest, particularly at a time when social conditions throughout the region are if anything deteriorating, that social deprivation could not be a major radicalizing force, but a political settlement would greatly reduce its impact. A political analysis would suggest that the best antidote to Marxism–Leninism is established democracy; this is not just a matter of liberal faith as there is abundant historical evidence that revolutions are directed against autocrats rather than democrats. However, as President Carter found to his cost, attempts to nudge autocracies in the direction of democracy risk creating precisely the short-term instability and danger which it should be the long-term objective of US policy to avoid.[4] Moreover, as Salvador's Duarte is currently proving, sustaining a democracy can be an expensive proposition.

In Central America democracy has to some extent replaced autocracy as the norm, although Panama is an important exception. In a sense, however, the horse has already bolted. The problem of US policy towards Nicaragua and Cuba is of dealing with existing Marxist–Leninist systems rather than preventing them. Thus far the rulers of these countries have not been prevailed upon by Washington either by fear or favour to alter their chosen policies to any significant degree.[5] The ability of any US policy to reduce the potential unpredictability of these states will be very limited; nevertheless unless some wild miscalculations are made Washington here confronts a nuisance rather than a threat.

Nor is there any reason to believe that the Soviet Union is likely to want to raise the stakes within Central America. What Havana – and therefore, to some extent, Moscow – could not afford to see was a clear-cut Sandinista defeat at the hands of the contras. A semi-compromise, based on maintaining the status quo in Central America, may in fact suit the Soviet Union rather well – enabling them to improve relations with the United States and concentrate their political efforts closer to home without suffering either loss of face or serious disaffection from Cuba. There can be no doubt that helping Central American revolutionaries is currently a very low priority for Gorbachev and it is likely to stay that way.

However, Soviet policy has to manoeuvre within strict limits. It is hard to see how Moscow could, or would ever want, to abandon Cuba. Yet if Cuba remains, as it has been, financially dependent but substantially independent in foreign policy terms, then the Nicaraguan regime will remain underpinned by at least one close foreign ally. The Soviet Union will find it difficult if not impossible to prevent the Cubans from aiding Nicaragua. The Soviets undoubtedly want to push the Sandinistas more in the direction of alliance with the major Latin American republics and, to the extent to which this is feasible, with West European social democracy. This is an important diplomatic game but it does have a corollary which Washington may find less reassuring. The Soviet Union cannot and may not even want to control the activities of local Marxist governments and Marxist movements.

What this means is that, whereas the Soviet Union will probably not

65

deliberately aggravate problems which the United States faces in Central America (although the Cubans may still try to do so), they are unlikely to be able (or want) to damp them down very much either. Washington must still face the fact that the events of 1979 and 1980 enabled insurgency movements, particularly in El Salvador, to put down roots which will not easily be eradicated.[6] The democratic reform strategy in El Salvador is alive but not well, and the problems in that country may not be conclusively solved even by a successful political settlement in Central America. If some form of power-sharing could be agreed between the government and the insurgents, then a comprehensive settlement might look promising (at least on paper). However one would have to be a supreme optimist to have very much confidence in such an outcome. Experience of other democratic countries which tried to negotiate peace settlements with entrenched guerrilla movements (e.g. Colombia) has not been encouraging, and conditions in El Salvador are particularly difficult. There is an entrenched right-wing. Duarte is no longer a popular president and some of the hard-line Marxists within the Salvadorean insurgency are very hard indeed. It is therefore difficult to see how Duarte (or his eventual successor) could find it possible to offer the insurgents anything which they might find it worthwhile to accept.

What is more likely, therefore, is that the Salvadorean insurgents will adopt a low profile until the pressure is taken off the Sandinistas. Some of the insurgents may accept an amnesty and reintegration into politics. El Salvador would then still have an insurgency which Washington would need to help to contain even after other parts of Central America (Nicaragua, Honduras, possibly Guatemala) were declared 'at peace'. Inevitably Washington would find this frustrating and some hard-liners within the US would then want to raise the stakes by putting renewed pressure on Nicaragua. It might be too pessimistic to see history repeating itself exactly, but El Salvador is likely to prove a difficult area for the United States for some years yet.

A successful peace process would also open broader economic and financial questions. Even if socio-economic factors were not paramount in creating the revolutionary situation in Central America, they are surely of considerable account. A sustained reduction of social tension throughout the region would have to involve a combination of economic growth and social reform. If the Central American democracies, after the peace process were concluded, were allowed to become dependent once more on international markets and national oligarchs, conflict (if not necessarily revolution) would still threaten. One could only be confident in predicting that this would not happen if the United States retained its interest in the area but acted with a degree of enlightenment which it has showed at best sporadically up to now. Washington's past record suggests that it is more likely, once immediate security concerns are relieved, to resort to a policy of 'benign neglect'.

However if the United States, and its Latin American allies, did retain a reform-and-development commitment to Central America the domino effect might work in reverse. A Sandinista government without armed enemies would be a government with little foreign aid, and with a serious problem of demobilization. It would need money and would probably have to come to some arrangement with private capital to avoid major disaster (just as some allegedly Marxist–Leninist systems in Africa have done). Even dedicated Sandinistas might then be seduced and softened by the prospect of affluence. Revolutionary purists would be disappointed and security concerns relieved.

FUTURE SHOCK: NARCOTICS

In the long run, the developed democracies may have as much to fear from Caribbean pirates as from Central American Marxists. The risk of piracy stems from the twin problems of drug traffic and drug addiction. There may be something to be said in the long term for some kind of regulation-cum-legalization of at least the softer drugs, which would perhaps reduce some of the secondary problems of addiction. In the foreseeable future, however, this is not really an option. We are faced instead with a particularly high-risk game of 'cops and robbers' which involves, but certainly is not confined to, the Caribbean and Central America.

The main security implications of the narcotics trade (from the point of view of the region) can be set out easily enough. Narcotics generates very big money; drug smugglers may now be earning as much as the OPEC cartel. Although the Colombian 'godfathers' are some way ahead of the competition, any drugs trade at all in a small and relatively poor country will create a class of local criminals with real economic power. The simplest way for economic power to convert itself into political power is straightforward corruption, although more violent forms of illegality are certainly not excluded. Not all Caribbean politicians are dishonest or easily intimidated, but the proliferation of national sovereignty makes it all but certain that some governments will be corruptible at some time. Moreover the doctrine of national sovereignty makes international control of the drugs trade very difficult; Britain, France and the Netherlands can still exert some control over their direct dependencies but this control has its limits.

There are also some secondary problems. Drug traffickers require banks, preferably away from the operation of anti-drug laws in the consumer countries and away from the immediate trade itself. They may also engage in secondary economic activities such as non-drug smuggling and, under some circumstances, even legitimate business enterprise.

One security concern springing from all of this is ordinary crime. Drug barons are not known for the peaceful way in which they handle disputes among themselves, nor for the gentle way in which they treat unsympathetic authorities. The narcotics trade itself creates an addiction rate and addicts, desperate to finance a habit which they are unable to afford, are often a source of secondary crime.

More important in the long run, however, may be the political issues. At present these are still of limited consequence, but various permutations of narcotic politics are likely to come into the open during the next decade. One can easily think of three different patterns of narcopolitics.

In the first, which is now the most common, the authorities declare themselves wholly hostile to the narcotics trade; this, unaccountably, continues to flourish and police round-ups fail to arrest major suspects. In practice there is a broad implicit consensus between government and narco-plutocrats. The latter understand that the government will be formally hostile to the drugs traffic and will mount the occasional police action to reassure foreign governments (mainly Washington) that their intentions are serious. The government will understand that policing has its limits; drug money finds its way into the security services and into the local economy, and arrests are few and far between. Imperceptibly, however, the political system becomes increasingly 'hooked' on drug money, and large areas pass out of the control of the central government.

The second permutation occurs when governments take major and genuine steps to stamp out the drugs trade. At the minimum there is major political scandal; some of those implicated in the trade will be found to be Cabinet ministers, police chiefs etc. At the maximum there is violence as threatened *mafiosi* seek to assassinate or intimidate law enforcement officials. Since the impetus to a crackdown on the trade comes mainly from abroad (i.e. Washington), there is the danger of some anti-foreign feeling. The most likely medium-term outcome, however, is that the traffic will move to another area, possibly just until the initial hue and cry dies down. There are already signs that drug traffickers have sufficient power to establish bases on smaller outlying islands and restore the age of piracy.

68

The third permutation is the most sinister and most interesting. This occurs when the drugs trade takes effective control of a government which comes under the scrutiny of the international press. Washington, in particular, comes under pressure to take some form of action, not least from police and judicial authorities within the United States. However attempts to pressure (and *a fortiori* remove) the government of an independent country (even if it is no more than a Caribbean island) are difficult and can be counter-productive. If such attempts are made and do not work we may yet see, by the mid-1990s, forcible efforts by Washington to limit the doctrine of international sovereignty in as far as it is used to protect drug traffickers.

FUTURE SHOCK: POVERTY

There is no direct or simple relationship between poverty and political violence or revolution. Still, it would be hard to deny that such a relationship does often exist and foolhardy to discuss security issues without considering their socio-economic context. Taken as a whole, the Caribbean and Central American countries are experiencing the classic 'modernization' problems (high birth rate, falling death rate, rapid urbanization etc.) at a time when, largely because of unfavourable world conditions, there is not the economic growth which may help resolve them.

It would be rash to predict an immediate upturn in the main Caribbean economies; dogmatic to predict that an upturn can never occur. The Caribbean Basin Initiative (CBI), for all of its faults, has delivered some new foreign investment in the region, although the effect of this has been more than offset, so far, by post-recession shakeout in activities such as oil refining. Even if the closer integration with the US economy which the CBI promises does have some undesirable side-effects, these are bound to seem minor in comparison to the benefits that increased economic growth might bring. However an impending US recession, and a threatened revival of protectionism, may limit the possibilities of even dependent development unless further steps are taken by Washington which will have the inevitable effect of making the region still more dependent on the US economy.

In Central America itself, economic prospects are themselves heavily dependent on the possibility of a political settlement to the regional conflicts. However a political settlement must be followed by economic recovery if the societies in question are to transcend the familiar vicious circle of economic decline, popular unrest and repression. To the extent that repression encourages armed subversion there is the danger of a return to a pre-revolutionary situation. This time round, however, the democratic governments are under intense pressure to accede to some popular demands rather than repressing them. This can only happen if US aid is provided to cover the cost. Specific US support for democratic governments in Central America is indicated above all by the blank cheque; the indications are that US governments will still be signing these in the middle 1990s.

One traditional response to hard times is migration, sometimes legal but more often not. It is still too early to say how the Simpson–Rodino law will influence patterns of migration to the US but early developments are ominous. There are estimated to be, for example, at least 300,000 Salvadoreans working illegally in the United States; many of these may continue to evade capture, but large-scale repatriation would create horrendous problems for the political authorities. Apart from the question of what to do with the returnees themselves, there is also the fact that dollar remittances are, along with foreign aid, the main sources of hard currency available to Salvadoreans.

CONCLUSION

It is not unusual for a great power to be faced with difficult and troublesome neighbours, and to make serious mistakes in trying to deal with them. The Soviets in Afghanistan, the British in Ireland, the French in North Africa come immediately to mind as examples; as with the last two of these cases, there is also a post-imperial element in the US predicament. Washington would once simply have sent in the marines. However, between 1941 and 1959 at any rate, the United States was fortunate that its ability to pursue global political objectives was not embarrassed, let alone compromised, by more local difficulties. The Cuban Revolution was a major trauma but one which was soon afterwards overtaken by the scale of the US commitment to Vietnam. The Vietnam defeat, and frustrations stemming from setbacks in other parts of the world encouraged the Republican right (and particularly the Reagan Administration) to see the later Central American conflict as one which they could simply 'win', essentially by engineering the overthrow of the Sandinistas without a direct commitment of US troops. This gamble has apparently failed but not as disastrously as the United States failed in Vietnam. The United States remains a major influence in the region (although its influence is not what it was) and the generalized triumph of insurgency in Central America – both hoped for and feared in 1980 – now seems a remote prospect. Equally remote however is the prospect of Washington being able to declare that it has 'won' and turning its attention to other areas. On the contrary, for US policymakers, Central America and the Caribbean is here to stay.

One positive feature of this change is that we may see a reduction in the 'born again' qualities of US policy which have so infuriated even well-intentioned critics (i.e., a refusal by US policymakers to consider past history or to regard it as important, coupled with a belief that deep structural problems can simply be 'solved' overnight by a change in US policy) and also contributed to subsequent disillusionment as it becomes clear that the world is not as simple as it once looked. Since informed US opinion (in contrast to its attitude towards Vietnam) is not willing to consider withdrawal from the area even as an option, Washington is likely to accumulate experience and, one hopes, understanding as it tackles the continuing problems in a less triumphalist spirit. A less positive feature is that there is nothing in prospect which will reverse the slow and perhaps inevitable trend for the United States (like the Soviet Union) to relate its foreign policy more to 'backyard' or sphere-of-influence concerns and less to the more universal global commitments which it sought and felt able to sustain during the 1945–75 period.

NOTES

1. For a collection of recent articles on Nicaragua see J. Valenti and Esperanza Durán (eds.), *Conflict in Nicaragua* (London: Allen and Unwin, 1987).
2. Laurence A. Whitehead, 'Explaining Washington's Central American Policies', *Journal of Latin American Studies*, vol. xv, pt 2, November 1983.
3. For a different emphasis see W. LeFeber, *Inevitable Revolutions: The United States in Central America* (New York: W. W. Norton, expanded edn, 1984).
4. This is at least a partial rebuttal of the critique of President Carter's foreign policy in Jeane Kirkpatrick's notorious 'Dictators and Double Standards' in *Commentary*, 68, November 1979. There may come a point when authoritarian regimes can no longer sustain themselves (or be sustained) in power and when a 'respectable' opposition does not exist either. Should Washington then send in the Marines, or take a chance with the rebels?
5. Nevertheless Washington has done business with revolutionary regimes which it did not initially welcome. See Cole Blasier, *The Hovering Giant: US Responses to Revolutionary Change in Latin America* (Pittsburgh, Pa.: Pittsburgh University Press, 1976). Recently declassified US government documents also show that there was more contact between Washington and Havana during the 1960s than published sources have indicated.
6. For an account of the events leading up to the conflict see James Dunkerley, *The Long War: Dictatorship and Revolution in El Salvador* (London: Verso, 2nd edn, 1985).

Part II: The problem at the state level

5   Cuba: a client state

Alistair Hennessy

A REVOLUTIONARY STATE

No one outside Cuba foresaw the Revolution or had the remotest idea of the influence which this hitherto despised and neglected island would exert on world affairs. Not even that great prophet Simon Bolívar, seen by Cubans as their precursor, anticipated this future. For him Panama would be the centre of the world and, with its strategic and geographical position, it was to become so – at least for the United States – but for Panama itself its global impact is limited to flags of convenience. What brought Cuba from the backwaters of colonial obscurity was the brutal crop of sugar which was to make it the richest colony for its size possessed by any colonial power, richer and more advanced than Spain itself, which could only bequeath to its colony a war of independence which was to make Cuba unique among Spain's ex-possessions by developing a sense of nationality before the achievement of statehood. Sugar wealth created a vibrant culture and an intelligentsia whose marginalization in the frustrated years of pseudo-independence was to give added strength to a sense of redemptive nationalism. With hindsight it can now be seen how the unique trajectory of Cuban history inculcated a belief in a messianic destiny deriving from the idea of a permanent revolution with its origins as far back as the outbreak of the war of independence in 1868.

A characteristic shared by all nations which have experienced successful revolutions is the tendency to couch their policies in terms of moral and philosophical absolutes and to proselytize with missionary zeal among the less fortunate. This is something at least which the Russians, Americans and Cubans have in common and, had the Americans known their Cuban history better or had they not assumed Cubans wished to be Americans, they might have avoided the mistake of believing them to have no minds of their own and to be simply sounding-boards for the ideas of others.[1]

A SMALL STATE WITH GLOBAL INFLUENCE

To describe the Cuban Revolution and Fidel Castro's role in it as unique is obvious and banal, and yet familiarity with the obvious may prevent us from appreciating just how unique a phenomenon it has been. To find comparable examples of small states exercising influence on a global scale we would have to go back to the sixteenth- and seventeenth-century sea-borne empires of Portugal and the United Provinces, and to the eighteenth century of Britain – states which owed their position and influence to the mastery of the technology of sea power. The rise of continental super-powers brought to an end the old European world empires and to the small state able to be an autonomous actor on a global scale.

There are, however, a number of courses open today to small powers with great power ambitions. There is the possibility of exploiting new productive processes based on high technology – the Japanese way – or of utilizing the technology of miniaturized terror which can put all powers, great and small, at risk – the Libyan way. A third possibility is to elaborate ideologies of sublimation, and to compensate for lack of material power by seeking to become a moral or cultural force – the post-imperial alternative open to Britain and France. There is, finally, the possibility of exploiting a favoured geographical and strategic location in order to exert leverage on a superpower and so gain concessions which will facilitate an otherwise impossible course of action. The case of Cuba may well be the first and last example of a small power able to pursue this alternative and through it to exert an influence out of all proportion to its size.[2] Leverage to gain concessions is one thing; it is quite another to take advantage of these concessions to initiate an autonomous foreign policy and to aspire to and succeed in playing a global role.

Cuba's leverage on the Soviet Union derived from its proximity to the United States and its potential as an irritant in a part of the world where Soviet policy had hitherto been remarkably unassertive and low-key. The nature of the relationship between Cuba and the Soviet Union is unique among the Soviet Union's allies, as geographical distance meant that it could not be subjected to the type of pressure exerted on Czechoslovakia, Poland or Hungary. By representing and articulating the needs and aspirations of the Third World, Cuba also enjoys a privileged position through enabling the Soviet Union to benefit from Castro's insights and contacts as well as from his charisma. It is a complementary not a subordinate relationship.

If a theme may be discerned in the labyrinth of Cuba's foreign policy it is

Fidel Castro's ambition to make Havana the centre of the Third World – an aspiration symbolized by the Tricontinental Conference of 1966 – and by doing so to divert the thrust of world politics away from East–West conflict to a North–South confrontation and so revolutionize the terms of international discourse.

The Tricontinental might have developed into a Third Bloc but the history of international affairs is littered with the wrecks of third parties and middle positions. However much the Cubans might have wished to repudiate both superpowers in the interests of the solidarity of small, poor nations, they were prisoners of their Revolution. The third position proved impracticable because of Cuba's lack of economic resources and resultant dependence on Soviet support, and the wide disparities, ideological and otherwise, of Third World nations, but the crucial factor was the inability to devise a form of economic co-operation between Third World nations which were in competition with each other for the trade of the First World.

The failures of the 1960s led to a fundamental reformulation of Cuban aspirations which was to culminate in Castro's attempt to swing the Non-Aligned Movement behind the Soviet bloc – a policy which would seem to have been implicit since 1972 when Cuba was admitted as the first non-European state into the Council for Mutual Economic Assistance (CMEA).[3] This constituted a watershed in Cuban–Soviet relations as, together with agreements signed then, it was to provide the economic security to enable Cuba to pursue an active and successful forward policy markedly distinct from the essentially defensive policy of the 1960s.

EXPORTING THE REVOLUTION

It may seem paradoxical to suggest that Cuban policy in the 1960s was defensive when it was distinguished by the attempt to export revolution to the rest of Latin America by guerrilla activity. Yet the *via armada* stemmed from a defensive response to the isolation of the US blockade as much as from the view that certain countries – Venezuela, Guatemala, Peru and Bolivia – were ripe for revolution. Cuban miscalculation of the revolutionary potential of Latin America and the subsequent unsuccessful guerrilla campaigns, culminating in Guevara's death in Bolivia in 1967, revealed how much they were out of touch with Latin American realities and how bemused they were with their own revolutionary tradition and the exportability of their model of revolution. The *via armada* was also in direct contradiction to the Russians' own distrust of Cuban 'voluntarism' which ran counter to their long-established policy of building alliances through orthodox communist parties working in co-operation with other progress-ive forces (and in Castro's view being corrupted by them in the process). But more important from the Soviet standpoint was Moscow's wish to avoid a confrontation with the United States at a time when they were distracted by the Sino-Soviet conflict and the threat on their Asian frontier. Such grudging support as Moscow might give to particular guerrilla activities was to dissuade the Cubans from being seduced by the Chinese, although with hindsight, there seems to have been little chance of that happening.[4]

Nevertheless, the Soviet Union owes a considerable debt to the Cubans for their support in the competition with China for influence in the Third World not only in Latin America but later, and more seriously, in Africa. In these days of post-Mao revisionism we tend to forget how large the Sino-Soviet conflict loomed in the 1960s and 1970s.

To practical considerations of survival must be added strong ideological motives which were another factor impelling Cuba into a forward policy in Latin America. The questions of whether the break with the United States was inevitable and who was responsible are highly controversial and likely to remain so. What is important to recognize is the nationalist thrust behind the Revolution and that this has been expressed in universalist and internationalist terms. The highly developed sense of nationalism gener-ated by the war of independence was exemplified in the writings and influence of José Martí. Without recognizing the extent of his influence on subsequent Cuban thinkers and politicians, and especially Castro, it is difficult to appreciate the imperatives sustaining the momentum of the revolutionary process. Ideology has played as large a part in the Cuban as in the Russian Revolution.

Martí was a Latin American and not a purely Cuban figure. Indeed, through a life spent in exile in Latin America and the United States he was better known there in his lifetime than in Cuba.[5] The insistence on Martí's legacy in the Revolution's ideology is therefore a way of generalizing the revolutionary experience to the rest of Latin America. Martí's perceptive-ness in predicting the United States' domination of Latin America imparts an anti-imperialist and anti-American character (with all its ambiva-lences) to Cuban nationalist ideology. Finally, and I would argue the most important legacy, though most under-estimated by foreigners, has been the moral categories of his thought. However much Castro declares himself a Marxist–Leninist, Martí's moralism always intrudes and this is a guarantee of his heterodoxy and originality as well as of his unpredictability.

Lacking a pre-colonial past to mythologize, as the Mexicans have done, and exposed to a century and a half of influences from the United States, Cuban nationalism has often been expressed in negative opposition, first to Spain and what it represents and latterly to the United States. Martí's thought, therefore, with its redemptive overtones, became the focus for a positive nationalist credo. With such a highly developed nationalist spirit it is imposssible to avoid the problem of the influence of political culture in assessing the relationship between Cuba and the Soviet Union separated by a chasm of cultural differences. Much has been written about Castro's *caudillo* qualities and his charisma and both have been explained in terms of Cuban political culture.[6] In a very real sense it has been Castro's revolution and the slow process of institutionalization is evidence of the great personal influence he has exercised even up to the present. But this must raise doubts about the viability of the regime when Castro ceases to be leader and the possible risks involved for the Soviets should a succession crisis encourage an attempt at destabilization from either outside or within. This is why the problem of the Party and its role assumes a disproportionate importance.

The Cuban Revolution is unique in being the only case where an existing communist party has been absorbed by, rather than dominating, the revolutionary process. The tensions between Cuba and the Soviet Union in the 1960s were not only due to differences in foreign policy but also to domestic tensions between the established communist Party (PSP) and the *fidelistas*. The PSP had played an unheroic role in the struggle against Batista, only joining Castro once it was clear that the 'bourgeois putschists' were winning. Their members could be distinguished from the *fidelistas* by the bureaucratic cautiousness of age. Nevertheless, they had their uses: they had a faithful following among those unionists who admired their dedication; their network of cells was intact so they could help to fill the administrative vacuum left by the largely middle-class emigration; and they were crucially important in two respects – as links to Moscow and as instructors in the EIRs (Schools of Revolutionary Instruction) which were established to give some ideological backbone to the Revolution.

When Castro publicly announced himself to be a Marxist–Leninist, victory seemed to be theirs, but it was illusory and the PSP, or certain members of it, overreached themselves by attempting to gain control of the new grass-roots party (the creation of which was one of the most original features of the Revolution). The purge of Aníbal Escalante in 1962 left no doubt as to who was in control. There was little that the Soviets could do with an ally in which they had made such a substantial economic and political investment. Castro's growing popularity in the Third World, reaching a climax in the Tricontinental Conference of 1966, as well as the threat from growing Chinese influences, left the Soviets no option but to accept the purge of their most loyal, and subservient, supporters in the PSP and to accept the *fait accompli* of a new party in which the 'old' communists would be in a permanent minority.

Meanwhile, in the wider world, the *via armada* was proving to be counterproductive by 'revolutionizing the counter revolution' in Debray's phrase, sealing off Latin America from further Cuban incursions. But failure was offset by moral triumphs. Throughout Latin America the left had been galvanized, and, if no longer a model, Cuba remained an example of successful defiance of the United States from which the Soviets, in spite of their opposition to the Cuban line, were major beneficiaries. Cuba was a beacon for the Third World and Havana's moral ascendancy was crowned by the Tricontinental. This put the seal on Cuba's credentials as the heir of the Bandung tradition and marks the opening of the attempt to pre-empt Third World leadership.

Although Cuba had joined the Non-Aligned Movement in 1961 it was highly critical of many of its assumptions, in particular of its attitude towards the Soviet Union as an imperialist power. By 1970, however, Cuba became more forthright in its pro-Soviet attitude when Raúl Roa, at the Lusaka Conference, expressed what was to develop later into the radical critique of the 'two imperialisms' thesis. This thesis was favoured by many non-aligned nations who feared Soviet imperialism as much as that of the United States, but Roa argued that

The real division of the world is between exploited and exploiter countries: between oppressed and oppressor countries ... Let us not place the developed socialist countries and the developed capitalist countries under the same flag. The socialist countries are the strongest support and the most pugnacious force of the anti-imperialist front, we cannot leave them out or isolate them if we expect to engage in a battle with the imperialist countries headed by the United States.[7]

However, the Cubans could not pursue this line, distracted as they were by the death of Guevara, and the acknowledged failure of the *via armada* and the Cuban model. This came ironically at the very moment when the theoretical justification of that model, Régis Debray's *Revolution in the Revolution*, was published in Havana.[8]

A turning point was 1967. Heroic achievement abroad was to be succeeded by heroic achievement at home in the battle to secure the ten million ton sugar harvest in 1970. The failure of that too finally put the seal on Cuban dependence on the Soviet Union, hastening the process of domestic sovietization and of economic integration into the Soviet bloc. Cuba's ability to pursue a successful revolutionary policy abroad was minimal precisely when the impact and reputation of the Revolution was at its greatest but when it was also most at variance with Soviet policy at home and abroad. When Cuba was in a position to make another bid for leadership of the Third World in the late 1970s, capitalizing on its remarkably successful intervention in Angola, circumstances had changed. Cuba was then to be even more heavily dependent, both economically and ideologically, on the Soviet Union, but paradoxically at the same time this dependence enabled it to pursue a successful global policy which had been impossible a decade previously.

Cuban radicalism in the 1960s had not only isolated Cuba from Latin America but had forced it into closer dependence on the Soviet Union and to the recognition that Salvador Allende's electoral victory in Chile in 1970 had vindicated the Soviet Union's more cautious policy. The next year Castro was able to break out of his Latin American isolation for the first time in eleven years with visits to Chile, Peru and Ecuador, in the course of which he admitted publicly that there were alternatives to the *via armada*. This presaged a shift in the attitudes of Cuba towards Latin America and vice versa. Cuba was now admitted to a number of Latin American organizations, the most important of which was the Latin American Economic System (SELA) founded in 1975 to present a united economic front against the United States. At the same time as this rapprochement reflected a convergence of Soviet and Cuban foreign policies, so domestically the process of industrialization was quickening, culminating in the First Congress of the Cuban Communist Party in 1975.

By 1975 Cuba had acquired a new confidence and sense of security stemming from the generous economic agreements signed in 1972, by a buoyant market for sugar and by diplomatic recognition by both Latin American and Caribbean countries. But perhaps the most striking conse-quence of international acceptance was a mellower attitude towards East–West détente which the Cubans had always feared and distrusted since the Missile Crisis had left Castro with a deep sense of betrayal. The spirit of détente extended to US–Cuban relations in a series of secret meetings in 1974–5, but any hope of rapprochement collapsed when Cuba intervened in Angola.[9]

INTERVENTION IN ANGOLA AND ETHIOPIA

Intervention in Angola provides the clearest case of Cuban global and Third World policy overriding the more mundane consideration of normalizing relations with the United States. It is invariably argued in Cuba and widely agreed by regional specialists that the decision to intervene was a Cuban one. This is consonant with Cuban views of international solidarity, and the original sea and airlift, which was crucial in securing the independence of Angola in the face of South African invasion, was a Cuban operation.[10] However both the effectiveness of the troops once they had arrived, and their continued presence in Angola, depended on close co-ordination with Soviet logistical support.

Cuban interest in Africa was not new. There had been a tradition of involvement going back to Algeria in 1962 (an important contact because of Algeria's position in the Non-Aligned Movement) and, more particularly, in Angola. Castro had first met Agostinho Neto, the Marxist leader of the Popular Movement for the Liberation of Angola (MPLA), at the Tricontinental Conference after which training started for MPLA officers in guerrilla tactics. Because of Soviet doubts about supporting Neto the Cubans were the MPLA's most reliable friends.

In 1978 there was to be a further Cuban intervention; this time in Ethiopia in the war against Somalia. But the two cases were very different. In the latter, Cuban troops were directly under the control of Soviet officers and the description 'the Gurkhas of the Russian Empire' may be applicable in this case. Once Somalia had been defeated, largely due to the Cubans, and after the failure of Castro's mediation efforts, the campaign against the Eritrean liberation movement caused the Cubans some heart-searching which led to a gradual withdrawal.

Whatever the initial impetus to intervene it was compatible with Soviet aims and underlined the usefulness to them of Cuban involvement in a continent where their policy had until then been comparatively ineffective. A major gain for the Soviet Union was that Cuban intervention finally swung the balance away from the Chinese in the Sino-Soviet struggle for influence in Africa.

What have the Cubans gained? Foremost has been the opportunity to turn declarations of international solidarity into action and in doing so to seize the initiative in defending the 'last great cause' – to borrow a phrase used of the Spanish Civil War – where issues, however complex, may be reduced to a stark confrontation between good and evil. The tangible spin-off from the credit accruing to Cuba's action was to facilitate the election of

Castro as chairman of the Non-Aligned Movement in 1979, when he used his term of office to try and swing the movement behind the Soviet bloc – an ambition which was to be wrecked by the Soviet intervention in Afghanistan.

There have been other more mundane but no less tangible gains: the combat experience afforded to field troops; the opportunity for civilians to participate in extensive aid projects (and perhaps to ease under-employment of technicians in Cuba); the chance for a post-revolutionary generation to recapture the élan of the early days of the Revolution; the opportunity to compare the gains of the Revolution at home with the underdevelopment of colonial exploitation; the opportunity to capitalize on Cuba's African heritage; the possibility of new sources of raw materials, especially oil, which would relieve pressure on the Soviet economy and reduce transport costs; and finally it has served to increase Cuba's leverage on the Soviet Union. Whether the African involvement, with no end in sight and a deteriorating economy at home, has resolved intra-elite rivalry between *fidelistas*, technocrats and the military, or exacerbated them, is a moot point.[11]

There is, finally, a range of issues related to even wider geopolitical considerations. South Africa is not only an arena of moral conflict but is also an Achilles heel of the West's economy, and this, coupled with its strategic control of the sea lanes to the East, gives added significance to the Cuba–Soviet presence in Angola and, in relation to Soviet global naval strategy, Luanda is a compensation for the loss of Mogadishu. Furthermore, its use by the Soviet navy acquires new meaning in the context of the growing geopolitical sensitivity of the South Atlantic with the looming review of the Antarctic Treaty in 1992. Cuban support for Argentina during the Falklands/Malvinas War, apart from its assertion of Latin American solidarity, has a wider resonance when Cuban presence in Angola and the activities of their ocean-going fishing fleet are taken into account. One aspect of the much heralded renewal of diplomatic relations with Brazil could be seen as strengthening the Cuban presence in the South Atlantic, opening up possibilities of Brazilian support in Angola where Brazil has economic interests.

CUBA'S LOW PROFILE IN THE CARIBBEAN

The early years of the Revolution were marked by a remarkable absence of Cuban activity in the rest of the Caribbean. It was only from the early 1970s that diplomatic relations were established with the English-speaking Caribbean and then it was on the latter's initiative. This low profile of Cuban activity can be explained by its isolation from even near neighbours due to the fragmentation of the islands, their cultural diversity and their links to ex-colonial metropolises rather than to each other. Since the mid-1970s, however, Cuban interest in the rest of the Caribbean has expanded rapidly and finds its most striking expression in a new assertion of its African heritage and in cultural co-operation, as in the holding of Carifesta in Havana in 1979.

The massive intervention of the United States in the Dominican Republic in 1965 (where the rising was urban and did not follow the Cuban model) was to make it quite clear that the United States would intervene to prevent a repetition of the Cuban experience. In a rational world Venezuela and Cuba would have been natural allies, having overthrown their dictators within a year of each other, but deep personal, economic and ideological differences prevented the earlier dream of the Caribbean Legion, of a social-democratic Caribbean purged of dictators, from being realized. In any case the Caribbean had a low priority when set against the mirage of revolution spreading throughout the mainland and turning the Andes into the Sierra Maestra of South America.

Other factors have inhibited Cuban advances – the islands have always had close links with the United States through migration and trade and these have been getting stronger. The economic and cultural pull of the United States has been difficult to resist. There is a further factor which tends to be overlooked. European powers – Britain, France and the Netherlands – have strong residual links and interests in their ex-colonies, dependencies and *départements*, and through Commonwealth and EC contacts the European presence is far stronger than in Latin America. Any forward policy might alienate powers which since the early 1960s have played a considerable, although little acknowledged, role in ensuring the Revolution's survival (and in this respect Canada too should not be forgotten). The refusal of Europe – and Canada and Mexico in the Americas – to join in the blockade in the early 1960s meant that Cuba had an important diplomatic and commercial lifeline and could command widespread sympathy. This sympathy was not confined solely to the West European left. Throughout the Franco period, for example, Spain not only provided the one direct air link to Europe, but was a leading trading partner, contributing, as in the case of building the fishing fleet, to one of the most successful sectors of the Cuban economy.

This European involvement has increased, particularly since Grenada (1983) when it was felt in some Commonwealth Caribbean circles that the crisis should have been resolved within a Commonwealth framework and not by US intervention. There is too a new awareness of the Caribbean in Europe, prompted by the presence of large communities in Britain, France and the Netherlands who constitute in those countries a political challenge and a highly visible (and audible) cultural presence. Family ties are a guarantee that these links will not be weakened.

There was a clear link between the Grenadan and Cuban Revolutions but this was due to Maurice Bishop's admiration for Cuba's achievements and not to Cuban initiatives. Castro had a closer empathy with Bishop than with any other Caribbean leader, and this sense of personal affinity – a factor never to be under-estimated in Castro's motivation – as well as the opportunity to make Grenada an example to the smaller islands of what might be achieved with Cuban co-operation (the more so after Manley's defeat in Jamaica in 1980), prompted a flow of aid which proportionately was higher than that given by Cuba to any other country. Whether the purpose of military assistance was offensive, as its scale might seem to indicate, or defensive, as the Cubans protested, the real threat came from the example which a successful socialist society would offer to the rest of the Eastern Caribbean.[12]

The precise reasons for differences in approach towards the PRG between Cuba and the Soviet Union are unclear. Moscow's attitude was more cautious. Bishop was closer to Castro's *modus operandi*; Coard was closer to Moscow's. As in the earlier case of Neto in Angola Moscow may have had misgivings about Bishop's orthodoxy and doubts as to his judgement. However useful as an irritant to the United States, Grenada's outspoken expressions of support for Soviet policy (in Afghanistan for example) were provocative and bound to provoke the predictable reaction, with the precedent of the Dominican Republic of 1965, of US intervention, an eventuality which neither the Soviet Union nor Cuba could or would resist. In the end Grenada was expendable to both.

The Cuban reverse in Grenada was to be followed by the expulsion of their ambassador from Suriname and this, together with the death of Burnham in Guyana, marked the decline of Cuban influence in a region which was beginning to assume a geopolitical sensitivity involving both Brazilian and French security.

The ramifications of the Grenada failure have been widespread. There is now a greater awareness of the need to reformulate strategies for the development of small states which involve indigenous and not imposed ideological solutions. It has given an impetus to the revival of European concern with the region, based both on an awareness of national interest

85

and on the pragmatic moderating role which Europe might play. It has underlined the need for integration among the smaller islands, not only as a safeguard against another Grenada but, more importantly, to strengthen them against destabilization in the form of the new piracy of drug smugglers and recyclers of dirty money. It also gave a boost to the Caribbean Basin Initiative. And, finally, it has led to a realistic assessment on the part of the Cubans of the advantages of multilateral co-operation with other Latin American countries for the solution of regional security questions, which finds its main expression in a cautious policy in Central America.[13]

Although in the 1960s Cuba had shown an interest in the potentialities of Guatemala for guerrilla activity it did not have a high profile elsewhere in Central America. The revolts in El Salvador and Nicaragua, like Grenada's, were inspired by Cuban example, but they owed little to active Cuban involvement beyond providing a haven for political exiles and training for small numbers of guerrillas. Cuba's most important political contribution to the overthrow of Somoza was Castro's contribution to the merging of the three Sandinista factions early in 1979. In any case, other Latin American countries, Mexico, Costa Rica, Panama and Venezuela, all had an interest in the overthrow of Somoza and contributed financially towards the Sandinistas' success. Cuban support has since been extensive in terms of medical, technical, teaching and military advisors.

In contrast to the Cuban Revolution, the most striking feature in Nicaragua has been the extent of international involvement, exemplified not only in the Contadora initiative but also in a European presence. What Cuba had been to European liberals and the left in the 1960s, so Nicaragua is today, but with the difference that the support is not ideological so much as practical, expressed in grass-roots aid projects by government and private agencies as well as by a belief that the EC and the Socialist International have moderating roles to play. Cuban influence has also moderated Nicaraguan policies, by warning their leaders not to imitate their model, ironically in a similar fashion to Soviet attempts to moderate the pace of Cuban change in the early 1960s. Support for a mixed economy, for example, derives from the view that, given the limits of Soviet economic aid, the regime's survival will be largely dependent on trade with Europe and the non-communist countries, and, from this perspective, political pluralism is a necessary prerequisite for Latin American and European political, religious and diplomatic support.

Predictably, hardliners in the State Department and elsewhere have interpreted this as Trojan Horse tactical pragmatism, adducing the increasing centralization and restrictions on freedoms of expression as evidence of the Sandinistas' 'real' motivation. Fear of Cuban influence has conditioned United States' responses, influenced by the powerful exile lobby and by frustrations experienced in other parts of the world. With almost all Third World conflicts viewed through the prism of East–West rivalry Washington became convinced that Soviet proxies in Havana, acting through puppets in Managua, were intent upon spreading revolution throughout Central America.

There is, furthermore, the apocalyptic view of the 'domino theory', that Mexico will succumb to revolutionary contagion and – as the Mexican issue is of far greater concern in practical, as distinct from ideological terms, to the United States than either Central America or Cuba – the 'backyard syndrome' determines the decision to resort to the military solution of the 'contras'. In reaction to the growing military threat the contras pose, Nicaragua has shown signs of becoming an authoritarian garrison state and so, as in the case of Cuba, yet another example of a self-fulfilling prophecy. What, then, is the relationship of Cuba to the USSR?

CUBA'S RELATIONSHIP WITH THE USSR

Cuba's major concern has been to ensure the survival of its own Revolution by a variety of means which have shown a remarkable consistency for nearly thirty years. Security has been achieved by the Soviet alliance which, in spite of disagreements, has remained the corner-stone of Cuban policy. The increasing dependence of Cuba on Soviet economic, diplomatic and military support, and the sovietization of Cuban society, with tight controls over freedom of expression, have given credence to the view that Castro was a 'crypto-communist' from the beginning and deliberately dissimulated and misled his early supporters. The argument over the direction the Revolution took in the early days and the radical departure from the original reformist aims based on the 1940 Constitution is not likely to be easily resolved but there is no *prima facie* reason to deduce from the convergence of the 1970s that it was implicit from the beginning. The failure of the *via armada* made it inevitable that Cuba would be unable to play a role independently of the Soviet Union; not that any Third World revolution can survive without the protection and support of a Great Power with similar aims in view. What was in doubt once links with the Soviet Union were established was the degree of freedom which a closer association would allow.

Sugar and oil have been the basis of the economic nexus. Cuba exports

87

Alistair Hennessy

sugar to the Soviet Union at above world market price; oil is imported at below world market price for domestic market and resale for hard currency on the open market.[14] When the price of oil was buoyant as in the early 1970s and the domestic economy expanded, the burdens both of domestic social reform and a global foreign policy could be borne with mutual benefit to both the Soviet Union and Cuba. But the fall in prices has put a considerable strain on the relationship, as the Soviet Union wishes to see maximum benefit derived from its outlay. Granting or withholding extra funds can and has been used either to restrain adventurism abroad, as in the 1960s, or to compel economic efficiency at home, in the 1980s.

The advantages to Cuba of an economic relationship in which it receives 50% of all aid given by the Soviet Union to recipients outside Eastern Europe are obvious and, although it has resulted in new forms of dependency, these are more predictable than those they have replaced. However, there are disadvantages. The relationship can be a straitjacket by restricting Cuba's ability to sell in the open market when the price of sugar is high and by tying the Soviet Union to a burdensome aid programme when the price of oil is low. The relationship, too, has made it difficult for Cuba to diversify its trading pattern and to benefit from trade with non-communist countries which has to be paid for in hard currency.

In any case a diversification of trading partners depends on diversifying the domestic economy and although attempts to do so have been made, these have still not substantially altered Cuba's trading pattern. Attempts to do so now, and to expand new areas of economic activity such as tourism, will require a modification of domestic and foreign policy objectives as well as the acquisition of new skills.

President Castro's speech at the Third Congress of the Communist Party of Cuba in February 1986 was a litany of criticisms of bureaucratic inefficiency, absenteeism, absence of self-criticism and lack of democracy. This was a reflection of Gorbachev's similar critique of the Soviet economy.[15] Castro's exhortation to Cubans to mend their ways was rewarded by a projected increase of 50% in Soviet economic and trade aid to Cuba over the 1986–90 period. But the price for this will be an improvement in economic performance. To achieve this the option of liberalizing the economy seems to have been rejected in favour of tighter controls and further austerity. Castro's own contribution has been an exhortation to the people to revive those values which have made the Revolution distinctive and to regenerate the economy by means of moral and not material incentives. It is difficult to imagine him changing priorities or modifying the commitment to revolutionary proletarian solidarity, but not to do so may entail even greater risks than in the past. What would be the Cuban response to challenges in Southern Africa, either in the form of a deteriorating situation in Angola or of an escalation of conflict in South Africa, either of which could make further demands on Cuban resources? Could Cuba afford to stand by if the balance swung against Nicaragua – the only successful mainland revolution in Latin America in twenty-nine years? But any overt action in the Americas involves a risk of United States intervention or another reverse comparable to Grenada, as there is no reason to suppose the Soviet Union would risk a confrontation with the United States any more in the future than it has in the past.

CONCLUSIONS

In an analysis of Castro's personality and motivation and the influence of each on future options, Eduardo González has interpreted Cuba's past foreign policy in terms of swings between periods of revolutionary maxi-malism and defensive tactical pragmatism, 'using political initiatives to disarm or confuse adversaries'.[16] The prudence of the latter is conditioned by constraints on the former caused by Cuba's domestic situation, the foreign policy postures of the United States and the Soviet Union, possible openings in the Third World and the position of Cuba's own clients. Of these, the attitude of the Soviet Union is critical, as it sets the basic parameters for Cuba's behaviour. González surmises that Cuba's capacity to think and act globally should not be under-estimated, as it was in the 1970s, and that Castro's audacious *modus operandi* could lead to a renewal of Cuban military or guerrilla involvement in the Third World.

In this scenario southern Africa figures prominently, but as with the Soviets in Afghanistan so the Cubans in Angola have become bogged down in a war of attrition where disadvantages may soon outweigh advantages. Cuba's attraction for the Third World does not lie in military operations, in which it can be too easily seen as a surrogate for the Soviet Union, so much as in its less publicized (at least in the West) but more impressive civilian aid programmes, and the lessons which these imply for inter-relationships and mutual co-operation within the Third World. Although the bulk of this aid is at present directed to Africa, Cuba is an integral part of the Americas and it is there ultimately that its destiny lies. Africa became a theatre of conflict when Cuban involvement in Latin America was restricted. Changes of regime and the move to democracy there have opened up the possibility of new relationships. The nature of these is bound to be very different from those of the 1960s and 1970s.

They may involve compromise and conciliation, but lower-key activity based on revolutionary pragmatism may prove a more effective, though less ambitious, way of transmitting the formidable achievements of the Cuban Revolution to a continent where the example, if not the model, is still capable of generating an enthusiastic response. It may be that, as the focus of world politics shifts to Central Asia and the Pacific, a Cuban policy towards Latin America closer to traditional Russian attitudes of cautious pragmatism could prove to be an effective way of perpetuating one of the most successful examples in international affairs of co-operation between a superpower and a client state.

NOTES

1. Before 1959 there were scarcely any academic specialists of Cuba in the United States. One of the most perceptive analyses of the early years of the Revolution is R. Welch, *Response to Revolution: the United States and the Cuban Revolution, 1959–61* (Chapel Hill, NC: University of North Carolina Press, 1985).
2. Israel is another example of a small state with a global presence, represented by aid policies, etc., subsidized by a superpower. For many Third World countries its position *vis-à-vis* the United States is regarded in much the same light as the United States regards Cuba.
3. For Cuba's role in the Non-Aligned Movement see H. Michael Erisman, *Cuba's International Relations: the Anatomy of a Nationalistic Foreign Policy* (Boulder, Colo.: Westview Press, 1985), and W. LeoGrande, 'Evolution of the Non-Aligned Movement', *Problems of Communism*, January–February 1980. For Cuba and CMEA see Cole Blasier, 'COMECON in Cuban development', in Cole Blasier and Carmelo Mesa-Largo (eds.), *Cuba in the World* (Pittsburgh, Pa.: University of Pittsburgh Press, 1979).
4. For the Chinese and Latin America see S. Frederick d'Ignazio III and Daniel Tretiak, 'Latin America: How Much do the Chinese Care?', *Studies in Comparative Communism*, I, spring 1972.
5. There is a vast Cuban bibliography on Martí. The best coverage in English is in C. Abel and N. Torrents (eds.), *José Martí: Revolutionary Democrat* (London: Athlone Press, 1986), and P. Turton, *José Martí: Architect of Cuba's Freedom* (London: Zed Press, 1986).
6. The concept of political culture in communist states has been fully discussed in Archie Brown and Jack Gray, *Political Culture and Political Change in Communist States* (London: Macmillan, 1979), where political culture is defined as 'the subjective perception of history and politics, the fundamental beliefs and values, the foci of identification and loyalty and the political knowledge and expectations which are the product of the specific historical experience of nations and groups' (p. xv). There is a chapter on Cuba by Francis Lambert. The most thorough analysis of changing Cuban political culture is still R. R. Fagen, *The Transformation of Political Culture in Cuba* (Stanford, Cal.: Stanford University Press, 1969).
7. LeoGrande, 'Evolution of the Non-Aligned Movement'.
8. Régis Debray, *Revolution in the Revolution?* (Harmondsworth, Middlesex: Penguin Books, 1969).
9. The Cubans also persisted in supporting Puerto Rican *independentistas* during rapprochement which was an added irritant.
10. From a large literature on Cuba in Africa see C. Mesa-Lago and J. Belkin (eds.), *Cuba in Africa* (Pittsburgh, Pa.: University of Pittsburgh Press, 1982). A. M. Kapcia, 'Cuba's African Involvement: A New Perspective', *Survey*, XXIV, no. 2, 1979), is one of the best short analyses. See also the forthcoming controversial Carlos Moore, *Cuban Race Politics: The Shaping of Cuba's African Policy* (Berkeley, Cal.: University of California Press, 1987).

For Russian policy in Africa see C. Legum, 'The African Environment', and D. E. Albright, 'Soviet Policy', *Problems of Communism*, January–February 1978; Jiri Valenta, 'The Soviet–Cuban Intervention in Angola', *Studies in Comparative Communism*, XI, nos. 1 and 2, spring/summer 1978; also W. J. Durch, 'The Cuban Military in Africa and the Middle East: From Algeria to Angola', in the same issue.

11. For an hypothesis on the divisions within the Cuban elite, see E. González,'Institutionalization of Political Elites and Foreign Politics', in Blasier and Mesa-Lago, *Cuba in the World*, and his 'Complexities of Cuban Foreign Policy', *Problems of Communism*, November-December 1977.

12. For a balanced treatment of the controversial Grenada affair, see Tony Thorndike, *Grenada, Politics, Economics and Society* (London: Frances Pinter, 1985).

13. From a large literature on Central America see Jorge Domínguez, 'Cuba's Relations with Caribbean and Central American Countries', *Cuban Studies*, XIII, no. 2, summer 1983.

14. Details of oil and sugar are in J. F. Pérez-López, 'Sugar and Petroleum in Cuban–Soviet Terms of Trade', in Blasier and Mesa-Lago, *Cuba in the World*. See also his 'Cuba's Economy in the 1980s', *Problems of Communism*, September–October 1986.

15. For reactions to Gorbachev, see W. Raymond Duncan, 'Castro and Gorbachov', *Problems of Communism*, March–April 1986.

16. Eduardo González and David Ronfeldt, *Castro, Cuba and the World* (Rand Publication R-3420, Santa Monica, Cal., 1986). For an overview, see R. Pastor, 'Cuba and the Soviet Union: Does Cuba Act Alone?' in B. Levine (ed.), *The New Cuban Presence in the Caribbean* (Boulder, Colo.: Westview, 1983) and P. Shearman, *The Soviet Union and Cuba* (London: Royal Institute of International Affairs, 1987).

6   Nicaraguan security perceptions

Eduardo Crawley

There was [in 1979] a powerful reason which demanded that the vanguard [the FSLN] should grant priority to the prompt organisation of its military apparatus: the perception that the main danger the revolutionary process would have to confront was *a direct aggression from the United States* ... Two potential enemies were identified: North American imperialism and the reactionary forces of the region; and also, though as a lesser danger, the incipient counter-revolution which was beginning to manifest itself in the bands of ex-*somocista* guards operating out of Honduras.[1]

This description of Nicaraguan security perceptions in the very early days of the revolution was published in mid-1986 by the Coordinadora Regional de Investigaciones Económicas y Sociales (CRIES), an independent but openly pro-Sandinista think-tank based in Managua, as part of one of the most comprehensive surveys of the war in that country. It reflects a widely held view of what the Sandinistas had expected from the outset – and it is completely inaccurate.

In 1979, when the Sandinistas took power, Jimmy Carter was in the White House, Ronald Reagan had not yet emerged clearly as a winning candidate committed to rolling back the 'Red tide' in the Caribbean Basin, and the term 'contra' had not even been coined. It is, of course, true that even with the Democrats in office, the US had done its utmost to prevent a Sandinista victory, and that in practical as well as ideological terms the Sandinistas considered that they had been fighting the US (Somoza being only the local representative of *yanqui* imperialism). But in equally practical terms, the Sandinistas were convinced that in July 1979 they had inflicted a decisive, if not completely irreversible defeat on the US.

It was in the last stages of the insurrection that the US was the main, immediate enemy:

As soon as the crisis of Somozism began, we realized more clearly that the real enemy that we would have to confront was the imperialist power of the United

92

States; the treachery and demagoguery of the reactionary local bourgeoisie being less important.[2]

The threat from this 'real enemy', however, was one to which the Sandinistas responded on a political and diplomatic plane – and did so with such success that they would continue to consider diplomacy and propaganda their most effective weapon for most of the ensuing years. In their own words:

[The FSLN] had to skillfully combine domestic and foreign alliances with a spectacular worldwide diplomatic struggle to neutralize the interventionist policies that imperialism was pursuing to make our Sandinist revolution fail ... The alliance that took the form of the National Reconstruction Government, the cabinet and, to a major extent, the FSLN's basic program ... was designed to neutralize Yankee interventionist policies in the light of the imminent Sandinist military victory.[3]

By staving off US efforts to control the transition through negotiations with Somoza or the despatch of an inter-American peace force, the Sandinistas reduced the problem to one of defeating the National Guard. And when the Guard collapsed in July 1979, they considered their victory as all but total.

By defeating the Guard, we were attacking the foundation, and of course the building, Somozism, fell to pieces ... By defeating the National Guard and toppling the dictatorship, we also dealt a decisive blow to the power of the bourgeoisie ... Because of the kind of victory that we achieved over the dictatorship, the defeated National Guard cannot possibly organize an attack on us for the time being, especially since it would have to have strong backing from a bordering or neighboring country. Some National Guard detachments that maintain ties with hard-core commands might gain the support of unofficial right-wing military groups or White Hand-type gangs and could possibly engage in terrorist activities or very limited banditry ... Imperialism's military base in Nicaragua has clearly been destroyed; interventionist aggression is not knocking on our door for now.[4]

PERCEIVED THREATS AND POLICY RESPONSES

In the first few months after taking power, the Sandinistas felt that the revolution would be most threatened from within Nicaragua's borders. They identified three enemies:

(1) The *vendepatria* bourgeoisie, 'the counter-revolution's main tool'. This sector was likely to receive support from the US, but mainly in the form of 'financial pressures ... to undermine the economic and social foundation of the Sandinist Revolution'. In the FSLN's view, the US would press for an agreement with the IMF, attempt to make Nicaragua dependent on aid (preferably channelled through the local private sector),

93

'infiltrate' the state apparatus and fund 'the bourgeoisie's trade unions, associations and parties'.[5]

(2) The 'vestiges of Somozism', by which they meant not so much the remnant of the National Guard still bearing arms as people associated with the old regime 'who have infiltrated mass organizations and the Armed Forces'.[6]

(3) The far left and 'lumpen-proletariat elements', who could help a 'spontaneous counter-revolutionary uprising'.[7]

In its directives to FSLN cadres, the Sandinista leadership underlined the importance of the political struggle even over the admitted need to organize a new regular army. Similar criteria were applied to foreign policy: consolidating the revolution at home took precedence over 'strengthening the Central American, Latin American and worldwide revolution'[8] – indeed, the former was seen as a necessary condition for the latter.

In Central America, within that context, priority was given to 'the need to counteract the aggressive policy of the military dictatorships in Guatemala and El Salvador'; the attitude towards Honduras was to be limited to underlining 'differences', while Costa Rica and Panama were described as 'friendly'.[9] None of the neighbouring countries was deemed likely to risk the 'chancy adventure' of actively supporting a counter-revolution in Nicaragua; El Salvador and Guatemala because of their own internal upheavals, Honduras because its domestic political scene virtually imposed neutrality.[10]

It must be noted, though, that the longer-term view – beyond the consolidation of the Nicaraguan revolution – was that survival of the Sandinista regime depended on revolution spreading throughout Central America.[11]

In the firm belief that they faced no immediate military threat, the Sandinistas set about organizing the country's new army with a view to its long-term strategic aims. It was to be a conventional army and a heavily politicized one. As the FSLN leadership described it, 'an unprecedented partisan army'.[12]

When the Sandinistas took power, their armed forces were a relatively small hodgepodge of groups with brief and widely varied military experience. Out of a total of about 15,000 combatants, as many as 10,000 were members of irregular, often improvised militias. Some 3,000 had fought as guerrillas in the north and east of the country. Only around 2,000 had served in the more 'conventional' units of the southern and north-western fronts.[13]

In August 1979 the first formal units of the Ejército Popular Sandinista

(EPS) were created. A month later, the blueprint submitted to FSLN cadres foresaw the development of a regular army deployed mainly in 'strategic zones' (among which the northern, southern and Atlantic coasts were identified as 'highly sensitive'). Around a small, professional nucleus the bulk of this army would eventually be formed by conscripts; the large urban-militia army would be 'eliminated'.[14]

A small number of combatants was deployed immediately for border patrol duty in the Tropas Guarda Frontera (TGF). Apart from preventing cattle-rustling and smuggling, the TGF were charged with intercepting and neutralizing the remnant of the National Guard attempting to set up base in Honduras. Months later other units were formed specifically to track down and destroy the bands for former guardsmen: the Pequeñas Unidades de Lucha Contra Bandas Somocistas (LCBS).[15]

For the mainstream development of their armed forces, the Sandinistas made an early policy option. They rebuffed a Panamanian offer of military assistance, which would have provided 'back-door' access to the US model and US technology. Instead they called on the Cubans, who had become their main suppliers in the last year of the insurrection, and on the Soviets. As early as March 1980 Nicaraguan officials were in Moscow negotiating military as well as economic agreements.[16]

FIRST REASSESSMENT

The Sandinistas' early reading of threats to their security, reinforced by Cuban advice to avoid premature confrontation with the US, was not reviewed until well into 1980. The Nicaraguan leadership continued to consider the US as the greatest *long-term* threat, but events seemed to confirm their assumption that Washington would eschew military action and concentrate on financial and economic subversion. (Far from ingratiating itself with the Sandinistas by sharply increasing economic assistance to Nicaragua, the Carter Administration merely strengthened their early suspicions that this would be Washington's main avenue of attack.)

Together with the Cubans, the Nicaraguans had become convinced that the post-Vietnam US had become incapable of stemming the revolutionary tide which then seemed clearly on the rise in Central America. They were confirmed in this view by the evidence that a number of officials in the US foreign policy and defence establishments were recommending Washington's disengagement from the region's autocratic regimes and recognition of the revolutionary movements.[17] Indeed, also with the Cubans, they had succeeded in overcoming the initial caution of the Soviets and winning them over to the same view – to the point at which a high-ranking Soviet military official voiced his conviction that there were 'no prospects for imperialism to turn back history'.

These assumptions only became subject to revision, albeit partial, when Ronald Reagan, already committed to a platform which promised to 'support the efforts of the Nicaraguan people to establish a free and independent government', began to look like the possible winner in the US presidential race. From Reagan they could expect at least an attempt to 'turn back history' or, in the later jargon, to 'restore US hegemony'.

The Sandinistas' reaction to this perceived threat was to bring forward in time one of their long-term foreign policy tenets: that the survival of their own Revolution would ultimately be assured only by successful revolutions elsewhere in Central America – or, seen in more immediate terms, that a newer and hence weaker revolutionary regime in another Central American country would provide a more urgent and tempting target for a Reagan presidency, taking the heat off Nicaragua.[18]

Abandoning their previous policy of low-profile, mainly verbal support for the Salvadorean FMLN, the Sandinistas plunged wholeheartedly into supporting the 'final offensive' which the Salvadorean rebels expected to place them in power before Ronald Reagan took office in early 1981.

The Sandinistas still saw no immediate internal threat, but early in 1980 they shelved their plans to eliminate the militia army. Instead, they passed a law institutionalizing the Milicias Populares Sandinistas (MPS) as a means of securing 'popular participation' in the defence effort until such time as conscription was introduced. A voluntary force, the MPS were charged mainly with the defence of workplaces and backing up the small units chasing the bands of former guardsmen.[19]

The failure of the FMLN's 'final offensive' left the Sandinistas facing an indignant US, and without the advantage of another revolutionary regime to draw the fire of the incoming Reagan Administration. None the less, as in the final stages of the insurrection against Somoza, the FSLN's reaction to the threat was conducted mainly in the diplomatic and propagandistic arena. In public, support for the FMLN was toned down to the point of being denied several times, while privately the Salvadorean rebels continued to be seen as Nicaragua's 'shield'.[20]

Even after Ronald Reagan produced, in March 1981, the first 'finding' to back covert action in the region, the Sandinistas seemed worried only about the highly publicized training of anti-Sandinista units in the US.[21]

The contras began to be welded into an organized fighting force, across the Honduran border, in late 1981. Their first field units were sent into Nicaragua, to conduct hit-and-run operations, in December of that year.[22]

REACTING TO THE CONTRAS

As the contras emerged on the scene clearly backed by the US, the Sandinistas felt the need to make some adjustments to their original scenario. Their public statements of the day offer scant information on this exercise. Their practical decisions suggest strongly that they saw no need for drastic departures; but merely for strengthening the short-term component of their defence apparatus – the one devoted to meeting the contra threat – while continuing to build up a conventional regular army to meet the country's long-term needs.

The means chosen for that purpose was the creation of the Batallones de Infantería de Reserva (BIR). The manpower for these units was drawn from those elements of the militia (MPS) willing to sign on voluntarily for six-month stints of active duty. Much later analyses of this development recognized two main reasons for this step:

1   The LCBS were proving inadequate on their own to cope with expanding contra activity; and
2   the policy of *ad hoc* mobilization of MPS units in support of the LCBS was proving costly in both political and economic terms, in as much as it involved the unplanned withdrawal of people from productive activities.[23]

Contra operations, however, continued to increase in magnitude and frequency, and it was not long before the new BIR-based defence was being seen as sharing the same deficiencies as the previous one. The FSLN leadership also began to see the degree of support enjoyed by the contras in some parts of the country as indicative of political failings on their own part, particularly of the neglect of the landless peasantry.[24]

The need was felt to build up a more solid counter-insurgency component of the defence apparatus, a task for which Cuban assistance was sought. In June 1983, Cuban General Arnaldo Ochoa Sánchez (a veteran commander of Ethiopia and Angola) arrived in Nicaragua to oversee this effort.[25]

In August–September of that year the FSLN leadership pushed through the Council of State a law establishing – at long last – compulsory military service: the Servicio Militar Patriótico (SMP) which began with the call-up of around 10,000 youths of the 18–25 age group for two years of active duty, following which they would be integrated in reserve units. The new conscripts were put through two to three months of intensive training and assigned to small, highly mobile infantry battalions (first known as BLIR, later as BLI). These were deployed alongside the existing BIRs for anti-contra operations.[26]

The idea was still to keep the core of the regular army out of the counter-insurgency effort, readying itself for a more conventional defence task. At this time, considerable confusion crept into Sandinista defence thinking. This became evident in public through a number of contradictory interpretations of US intentions, ranging from the conviction that a direct invasion by US troops was imminent to the notion that a Reagan facing re-election needed to speed up a negotiated settlement to the Central American conflict because of increasingly adverse public opinion in the US.[27]

According to a later reading, the Sandinistas had come to believe that the Reagan Administration's attempts to 'restore US hegemony' in Central America would follow a 'Vietnam-type' pattern.[28]

Applied to Nicaragua, this meant that US action would unfold in three successive stages:

1   Economic warfare, culminating in a trade embargo and perhaps a naval blockade;
2   a brief period of support for irregular armed action against the Sandinistas, orchestrated so as to provide the motive for
3   direct US military intervention.

Confusion began to set in when the second phase (irregular warfare) preceded the first (a trade embargo was not imposed until two years later). And though irregular warfare was not followed as swiftly as expected by direct US military intervention, for a long while the Sandinistas continued to interpret successive US actions (manoeuvres in Honduras, the invasion of Grenada, naval exercises, the destruction of Nicaragua's oil depots and port facilities, the mining of harbours) as the signal that the third phase was finally about to begin.

When the invasion still did not materialize after a number of such preludes, the notion began to spread in Managua that the Reagan Administration was being held back by public opinion in the US and international opinion. This notion was reinforced by Washington's all-too-obvious concern to neutralize the prestige of the Contadora Group and reverse pro-Nicaraguan sentiment in European media and political circles, and by the US Congress' decision to cut off military aid to the contras. They also observed the reluctance of the neighbouring governments of Honduras and Costa Rica to admit publicly to harbouring and aiding the contras, and of the Hondurans to commit their own forces to shield the contras.

In this they believed their own conventional military build-up had acted as an efficient deterrent. The Sandinistas had created the largest land army in Central America, ostensibly to meet the threat of invasion, but clearly designed with a capability to project force deep into any of the neighbouring countries, including El Salvador.[29]

Though the possibility of a direct US invasion was never completely dismissed (and was certainly kept alive in public as a key weapon in the Sandinistas' diplomatic and propagandistic campaign), in 1984 the Nicaraguan leadership felt Washington was sufficiently constrained to allow more of the defence effort to be directed towards a 'strategic defeat' of the contras. The regular army began to be geared up to join the counter-insurgency effort, equipped with Soviet-provided air transport and helicopter gunships. Large counter-insurgency brigades (BLIs) were formed, combining battalions of conscripts, reserve and regular forces.[30]

In early 1985 the second call-up (of seventeen- to eighteen-year-olds) for SMP duty went out; those in the twenty-five to thirty age group were instructed to register for reserve duty, and a drive was launched to boost the volunteer militia units.[31]

Much of the population was evacuated from northern and southern border areas, so as to create 'free-fire zones' in which anyone moving could be deemed a contra.[32]

At the same time an important shift in long-term defence thinking began to emerge.

CHANGING THE SCENARIO

In the early days of open confrontation with the Reagan Administration, the Sandinistas had been only too happy to play publicly on US apprehension of 'another Vietnam' in Central America. They let it be known that, in case of invasion, rather than attempting a conventional defence of their cities (Nicaragua is basically a three-city country), they would retreat to the countryside and wage a protracted, costly guerrilla campaign against the intruders.

Visiting US military experts were told of plans for 'arming as many as one million people for nationwide guerrilla warfare resistance'.[33]

Politically, this line of talk evoked emotive memories of their national hero, Augusto Sandino, and his much-inflated guerrilla campaign against the US Marines over fifty years earlier, as well as of the mythology of the FSLN's long guerrilla campaign against Somoza (the least decisive element in his overthrow). But the very example of the contras had by early 1984 caused the Sandinistas to revise their assessment of how efficacious a guerrilla threat would really be.[34]

Accordingly, by late 1985 they had institutionalized the reserves, creating a second category of military service, the SMR, with a first call-up of 45,000 people in the twenty-five to forty age group. This was 'limited to Managua given the capital's strategic importance'.[35]

Country-wide, companies and battalions of local militias were organized into permanent territorial defence units (UPTs), with the dual purpose of providing a first line of defence of the cities and of allowing the counter-insurgency more freedom of action in the field.[36]

The campaign to inflict a 'strategic defeat' on the contras continued, growing in intensity, into 1986. Though cross-border 'hot pursuit' operations into Honduras had been recorded since as early as 1979, it was not until 1986 that major cross-border incursions were mounted.

The first of these, in May, seemed to confirm Nicaraguan assumptions that the Honduran military did not wish to become involved in direct clashes with the EPS – it was only belatedly, and under considerable US pressure, that the Honduran government even admitted an incursion had taken place, and despatched troops to the border. The second major incursion, in November–December, marked an important change in this situation. Following direct clashes between EPS and Honduran troops, the Sandinistas had to face the rapid deployment of Honduran units to the border, and retaliatory Honduran air strikes into Nicaraguan territory. The Honduran military warned that further incursions would meet with similar retaliation.[37] Coming immediately after the formal resumption of US military assistance to the contras, this shift revived fears in Managua that a direct US military intervention could be on the cards.

The subsequent eruption in Washington of the scandal over covert diversion of funds to the contras during the congressional ban did not quite erase this fear. Indeed, it resuscitated the old confusion over the US government's capabilities and intentions. On the one hand, the entire policy built by the Reagan Administration around the contras began to be seen as liable to collapse definitively. On the other, that very liability began to be interpreted as possibly providing a strong motive for the Reagan Administration to move even more aggressively, and more swiftly, against Nicaragua.

CONCLUSION

The signing of the 'Esquipulas II' peace-seeking agreement by the five Central American presidents in August 1987 did little to change the essential components of the Sandinistas' outlook. The three strands of their strategy, as developed in the mid-1980s, remained in place.

1   The publicly stated assumption that Nicaragua remains under the threat of direct intervention by the United States has been reiterated by the government. This must be seen on two planes: first as a very real fear, which informs part of the country's military planning, training and maintenance of international alliances; second, as a powerful tool to attract sympathy abroad for the second strand of the Sandinistas' strategy.

2   The assumption that political and public opinion in the United States (and elsewhere abroad) can be directed by diplomatic and propaganda efforts so as to (a) constrain the US government from more direct intervention, and (b) erode US congressional support for the contras.

3   Increasing use of the entire Sandinista military apparatus for counter-insurgency operations, avowedly with a view to the complete eradication of the contra threat, though more realistically with the purpose of holding the contras at bay until such time as the second strand, the diplomatic and propaganda effort, succeeds in depriving the contras of outside support.

There are no signs that the Sandinistas have abandoned their conviction that revolution is the answer for Central America as a whole. At most, their objectives in this field have been postponed until the immediate threats to the survival of their own regime are removed or sufficiently minimized. It is worth noting that immediately after the signing of the 'Esquipulas II' agreement, armed action by 'friendly' guerrilla organizations – the FMLN in El Salvador, the URNG in Guatemala – escalated to the point where government–guerrilla negotiations in these countries could be presented as the logical counterparts to the Sandinista–contra talks which the US and the other Central American governments were demanding from Nicaragua.

Without a 'final outcome' in sight as these lines are written, any assessment of the efficacy of Sandinista strategy is necessarily provisional. The situation, eight years after the Sandinistas came to power, is:

1   The contras, even with substantial US backing, have been unable

to gain a decisive advantage against the Sandinistas inside Nicaragua, but still remain a deadly threat.

2 The Sandinistas have lost much of the international support and sympathy that they enjoyed in the early years, but have retained enough to constrain the United States. Moreover, even though they have lost sympathy themselves, their portrayal of the Reagan Administration has gained acceptance, most significantly within the United States itself, and to the point that continued congressional support for the contra effort is in doubt.

3 The United States has not intervened directly with its own military force against Nicaragua. Though the Sandinistas themselves keep alive the possibility of such intervention, the mere passage of time, together with the erosion of support for the Reagan Administration's policy towards Nicaragua within the United States, and the international impact of the 'Esquipulas II' effort, have rendered it much harder for the United States to justify direct intervention.

NOTES

1. Raúl Vergara Meneses *et al.*, *Nicaragua país sitiado (Guerra de baja intensidad: agresión y sobrevivencia)* (Managua: CRIES, Cuadernos de Pensamiento Propio, Serie Avances Cuatro, Junio de 1986).
2. *Análisis de la coyuntura y tareas de la Revolución Popular Sandinista*, Tesis políticas y militares presentadas por la Dirección Nacional del Frente Sandinista de Liberación Nacional en la Asamblea de Cuadros 'Rigoberto López Pérez' celebrada el 21, 22, y 23 de Septiembre de 1979 (Managua, October 1979.) (The English version used here is taken from the photocopy of the translation pouched by US Ambassador Lawrence Pezzullo to the Department of State on 26 December 1979).
3. *Ibid.*
4. *Ibid.* 'White hand' (in Spanish 'Mano Blanca') is a reference to the right-wing terrorist organizations of that name which operated in Guatemala in the late 1970s and in El Salvador in the early 1980s.
5. *Ibid.*
6. *Ibid.*
7. *Ibid.*
8. *Ibid.*
9. *Ibid.*
10. *Ibid.*
11. Arturo Cruz Sequeira, 'The Origins of Sandinista Foreign Policy', in Robert S. Leiken (ed.), *Central America: Anatomy of Conflict* (Washington, DC: Pergamon Institute, Carnegie Endowment for Peace, 1984).
12. *Análisis.*
13. 'Nicaragua's New Army: Fighting to Achieve Peace', *Envío*, año 3, número 8, Octubre de 1983 (Managua: Instituto Histórico Centroamericano).
14. 'Nicaragua's New Army'; *Análisis.*
15. 'Nicaragua's New Army'; Vegara Meneses *et al., Nicaragua país sitiado.*
16. Vernon V. Aspaturian, *Nicaragua Between East and West: The Soviet Perspective*, paper

submitted to Conference on Conflict in Nicaragua: National, Regional and International Dimensions, London: The Royal Institute of International Affairs, 28–30 April 1986.

17. ESCATF/D, *Dissent Paper on El Salvador and Central America* (Washington DC, 6 November 1980), mimeographed.
18. US Department of State, *Revolution Beyond Our Borders: Sandinista Intervention in Central America*, Special Report No 132 (Washington DC, September 1985).
19. 'Nicaragua's New Army'; Vergara Meneses *et al.*, *Nicaragua país sitiado.*
20. US Department of State, 'Building the Peace in Central America', *Current Policy*, no. 414, Washington DC, 20 August 1982.
21. US Department of State, *Revolution Beyond Our Borders.*
22. Affidavit of Edgar Chamorro before International Court of Justice: Case Concerning Military and Paramilitary Activities In and Against Nicaragua (*Nicaragua* v. *United States of America*), 5 September 1985. See also: *Contrarrevolución: desarrollo y consecuencias. Datos básicos 1980–1985* (Managua, 1985).
23. Vergara Meneses *et al.*, *Nicaragua país sitiado.*
24. *Ibid.*
25. US Departments of State and Defense, *Nicaragua's Military Build-up and Support for Central American Subversion.* A 3-part Background Paper (18 July 1984). See also *The New York Times*, 19 June 1983.
26. 'Nicaragua Delineates its Concept of Defense', in *Envío*, año 3, número 27, Septiembre 1983 (Managua: Instituto Histórico Centroamericano). See also 'Nicaragua's New Army', and Vergara Meneses *et al.*, *Nicaragua país sitiado.*
27. 'Nicaragua Delineates'.
28. *Envío*, Diciembre de 1986 (Managua: Instituto Histórico Centroamericano).
29. US Departments of State and Defense, *Nicaragua's Military Build-up.* See also *El Nuevo Diario* (Managua, 12 June 1984); and Humberto Ortega Saavedra, *The Defensive Character of the Sandinista People's Army*, statement released in Managua on 13 April 1985.
30. 'What's What in Nicaragua's Military', *Update*, vol. IV, no. 5, 28 February 1985 (Washington DC: Georgetown University Central American Historical Institute). See also Vergara Meneses *et al.*, *Nicaragua país sitiado.*
31. 'What's What'.
32. 'Relocation Effort Launched in Northern Nicaragua', *Update*, vol. IV, no. 10, 10 April 1985 (Washington DC; Georgetown University Central American Historical Institute).
33. 'What's What'.
34. Own conversations with EPS officials in Managua, March 1985.
35. 'Reserve Registration Drive Launched: Defense of Managua First Priority', *Update*, vol. IV, no. 26 (Washington DC: Georgetown University Central American Historical Institute).
36. Vergara Meneses *et al.*, *Nicaragua país sitiado.*
37. These events have been covered in some detail in Latin American Newsletters' *Weekly Report* and *Mexico and Central America Report* throughout 1986 and in early 1987. For early records of 'hot pursuit' operations, see the annual reports issued by the Honduran government since 1982.

7 The security of small Caribbean states: a case-study of Jamaican experiences in the 1970s

Caroline Thomas and Julian Saurin

The policymaker in the developing state is faced with an array of problems often unfamiliar to his or her counterpart in the developed states, and the security equation must reflect these differences. The Third World state is usually far more insecure domestically than the developed state. The essential nature of the Third World is often contested. The process of forging loyalty to the state may be at an early stage. Indeed, the survival of the state itself may be threatened by secessionist or irredentist forces. Sometimes the type of political system adopted by the new state may not serve well the requirements of state-building which are vital if development and social transformation are to take place. The problem of meeting basic human needs is overwhelming and the inability effectively to address this intensifies domestic instability and thus plays a crucial role in the security question. These problems of internal insecurity for Third World states make the problem of their external insecurity all the greater, and vice versa.

Externally, the insecurity of Third World states is characterized by their almost total lack of control over the environment, and this undermines any hope of expression of sovereign autonomy. The overarching geopolitical structure of the East–West divide places massive constraints on independent action by Third World governments, and has vastly limited both the possibility and the recognition of indigenous developments and choices. Non-alignment is a privileged policy which few Third World states can materially afford. The search for security by Third World states is all-encompassing; it extends far more broadly than the pursuit of military alliances or the acquisition of modern weaponry, though of course these are very important. At its core the search for security is the search for the autonomous expression of sovereignty. Accordingly, the economic and social dimensions of security are paramount.

This chapter examines the great difficulties faced by a single Third World state in the Caribbean area, Jamaica, as its governments tried to exercise the rights inherent in sovereign statehood and adopt a strategy for increasing the security of the state. This strategy was opposed by other powerful international actors, both state and non-state. The Jamaican example in particular shows the intimate and intricate relationship between the domestic and international spheres of policy for such states. During the decade under review, the attempts of the Manley governments to increase the security of the Jamaican state and people were constrained – in some ways even controlled – by external agents. However, external opponents were not the only obstacle: Manley's policies faced significant domestic opposition as well. Indeed, the particular Jamaican political and economic experience of Westminster-style democracy casts doubt on whether, external factors aside, there is a hope of development in such a Third World state which frequently radically changes its economic course. The method of the political contest seems to create deeper divisions within the state rather than build bridges and forge a domestic social, economic and political consensus.

At the fortieth session of the UN General Assembly in 1985, President Alan Garcia of Peru asserted that his country would only permit 10% of its annual export earnings to be channelled into debt servicing. Explaining this, he remarked: 'What we should ask ourselves is how and by whom was our economy impaired and what historical answer must we give to this situation.'[1] Michael Manley asked a similar question over thirteen years earlier, and had proposed an answer.[2] Manley's democratic socialism was an attempt to improve domestic security by restructuring the Jamaican economy to satisfy the basic needs of the majority of its citizens and to insulate Jamaica to as great a degree as possible from the damaging effects of commodity price fluctuations, interest rate rises and loan conditionality. It was further intended to reorient Jamaica's external security in the direction of non-alignment, thereby taking the country out of its automatic position in the East–West configuration.

The efforts to improve external security had great repercussions on domestic security, and vice versa; each dimension fed off the other and to a large extent they became inseparable. Manley saw all these efforts as a legitimate expression of sovereign statehood, and he championed sovereignty as a right of Third World states as much as of developed states. During his eight years in office, however, it became increasingly clear that the successful exercise of such rights was dependent to a large degree on external factors, notably the attitude of the hegemonic power in the region, the US, international institutions such as the IMF, multinational corporations, the market, and even the weather, as well as the internal political configuration. In the face of such obstacles and sources of opposition, the attempt of the democratically elected Manley governments to carry out a reorientation of Jamaican security proved fruitless.

In October 1980 Michael Manley was heavily defeated in a national election that he himself had called eighteen months before it was constitutionally due. Jamaica was in a state of economic and social collapse. Manley had concluded that the time had come for the Jamaican people to make a choice. One option was to vote for the Jamaican Labour Party (JLP), led by Edward Seaga, which would mean an acceptance of IMF policies, greater integration in the international capitalist economy and stronger links with the US. The alternative was that of re-electing the People's National Party (PNP), led by Manley himself, which would mean a rejection of IMF policies, the adoption of a new, largely untried road to economic development, and the broadening of international links. In the event, 58% of the electorate voted for the JLP, and only 41% for the incumbent PNP.[3] Why was Manley's vision of a more secure future for Jamaica rejected by the electorate?

There were two basic problems for Manley. The first was the impossibility of implementing a democratic socialist programme while being dependent on foreign investments and exports for prosperity, and the general incompatibility between democratic socialism and Jamaica's continued existence in an international capitalist environment. The second was that in a democratic, two-party state like Jamaica, Manley never had the time or the free hand to give his alternative a real chance. The problems he faced were not just external, they were internal as well. Jamaica was and is a very weak state with major internal divisions and a lack of political consensus. Great political prudence is needed in such circumstances, especially if politicians are committed to the continuation of democratic as opposed to authoritarian rule.

DEMOCRATIC SOCIALISM AND THE SEARCH FOR SECURITY

Manley was swept to power in 1972, and re-elected in 1976 on the platform of democratic socialism. The latter represented a total reorientation of Jamaican security in the wider sense of the term. He rejected the Puerto Rican model of economic development. He wanted Jamaica to develop with regard to, and not regardless of, the social and economic needs of the people. A detailed study of his policies and proposals indicates that he wanted to take Jamaica down an independent, non-aligned path. Unfortunately, this is not how his policies were portrayed either at home or abroad. Internally, democratic socialism stood for a mixed economy, with a redistribution of income and development of a social welfare system to cope with the massive problems facing Jamaican society, notably widespread illiteracy and over 25% unemployment. It stood for increasing self-reliance. Externally, it stood for sovereign independence. While opponents both domestically (the JLP) and externally (the US) represented the policy in terms of Marxist dogma, Manley's democratic socialism included none of the class antagonism which is an integral part of Marxist theory. The reorientation of Jamaican security was *not* an attempt to shift Jamaica from the western camp into the eastern in an economic, ideological or military sense. Rather, the aim was to provide basic needs for all Jamaicans and to make the state less dependent on, and less vulnerable to, external agents. In essence, it was an attempt to exercise the rights inherent in sovereign statehood – to choose a social, economic and political path without external interference.

In the domestic setting, democratic socialism offered the government a framework in which to analyse problems, order priorities and define solutions. Important industries and public utilities were brought under governmental control. Contracts with the multinational bauxite companies were re-negotiated in an expression of sovereign rights and duties (see Chapter 2). Buses and telephones were nationalized. Compensation rather than expropriation was the norm. Foreign investment was welcomed so long as it was consistent with Jamaica's needs. Minor efforts at land reform were attempted. Job creation schemes were undertaken, e.g., in 1975, 25,000 jobs were created for street cleaners in Kingston.[4] In the same year a minimum wage was instituted for the first time and government help for unemployables was given. In the poorest districts, rents were rolled back to 1971 levels. Under the guidelines of the democratic socialist philosophy, massive strides were made in literacy.

Externally, democratic socialism stood for the desire to develop links with any country, regardless of the latter's ideological colour, so long as it would help Jamaica. Manley thought this was necessary both to demonstrate the independent exercise of sovereignty, and because as a developing country functioning in an international structure biased heavily against it, Jamaica needed all the help she could get – whatever the source. Under Manley's guidance Jamaica was to move in just a few short years from a well-entrenched position in the western camp to a position of prominence in the Non-Aligned Movement.

Yet far from rejecting friendship with the US, and the rest of the western world, Manley extended the hand of friendship to them and beyond. In 1973 he commented that 'the opposition has done its best to paint a middle of the road administration in the most lurid colours'.[5] Indeed, his announcement in late November 1972 that Jamaica would seek to establish closer trading links with Cuba (which, after all, was another developing country situated just ninety miles away), the expressed intention to recognize the People's Republic of China, and Manley's acceptance of a lift to the Algiers Non-Aligned Summit in 1973 in Castro's Soviet-built jet, were portrayed in the Western media and by the domestic opposition in the worst possible light. The suspicion was that Jamaica was lost to the communist camp.[6] Yet the general philosophy behind these isolated examples suggests a less alarmist interpretation. While government rhetoric might have indicated otherwise, the practical extent of the Cuban connection was very limited. Moreover, it must be seen within the wider context of Jamaica's international relations. Hence, when in March 1976 the JLP and the US were highly critical of Cuban aid being given to train Jamaican security forces, they forgot that for the most part this training was provided by British, Canadian and US forces, and that the Cuban aid in this field amounted to the training of eight of Manley's personal bodyguards. The Cuban role was exaggerated and misrepresented. Saul Landau reported in the *International Herald Tribune* on 28 August 1976 that 'The charge that Jamaica is a satellite of Cuba has no basis in fact or logic'. Rather, he saw it as the product of an irrational fear in the minds of men who were not willing to allow Jamaica to follow the path of non-alignment and democratic socialism. Such fear dictated that Manley's support for Cuban involvement in Angola was seen as the act of one already in the communist camp and under Soviet control, rather than the decision of an independent and non-aligned actor.

In 1975, Manley made a significant political statement which amounted to a classical liberal stand: 'The independence of a country cannot be bestowed by others but actively achieved by oneself.'[7] His actions were decided with this end in view. Hence, as well as traditional trading partners, the importance of which Manley certainly did not underestimate, he pursued links with a wide variety of countries belonging to both eastern and western blocks and the non-aligned group. It should not be forgotten that Jamaica's early interest in states other than the US and UK was encouraged by the UK's entry into Europe, which disrupted her most important export market.

The ideological setting of Manley's governments displayed definite traces of socialist attitudes, yet this was very far removed from an espousal of Marxist–Leninist doctrine. It is a pity that his democratic socialism was portrayed in a garb which did it little justice and so much harm. Yet both Manley and his governments must shoulder responsibility for this. They misread both the domestic and the external situations. Perhaps, they were simply inept at the art of politics. An outright statement of political beliefs and social and economic preferences which goes against the tide of power and convention is rarely met with understanding by adherents of the status quo. Despite the sweeping victory in the 1976 election, prudence was required in the application of domestic policies due to the nature of the opposition, and also the fact that Jamaican society was renowned for its violent nature.

Externally, in asserting Jamaica's sovereign right to independence and in expressing this right by developing links (albeit minimal), with the communist world, Manley acted in a manner which offended western – especially American – sensitivities. Had he been more politic in his behaviour, he might have had a greater chance of implementing at least some parts of his vision. His emotional attachment to the morality of the Jamaican cause – and for that matter, for the cause of all other dependent and developing countries – meant that he lacked a sense of realism. He seemed to be unconversant with the rules and the reality of the international political game. An illustration of this is that while the social aspects of his domestic policy were given so much rhetorical prominence, other elements, such as the promotion of the private sector, were not. Many people both within and outside Jamaica concluded that the latter was being disregarded. In fact this was certainly not the case. The dilemma of the Manley governments – like that of any democratically elected government trying to alter fundamentally the socio-economic structure of a state – was that they had to attempt the implementation of long-term goals by short-term policies since their life was limited. In attempting to create a more just and equitable society and thereby increase Jamaica's domestic security, Manley's governments gave the impression to those people who did not delve below the surface that they were neglecting the very sectors on which the Jamaican economy relied – at least in the immediate term – to survive.

Democratic socialism provides the backdrop to Manley's conception of security in both external and internal spheres; indeed under it the two spheres merge. Hence, Jamaican attitudes towards the international capitalist system and relations with its particular agents such as the IMF, the bauxite multinationals and the Western powers, must be understood within this context. Here, attention is concentrated on the relationships with the IMF, for that institution was perceived in Jamaica to be playing a massive role in undermining the government's attempts to increase security. Moreover, the experience of the power of the IMF helped shape the attempts of the Manley governments to pursue a new path in the search for a meaningful security policy for Jamaica.

THE IMF AND THE JAMAICAN SEARCH FOR SECURITY

During the 1970s the Jamaican economy was characterized by a spiralling deterioration, reflected in the growing shortage of foreign exchange. The early years of Manley's government saw massive rises in oil and grain prices. Bauxite production was dropping, due partly to a fall in demand for alumina in the US and then to the response of the multinationals to the levy imposed by Manley on bauxite production. The banana and sugar industries were hampered by inauspicious natural conditions. The bottom was falling out of the tourist industry largely due to reports in the American press of 'reds under the beds' and violence in holiday resorts. Money borrowed from commercial banks during the years 1972–6 was spent on infrastructural projects which showed no immediate return. Jamaica drew on the low-conditionality oil facility and the compensatory finance facility[8] of the IMF in the period 1975–6, to avoid having to follow the austerity measures which come as an integral part of accepting an IMF standby loan. During these two years, however, Jamaica's economic fortunes declined rapidly, and in March 1976, her foreign reserves became negative. Prior to this, Manley had been able to turn a deaf ear to murmurs of discontent emanating from the Fund about wage inflation, fiscal deficit, restrictions on trade and prices, and monetary expansion. Now, however, Jamaica became vulnerable to pressure from the Fund. This was anathema to Manley's government, which saw the economic orthodoxy of the IMF as being informed by a political philosophy with which it was at odds. Worse still, Jamaica, like all Third World states, had no influence on policymaking at the Fund. For both reasons, the conditions accompanying IMF standby loans were regarded as illegitimate interference in the domestic social, economic and political processes of Third World states.

Before the December 1976 national election, the IMF told Manley that he would have to carry out a 40% devaluation as the price of a two-year standby arrangement. The PNP government decided to see what result the election would bring before taking any decisions. In the event, the PNP were victorious, and the idea of a 40% devaluation was rejected because of the cost in human terms to the poor. Throughout the 1970s the Manley governments clashed with the IMF over the importance to be attributed to the human factor. Many people in Jamaica believed that 'the adoption of the proposed agreement would be inconsistent with the political mandate that the PNP had freshly secured'.[9]

Immediately following the PNP triumph the voices of progressivism grew louder. The left wing of the PNP in particular, denied the validity of the Fund's call for a 40% devaluation, and questioned the basis of a resort to the Fund. Manley has written that this group believed that 'an IMF programme for adjustment and recovery meant delivering Jamaica into a trap'.[10] They believed that the Fund's policies were designed to cure the ailments typical of developed capitalist economies; as such they failed to do justice to the developing countries in either a social or an economic sense. Socially, they increased domestic tensions, since developed countries were far better equipped than developing countries to offer comprehensive welfare services to cushion the poorer sectors of their population against the adverse effects of IMF austerity measures. Economically, the government felt that devaluation, far from increasing exports by making them cheaper, would have no influence on some of them. The reason for a fall in exports in bananas and sugar had nothing to do with their price, but rather with problems within those industries which led to shortfalls in production. Moreover, the sugar exported to Britain at the beginning of 1974 under the Commonwealth agreed price of £61 sterling a ton, was being sold at one-tenth of the world market price.[11] Similarly, in the case of bananas, apart from unfavourable natural conditions, market factors, such as the dumping of bananas from the Ivory Coast, Suriname and Martinique by Fyffe's in late December 1972, led to a massive slump in Britain (Jamaica's largest market) of West Indian banana prices from £102 to £72 pounds a ton.[12] By 1974 the Jamaican Banana Board was losing £20 on every ton shipped to Britain.[13] If devaluation were to result similarly in less foreign exchange earnings from bauxite, the situation for Jamaica would be catastrophic.

Differences prevalent in the PNP began to crystallize. An attempt during Manley's first government to define socialism provoked, in his own words, 'immediate controversy within our ranks'.[14] For the PNP, ideological differences were long-standing. As far back as the 1940s, right and left wings had emerged, and the ideological argument had never been resolved. The elucidation of the policy of democratic socialism, far from uniting the party and establishing a general consensus, seemed to make the division more acute. Members polarized around divergent interpretations of, for example, the role of the public sector in the mixed economy. In 1975, Manley convened a committee on policy following bitter internal wrangling and the suspension of a political education programme. This committee faltered along, with no real results. It was after the 1976 election that matters came to a head inside the PNP, focusing on the question of relations with the IMF. In this battle, the left wing of the PNP won out. While never formally breaking off negotiations with the IMF, the government rejected the 40% devaluation, and tried to mobilize resources elsewhere.

Any real improvement in security depended on Jamaica both economically and socially becoming less vulnerable to the external environment. The aim of the new path was to re-direct the national effort to save the economy, whilst maintaining the highest possible level of independent decision making within the hands of the government. For Manley, the matter extended far beyond pure economics and hit at the heart of the issue of sovereignty. In his speech to the nation on 5 January 1977, he said in reference to the IMF's terms: 'this government, on behalf of our people, will not accept anybody anywhere in the world telling us what to do in our country. We are the masters in our house and in our house there shall be no other master but ourselves.'[15] Manley perceived the problem in terms of a struggle to maintain Jamaica's political integrity as an independent actor while this independence was under attack from the IMF which sought to impose domestic economic (and by implication social and political) policies and priorities on a theoretically sovereign state.

On 20 January 1977, Manley made an economic policy statement in the Jamaican Parliament.[16] Some of the measures taken including a wage freeze and tax increases, were in keeping with the previous IMF recommendations, but there was no devaluation of the Jamaican dollar, and on this of course Manley parted ways with IMF demands. The latter saw such a measure as a means to stimulate exports and cut domestic consumption, while Manley felt it would increase inflation. In April the government introduced a two-tier exchange system, which represented a partial devaluation of 37.5%. During the first six months of 1977 Jamaica tried to get by without IMF help, but since commercial lending bodies increasingly took their cue from the IMF Jamaica did not find it easy to obtain loans without the IMF's seal of approval. With her foreign reserves almost exhausted, there was little alternative but to go to the IMF once more.

On 12 July a loan agreement was announced,[17] and in August, a two-year standby arrangement for $74 million came into operation. Jamaica had returned to the IMF fold. The IMF got what it wanted in terms of a tight incomes policy and a high degree of fiscal restraints, while the Jamaican government got what it wanted in terms of limited exchange adjustment. The arrangement amounted to a compromise, but the trump card was held by the IMF since continued disbursement of funds depended on the fulfilment of quarterly performance tests. These tests reflected the IMF's desire for fiscal restraint, and they related to such issues and areas as credit to the public sector, limits on new external medium- and long-term borrowing, net foreign reserves and net domestic assets of the Central Bank. In December 1977, Jamaica failed the IMF's quarterly test, and hence the July agreement was interrupted. David Core, the Finance Minister, argued that Jamaica only very narrowly missed one part of the test concerning domestic credit expansion. On 15 December, the net domestic assets of the Bank of Jamaica failed to be below the IMF imposed ceiling of 355 million Jamaica dollars by just 9 million dollars, or 2.6%.[18] Jamaican policymakers were angry because of the marginality of the shortfall and because they felt this was partly attributable to the fact that certain foreign loans which had been expected to flow in with the IMF's seal of approval had failed to materialize. As far as the IMF was concerned, this excessive expansion in domestic credit had financed the fiscal deficit which now reached 16.3% of GDP instead of the targeted 9.1%, and had increased wage-price pressure. The IMF concluded that the end result was a further decrease in Jamaica's external competitiveness. Of the 74 million dollar loan granted in July 1977, only the first tranche of 22 million dollars was drawn. The loss extended much further than the IMF loans, for other financial packages, such as $32 million from a commercial consortium, were dependent on continued IMF agreement to help Jamaica. Failure of the quarterly test also halted the disbursement of a newly negotiated $30 million World Bank loan.

The country was in such dire straits that the government was forced to carry through a 10% devaluation which the IMF demanded as a precondition of renegotiations. It agreed to this only because it perceived itself as having no alternative. In an ideal world, a state could choose between joining the IMF or staying outside. Unfortunately Third World states do not have this choice. Membership of and loans from the Fund not only help attract private foreign capital – the former is a prerequisite of joining the World Bank, and membership of the World Bank is a prerequisite for borrowing from the International Development Agency. In rejecting the exhortations of the IMF, therefore, Third World states cut themselves off from many other major sources of funding. Thus, the Jamaican government felt it had to agree to the conditions set out by the Fund. It had been unable to mobilize significant funding from alternative sources. The Fund stipulated that the linking of the wage rate to the exchange rate was to be the basis of the new programme. In its control over foreign exchange, the IMF had ultimate control over a theoretically sovereign country. The new package took five months to sort out, and there was much bad feeling in Jamaica because it was widely believed that the country had been singled out for harsh treatment. The three-year extended fund facility loan concluded in May 1978, represented a $240 million package, or 270% of Jamaica's quota. Manley described it as 'one of the most savage packages ever imposed on any client government by the IMF'.[19] Overturning previous government policies, it aimed to reduce consumption and stimulate exports by pushing private sector export-led growth and minimizing government intervention. The two-tier exchange rate system established in April 1977 was abolished, and there was an immediate 15% devaluation on the lower unified rate, coupled with a crawling peg arrangement whereby the Jamaica dollar would be further devalued by 2.5% every two months for six months. The Fund also insisted on the biggest tax package in Jamaica's history. Wage increases were limited to 15% of an employer's total existing expenditure on wages. The objective was that funds released would find their way into savings to boost investment and lead to self-sustained growth.

Commenting in *The Times*, Michael Leapman wrote that

The story of Jamaica's decline into brutal austerity is an example of how little freedom of political manoeuvre can be enjoyed by theoretically independent countries which rely on overseas investment ... To keep Jamaica afloat, he [Manley] has been forced to adopt policies which hit hardest the poor people he so eloquently champions ... it is an unhappy irony that the advocate of the new economic order has fallen victim to the old IMF squeeze.[20]

Domestic reaction to the package was unfavourable. The left of the PNP saw its acceptance as a grave mistake, believing that Jamaica should have continued in the search for other sources of finance. The JLP felt the terms were too harsh, and should be renegotiated. The trade unions were bitter and divided. Having borne the austerity implicit in and consequent upon IMF demands, Jamaicans found that their country made little progress. It is surprising to note, therefore, that despite the hardships incurred, support for the IMF's policies did not completely tail away. A poll published by Carl Stone in September 1978, showed that 46% of Jamaicans favoured the loan, while 40% opposed it. By early 1979, the climate of opinion was changing, but the irony is that it was becoming anti-Manley, rather than anti-IMF.

There was no marked improvement in the economy in 1979, and the government's search for commercial funding was hampered also by an ill-timed speech by Manley at the Non-Aligned Conference in Havana in which he spoke out against the US blockade of Cuba and called for an independent Puerto Rico. At this very moment Eric Bell was trying to negotiate a loan package from a group of commercial bankers. The bogey of communism was raised yet again and Bell's efforts were in vain. Manley's ill-timed speech provides another example of his lack of political prudence.

As 1979 drew to a close, Jamaica became something of an embarrassment to the IMF as its policies did not appear to be working. Some of the tough constraints were loosened up. As December approached, failure of the quarterly test was anticipated. The prediction came true, the only thing in contention being whether the failure was due to internal factors (as claimed by the Fund), or external factors (as claimed by the government). Negotiations continued with the Fund until early February, when the government wanted wage rise limits of 10% and £38 million sterling of public spending cuts (the equivalent of wiping out the few remaining food subsidies and abolishing the adult literacy programme). Manley believed there was a basic level that could not be disregarded in terms of the provision of services to the poorer sections of society – which in the Jamaican context meant most of the population. Also, the Fund was demanding an estimated 323% drop in real expenditure in the country over the period 1980–1, and this would have entailed massive job displacement in a country where unemployment was already well over 25%. Moreover, the political repercussions would be vast since unemployment in the fifteen to twenty-nine age group was running at 40%. Such factors held no place in the IMF formulation of a package which seemed to take place in a social and political vacuum.

In early February, Manley announced that he had decided to call an election on the issue of the IMF, in an effort to settle an economic path for Jamaica once and for all. Addressing the nation on 3 February, he said 'I believe that the country needs to settle its economic strategy and that when it is settled it will be easy to understand what part the IMF should play; or whether it should play any part at all. What must be brought to an end is the present state of confusion, because the country has to settle on a path and understand the efforts, the discipline and the sacrifices that are necessary to that struggle.'[21]

Two immediate problems facing the government were that of obtaining funds from other sources (which had already proved extremely difficult) and educating the people of Jamaica (and especially members of the PNP) politically, to understand democratic socialism, and to engender in them in a few short months the feeling of unity, purpose, courage and determination necessary for the pursuit of a self-reliant policy, should the PNP win the election. Whichever party won, and whichever path was followed, the way ahead would be extremely difficult.

On 30 October 1980, the PNP suffered a resounding defeat at the national polls. Of the million who had registered, 86.9% voted; of these 58% voted for the JLP, and 41%[22] for the PNP. The electorate had been presented with a clear-cut choice, and so on the face of it the result can be interpreted as a green light for IMF borrowing and the policies that implied. Perhaps though it was more a reaction against something than for something else. The PNP had devoted far too little attention to educating people and familiarizing them with the goals and policies of democratic socialism. The slogan had won hearts in 1976; since then, living standards had continued to drop substantially. There was no deep-seated compelling ideology to justify the sacrifices. A literacy programme is not enough to instil devotion to a party when there are problems obtaining enough to eat. Another factor influencing the election result was the great increase in violence during Manley's years in office.[23]

In trying to make the Jamaican people and state more secure by transforming the society and economy, Manley fell between two stools. In a democratic and divided society like Jamaica, with weak institutions of state, the task he undertook was impossible of achievement for internal as much as for external reasons. Unless Manley was willing to adopt a more authoritarian type of government, it would be difficult for his policies to have a real chance; and were he to do that, he would anyway be betraying democratic socialism. Whoever is in government the control that can be exercised over the economy is marginal: the whims of an oil cartel, a fickle international demand for bauxite, contrary behaviour of multinationals, and the vagaries of the weather hold sway. Manley and the IMF represented divergent and incompatible interests. The IMF's insensitivity to the social and political consequences of its policies amounted to disruptive behaviour in the Jamaican political process, if not outright interference. Indeed, the Fund blatantly interfered in that process by providing the JLP with figures about the financing of the foreign exchange gap. The JLP made its ability to close that gap a major plank in its election campaign. Without a doubt the Fund violated the Charter of Economic Rights and

Duties of States: 'Every state has the sovereign and inalienable right to choose its economic system as well as its political, social, and cultural systems in accordance with the will of its people, without interference, coercion or threat in any form whatsoever.'[24] Clearly, the IMF acted against the dictates of this Charter, and intervened in Jamaican domestic affairs, violating her sovereignty. The development of strong states and governments, the price of which is often the shelving of the Western-type liberal democratic political process, in many cases may be a necessary (though not sufficient) condition for decreasing vulnerability and increasing the security of dependent and incohesive states.

CONCLUSION

An essential dilemma facing the governments of dependent Third World states is how to increase their country's security given the seemingly irreconcilable contradiction between the demands of functioning in the free-market system established and founded by western states, and the domestic political requirements of liberal democracy. A state such as Jamaica is caught in the double bind of having to conform to the principles and practices of the *laissez-faire* international economy in which it must struggle for economic survival, despite the often cruel effects on its own population, whilst simultaneously wishing to fulfil its obligations to its own citizens. As Macpherson has pointed out, 'liberal can mean freedom of the stronger to do down the weaker by following market rules; or it can mean equal effective freedom of all to use and develop their capacities. The latter freedom is inconsistent with the former.'[25]

In an attempt to resolve this dilemma, an alternative path of domestic development and external orientation was adopted by the Manley governments which entailed above all a revaluation of desirable national objectives and a reformulation of national security.

The Manley governments addressed what they perceived to be the needs of the majority of Jamaican citizens, rather than the needs and preferences of Wall Street bankers, Alcoa shareholders, IMF executives or Pentagon planners. The democratic socialist philosophy which informed the domestic and external policies of the PNP from 1972 until the electoral defeat of 1980 was perceived by the US as a challenge to an order vital to the sustenance of its own hegemonic security in the region. In this context, the domestic social and economic programmes of the PNP governments were transformed into security issues for the US. The Jamaican experience of the 1970s characterizes the predominant economic dimension of insecurity

prevalent in Central America and Caribbean states today, and it characterizes also the US response to any attempt to lessen that insecurity by
decreasing dependence on traditional production and trading patterns and
partners and by rejection of IMF advice. The politics of affirmation as
practised by Manley were translated by the US establishment from a
legitimate attempt by a sovereign government to increase security by
improving the general condition and welfare of Jamaicans, to a
subjectively interpreted attempt at domestic and regional subversion.

For the new states of the Third World, security is much more than a
military condition. Security for them must mean the ability of the state to
pursue within its frontiers self-determined policies, free from intervention
and fear, for this is at the heart of sovereign statehood. Whilst these may be
politically possible in theory, given formal sovereignty, there is a psychological dimension of security which is firmly rooted in economic affairs,
and which transcends frontiers. It is this additional dimension, which lies
at the forefront of the Third World crisis of insecurity and which
differentiates their interpretation of the concept from that of the western
industrialized states. For dependent Third World states, the phenomenon
of neo-colonialism is the very subversion of security; it removes the
possibility of independent choice and control. It is for this reason that
Manley has argued that the dependence on foreign capital and the
unquestioning acceptance of the existing trade relationships as manifested
in his rival Edward Seaga's free-market philosophy 'begins with an
admission of national defeat'.[26]

The battles between the PNP governments and the IMF exemplify what
control of the economy meant for Manley as a basis for self-determination
and security. It has already been stated that in January 1977, Manley
asserted that 'the government on behalf of the people will not accept
anybody anywhere in the world telling us what we are to do in our own
house and in our own house there will be no other masters but ourselves.
Above all we are not for sale.'[27] In contrast, the JLP under Seaga has
sought to increase security not through control but through integration
and accommodation with the designs of the hegemonic power. For
Manley, security is the politics of affirmation; for Seaga, it is the politics of
accommodation. Affirmation, however, brings with it the approbation of
the dominant power, the US.

In the context of security, Mohammed Ayoob has pointed out that what
distinguishes western industrialized states from dependent Third World
states is that the former have a status of 'unconditional legitimacy'.[28] Just
as their economies are dependent, so the legitimacy of most Third World

states is contingent upon conforming to prescribed behaviour. It is in the legitimating process that the democratic socialist experiment encountered overwhelming problems, for Manley demanded not legitimation or permission from the capitalist world at large, but acceptance of PNP policies. While it is within the authority of Third World leaders to make such a demand, it is not within their power to see it fulfilled. Perhaps this is why so many of them adopt the path of accommodation so unquestioningly, despite the fact that it represents the route to lesser insecurity and disruption, not the route to real self-determination and security.

NOTES

1. Cited in 'Creditworthiness: at what cost?', editorial in *Third World Quarterly*, vol. VIII, no. 1, January 1986, p. vii.
2. For details see E. H. Stephens and J. D. Stephens, *Democratic Socialism in Jamaica: the Political Movement and Social Transformation in Dependent Capitalism* (London: Macmillan, 1986). See also Caroline Thomas, *In Search of Security: The Third World in International Relations* (Brighton, Sussex: Wheatsheaf, 1987), ch. 7.
3. Quoted by Michael Manley in *Jamaica: Struggle in the Periphery* (London: Writers and Readers, 1982), p. 207.
4. *The Sunday Times*, 11 May 1975.
5. *Financial Times*, 18 January 1973.
6. Manley, p. 108. He points to the double standards of people who 'had watched De Gaulle put France on a course which set the example of detente to the world: who had lived through the Ostpolitik of West Germany under Willy Brandt; who had seen peaceful co-existence unfold into detente and were to watch Kissinger and Nixon set up their marriage of convenience with China', become hysterical on hearing that Manley was to travel with Castro.
7. *Hsinhua*, Peking, 31 May 1978.
8. The low-conditionality facilities deserve special attention here for they demonstrate the ability of the Fund to respond to a changing perception of the needs of the international monetary system with the provision of different facilities carrying with them differing conditions. To this extent they demonstrate that the Fund has a certain degree of flexibility and creativity.

   Of the compensatory finance facility, de Vries has written in the IMF's official history that 'In 1963 a decision on compensatory financing introduced a new drawing policy, chiefly for the benefit of [less developed countries]. Under this decision, members can draw on the Fund's resources to meet payments difficulties arising out of temporary export shortfalls, provided that the shortfall is largely attributable to circumstances beyond the control of the member, and providing that the member is willing to cooperate with the Fund in seeking appropriate solutions for its balance of payments difficulties where such solutions are called for. This second provision is much less strict than the conditions generally stipulated for drawings of a substantial amount ... in other words, there was a recognition that even countries which had difficulty in meeting the Fund's standards should be able to obtain assistance to meet difficulties arising out of genuinely short-term export fluctuations.' In J. K. Horsefield (ed.), *The IMF, 1945–65* (Washington, DC: IMF), vol. II, pp. 33–4.

   Like the compensatory finance facility, the oil facility of 1974 also catered to the specific needs of developing countries. The conditions attached to the facility were minimal. First, borrowers were to consult with the Fund on their balance of payments difficulties and discuss policies. Second, borrowers were required to refrain from imposing restrictions on their international transactions. A year later, in 1975, this facility was replaced by another oil facility which was more demanding. As well as the qualitative commitments of the earlier facility, borrowers were now required to provide a quantitative description of the policies they intended to follow. These policies were subject to assessment by the Fund.

9. N. Girvan, R. Bernal and W. Hughes, 'The IMF in the Third World: the Case of Jamaica, 1974–80', *Development Dialogue* (Sweden), no. 2, 1980.
10. Manley, *Jamaica: Struggle in the Periphery*, p. 153.
11. *The Daily Telegraph*, 9 November 1974.
12. *The Guardian*, 9 January 1973.
13. *Financial Times*, 12 March 1975.
14. Manley, *Jamaica: Struggle in the Periphery*, p. 121.
15. Girvan *et al.* 'The IMF in the Third World', p. 123.
16. See *Keesing's Contemporary Archives* (Bristol: Long 1977), p. 28220.
17. *Financial Times*, 14 July 1977.
18. Girvan *et al.* 'The IMF in the Third World', p. 215.
19. *Ibid.*, p. 160.
20. *The Times*, 27 November 1978.
21. R. Kincaid, 'Conditionality and the Use of Fund Resources', *Finance and Development* (Washington DC: International Monetary Fund), June 1981, p. 20.
22. Manley, *Jamaica: Struggle in the Periphery*, p. 207.
23. Manley, *Jamaica: Struggle in the Periphery*; Stephens and Stephens, *Democratic Socialism in Jamaica*.
24. *Keesing's Contemporary Archives*, p. 26954.
25. C. B. Macpherson, *Life and Times of Liberal Democracy* (Oxford: Oxford University Press, 1977), p. 1.
26. M. Manley, 'The Caribbean Basin: Its Political Dynamic and Possible Directions', *Third World Affairs* (London: Third World Foundation, 1985), p. 244.
27. M. Manley in a broadcast to the nation, on 6 January 1977, cited in Stephens and Stephens, *Democratic Socialism in Jamaica*, p. 150.
28. M. Ayoob, 'Security in the Third World: the worm about to turn?' *International Affairs*, vol. LX, no. 1, 1984, p. 44.

8 United States' security perceptions

Martin C. Needler

Because at the moment United States' policy towards Central America seems so rigid and one-sided, it is all too easy to forget that, over the long term, this policy has been variable and ambiguous. The force of this observation can be brought home clearly by any visit to the Dominican Republic, where the United States is remembered not only as the country that supported Trujillo and Balaguer, and sent in Marines in 1965, but also as the country that in 1961 conspired to assassinate Trujillo and then to prevent the reimposition of the rule of members of his family, and which in 1978 forced the military to accept the results of an election in which Antonio Guzmán, the candidate of the Dominican Revolutionary Party, defeated Balaguer, the favoured military candidate.

Here clearly is one source of variability in US policy: the fact that different United States administrations do not perceive American interests and values in the same way.

In the present chapter it will also be suggested that other sources of variability lie in the facts that the United States adopts different strategies depending on whether it conceives of the threat of revolution in an area as remote or immediate; that, because possible threats to national security lie always in the realm of the hypothetical, the same situation can be defined in quite different terms, depending on the premises adopted; and that there is a lack of synchronization in the way in which different sub-regions in the area are evolving with respect to United States hegemony.

These are sources of ambiguity as well as of variability. A further source of ambiguity is the process of policymaking itself, in which various individuals and agencies participate, so that the outcome of the process may be an agreed-on formula masking differences which remain to make policy ambiguous and fluctuating. Particularly under a weak or preoccupied president, US policy cannot be understood as though it were made by the single rational actor of classic international-relations theory.

THE WAXING AND WANING OF HEGEMONY

Let us take up first the point about lack of synchrony. It has long been asserted that the Monroe Doctrine, the formal statement which presaged assertion of United States hegemony in the Western Hemisphere (see Chapter I), always applied to Central America and the Caribbean rather than to the hemisphere as a whole. It was this 'backyard of the United States' where the Marines were sent, customs receiverships were imposed, and the Navy established bases. South America was, despite the Monroe Doctrine, left to the British, who proceeded to occupy the Falkland Islands, mediate between Argentina and Brazil over Uruguay, and train South American naval officers. What has been less often remarked, however, is that even in the backyard of the United States, hegemony was in fact shared with the British, who retained a string of dependencies in the region, not only in the islands of the Caribbean but also on the mainland, in Belize (British Honduras) and Guyana, although the last is of course at the margin of the region under discussion.

It is clear that in some respects United States hegemony in the region is weakening. Revolution in Cuba and Nicaragua; increased assertiveness in Venezuela, and, for a time at least, in Mexico, flushed by their oil wealth, and even in Guatemala; the Carter–Torrijos Treaties to abolish the Canal Zone and return the Canal to Panama – these are the most obvious instances testifying to the waning of US power in the region. In other respects, the US presence in the region is expanding. Honduras and El Salvador, long ignored before, now find themselves being transformed into vassal states of the US. The British withdrawal from the region means that the former British possessions are now turning to the United States as hegemonic power, replacing Britain as the military guarantor of the independence of Belize with respect to Guatemala, for example. The United States did not even go through the formality of consulting with the British before occupying Grenada, which the British had until then still thought was in their sphere of influence.

VARYING PERCEPTIONS OF THREATS TO SECURITY

The second source of variability and ambiguity is the absolute arbitrariness of the definitions of national security interest and national security threat which are paraded to give plausibility to, and apparently sometimes even to motivate and to structure, United States policy in the region. Let us take as an example the way in which the United States government has chosen to interpret different stages in the Sandinista revolution. Somoza, particularly in his latter, post-earthquake days, was obviously unsatisfactory. The Carter Administration nevertheless waited until the last possible time, when a Sandinista victory was already assured, to launch a foredoomed attempt to cobble together a non-Somoza, non-Sandinista solution. When this inevitably failed, the appearance of a US defeat was created. There seems no ineluctable reason why this should have been so. The Sandinistas were, after all, in alliance with a broad middle-class sector of the population. Their revolution could have been embraced as a popular overthrow of a dictatorship and thus a victory for the Carter human-rights policy. If it was feared that the Sandinistas might evolve in a socialist and anti-Yankee direction, there seems no reason why the Bolivian model could not have been adopted. That is, the United States could have opened the aid spigot, filling the country with Agency for International Development (AID) officials to oversee projects and creating such dependence on the United States as to co-opt the new regime and render it harmless. Enough properties had been inherited from the Somoza family to keep the revolution busy indefinitely trying to administer them, creating both a reason and a pretext for postponing any other expropriations.

This was the policy adopted toward the Bolivian Revolution of 1952. This was potentially much more radical than the Nicaraguan, its middle-class political leadership barely maintaining the fiction of control of its mass peasant and miner base. Nevertheless, this neo-Trotskyite revolution was finally manipulated by the United States to its doom in 1964 (whether inadvertently or deliberately remains obscure).

Further opportunities for co-optation of the Sandinistas were missed by the Carter Administration, and the Reagan Administration came in with a mind-set that defined the Nicaraguan revolutionary regime, quite without any basis in fact, as necessarily a Soviet puppet. Yet even given the presuppositions of the Reagan Administration, the situations that arose could have equally well – indeed much better – been defined in more productive ways. Given the Reagan Administration's concern with public relations, and the clear demonstration in the opinion polls and in congressional votes that the American public has no stomach for war in Central America, it is remarkable how the Administration has repeatedly refused to treat as victories what were indeed victories for its policy, handed to it by the Sandinistas on the proverbial silver platter. The pressures and threats and support for the contras were supposed at one point to be designed to force the removal of Cuban and Soviet troops. But when the Nicaraguan regime accepted the Contadora agreements that would have required the departure of foreign troops, the Reagan Administration refused to accept its victory as such. When the Nicaraguans even scheduled competitive elections and allowed opposition parties to campaign, the Reagan Administration induced the major opposition forces to pose a series of what were thought to be unacceptable conditions. When all of the conditions except one, the postponement of the elections, were met, the Administration again refused to claim victory. The Sandinistas' pledge in February 1985 that they would not acquire Soviet MiGs and would send home a symbolic contingent of a hundred Cuban military began to make it difficult for the Reagan Administration to keep on insisting that it had not won a victory. There is clearly much latitude in how situations involving national security may be interpreted.

Part of the difficulty under which the Reagan Administration was labouring on this point may have been that policy towards Nicaragua was being set by a committee, some members of which had as their goal the overthrow of the Sandinistas, others only the exertion of pressure which would cause the Sandinistas to abandon their support for the Salvadorean insurgents – which, it was apparently thought, might make it possible for the insurgents to be defeated; while still other committee members doubtless shared neither of these goals, or at least thought them too difficult to achieve, or not worth achieving, but were unwilling to be seen as dissenting, or as insufficiently tough, or as lukewarm in their enthusiasm for the President's policy goals.

ALTERNATIVE PATHS TO HEGEMONY

Beyond problems of this kind, however, there lies a more fundamental source of variability in United States policy: the opposition – not, as it is usually interpreted, between the requirements of national security and naive altruism – but between two different concepts as to how security may best be achieved. The point was made by Helio Jaguaribe in his book *Political Development: A General Theory and a Latin American Case Study.*[1] There are two ways for a great power to exert hegemony in its sphere of influence. One is by control, which itself has different styles. The United States, with some exceptions, has chosen what the British used to call indirect rather than direct rule; that is, to leave intact the local structure of authority, while setting guidelines as to what the local government is permitted and not permitted to do, reserving for the imperial power the right of veto. The other method, adopted by hegemonic states since the days when the Spartans set up oligarchies and the Athenians democracies in the states that they conquered, is to establish governments in the dependent state based on the same principles and supported by the same social premises as the government in the hegemonic state. Policies of the dependent country will thus tend naturally to be compatible with those of the hegemonic power, with which the dependent state government will sympathize.

Now it should be noted that the indirect-rule model of imperialism may be more or less benign. For obscure psychological reasons as much as on other grounds, the more right-wing United States governments prefer to rely on threats, suborning of military officers, and covert manipulation of various kinds while more liberal United States' governments favour non-military economic aid – but the principle is the same. Even to Franklin D. Roosevelt, Somoza may have been an SOB but he was 'our SOB' and thus had US support and tolerance, as did Batista and Trujillo. In a period of fundamental social change, such as the one that has prevailed in the 1980s, however, this kind of indirect rule lends itself to the criticism raised by Rómulo Betancourt: 'It is not understood why the friendship of the dictators who will disappear is preferred to that of the peoples who will remain.'[2]

THE ELUSIVE MIDDLE GROUND

The United States is a liberal capitalist society. Its people have no sympathy with the socialization of property, on the one hand, nor with hereditary aristocracy and serfdom, on the other. In its occupation of post-war Germany, the United States promoted workers' rights and anti-trust legislation, and, in its occupation of Japan, land reform. When it looks as though some Latin American dictator the United States have supported is about to come tumbling down, the State Department knows what should be done: it looks for some middle-class centrist solution, perhaps a Christian Democrat who will promote land reform and small private property. The problem is always that the State Department, or the President, sees what is happening when the moment for such a solution is long past, in Cuba in 1958, in Nicaragua in 1979, or in El Salvador in 1981. The optimal objective that United States' policy could hope to reach in El Salvador now would be a coalition of moderate pro-government elements with moderate opposition elements in a broad-based national government for peaceful reform – in other words a Duarte–Ungo government. That was the option the United States let pass in 1972, without realizing that was the last chance for an acceptable peaceful solution in the country.

It may well be that the Reagan Administration in the United States was located so far to the right on the policy preference continuum that, other things being equal, it would prefer a Latin American country to be ruled by a hereditary class of wealthy landowners exploiting serf labour, rather than a middle-class democracy of small and medium proprietors. At the same time, there are, no doubt, other observers at the far left of the spectrum who would accept a dictatorship dedicated to reorganizing the economy and society in the interest of the poor without elections, press freedom, and other guarantees of civil liberty. Within the broad consensus represented by the rest of the political spectrum, however, a policy towards Central America can be devised that transcends the ambiguities of the US foreign policy tradition and at the same time embodies successful elements of the policies of both Democratic and Republican Administrations of the past.

ELEMENTS OF A US POLICY

Clearly we must start from the acceptance of United States' hegemony. The political, economic, and cultural presence of the United States is so overwhelming in the area that United States' policy will necessarily set the parameters within which the life of Central America will go forward. In setting these parameters, considerations of national security necessarily enter. These must be, in the first instance, realistic. It is simply foolish to let policy be derived from fantastic scenarios based on putative Cuban attempts to seize Mexican oilfields, Russian air and naval bases in Grenada, and the like. The deploying of Soviet missiles in Cuba might arguably represent a threat to US security. Submarine warfare against tankers bringing oil to the United States could represent such a threat. In itself, the existence of a revolutionary socialist government in Nicaragua is not a military threat to the United States.

The United States has an obligation to look after the property and economic interests of its nationals in the region. If these are expropriated, representations should be made to secure just compensation. It may transpire that such just compensation would be minimal or non-existent if, for example, interests were acquired illegally, taxes were evaded over the years greater than the value of the property expropriated, and the like. The interest of the US government in such cases is to see that due legal process, which may be due legal process according to the legal procedures of the host country, is observed.

In addition to national security and economic considerations, humanitarian concerns of the American people have become part of the structure of foreign policy under the rubric of 'human rights'. Under pressure from members of Congress, human rights' considerations became part of United States policy in Latin America in the latter days of the Nixon Administration, especially under the auspices of Assistant Secretary of State for Inter-American Affairs, William D. Rogers, who became Under-Secretary of State in the Ford administration. This concern proved very popular, and was seized on by Jimmy Carter to become one of the central elements in his foreign policy. Human rights provisions are now embodied in treaties and have thus become part of the international obligations of states. They are thus not exclusively a matter within domestic jurisdiction, but states may be called to account on human rights' questions by other countries signatories to those treaties.

It should be noted that human rights policy is not particularly leftist or exclusively liberal. In fact, it is historically no accident that human rights should have become central to US policy at the point when Americans were generally ready to concede that the pro-democratic policies of the Alliance for Progress had failed. Those policies, representing the liberal impulse to create societies throughout Latin America resembling the US ideal of its own society, petered out following the death of Kennedy and a certain amount of disillusionment that set in because the original rather grandiose goals of the Alliance for Progress were not fully attained. It might be noted that disillusionment is only possible when illusions are present in the first place. The sixties did in fact witness tremendous improvements in Latin America in economic and social levels. The Alliance for Progress was a 'failure' in large part only because its goals were set unattainably high.

If that programme, in its political dimension, had been successful, that is, if democratic societies had been created across the hemisphere, then no human rights' policy would have been necessary. Human rights' policy accepts the fact that all governments are not well-functioning constitutional democracies, that oligarchies, military juntas and authoritarian regimes continue to exist, however it attempts to secure a minimum of performance even by such regimes, in such respects as the abolition of torture, or of assassination of political opponents, or of the inhumane

Martin C. Needler

treatment of prisoners. It thus represents a *minimal* programme which can be accepted by all decent people. It is to be regretted that such a minimal policy still needs strenuous advocacy in the hemisphere.

THE STYLE OF POLICY

The eighteenth-century liberal heritage of the United States, which gave rise to the fundamental ambiguity that runs through United States' policy in Central America, has also had an unfortunate effect on what might be called the style of policy, as distinct from its substantive goals. The same year that saw the American Declaration of Independence, 1776, also witnessed the publication of Adam Smith's *The Wealth of Nations* and Jeremy Bentham's *Fragment on Government*. Adam Smith preached that if government only prohibited anti-competitive practices, then the self-interested behaviour of free individuals would automatically result in the greatest good for the greatest number. Bentham thought that the same results could be achieved in social behaviour only by rather more effort on the part of government; in questions such as the deterrence of crime, the free behaviour of individuals would in fact result in the greatest good after the government had first carefully engineered a set of rewards and punishments designed to produce the desired behaviour. Inspired by liberal ideas of this kind, mixed in strange ways with Puritan concepts of sin and salvation, American models of human behaviour tend to assume self-interest as the only human motivation, punishment and reward the only means of shaping behaviour. This has as unfortunate results in child-rearing as it does in foreign policy. Criticizing the 'engineering approach' to foreign policy, Dean Acheson once wrote 'we must be gardeners, not mechanics'. Human beings, including the leaders of foreign states, are motivated by political sympathies, pride and emotion as well as by an egoistic calculus. Moreover, the process of transparent manipulation which the rewards and punishments school implies creates its own backlash of resentment. And the world has its own way of allocating punishments and rewards that must be taken into account by statesmen above and beyond those assigned by the makers of US foreign policy.

What this means in the case of Nicaragua, say, or that of a possible revolutionary government in El Salvador, or even in the case of the revolutionary government of Cuba, is that 'engineering' policies based on threats of punishment may not achieve their ends in the short run and are overwhelmingly likely to be self-defeating in the long run. Unlike an engineering problem, a foreign policy problem is not solved once and for all, at which point the engineer can turn his attention elsewhere. Foreign policy involves continuing relations with other countries unlimited by time and a policy, even one apparently brought to success, on the basis of threats of punishment, will leave a residue of ill-will that will rebound to the disadvantage of the apparently winning state at some future point in time. Traditional diplomacy had its merits in this respect.

ALTERNATIVE POLICIES TOWARD REVOLUTIONARY REGIMES

The United States has historically followed two different policies towards revolutionary governments in the region. The government of Jacobo Arbenz in Guatemala was overthrown in 1954, in part due to CIA sponsorship of an exile invasion. As a result, since that time the Guatemalan military has engaged in intermittent campaigns of urban torture, repression and assassination, and massacres of Indian villagers, in order to keep the lid on the cauldron of rising expectations left by the overthrow of Arbenz, whose reforms seem, in retrospect, mild ones that the United States could easily have lived with. The attempt to overthrow Fidel Castro by an exile invasion failed miserably and later policies of attempted assassination and boycott have served to lock in Cuba's alignment with the Soviet Union.

Concerning the Mexican Revolution, the US ambassador on the spot, Henry Lane Wilson, took a similar attitude, conniving in the *coup* by General Huerta against Francisco Madero. During the fighting that followed, Woodrow Wilson intervened on two occasions, once with the Marine landing at Veracruz, and once with Pershing's punitive expedition against Villa. He also played favourites in the fighting among Villa, Zapata, and Carranza by granting Carranza recognition and permission to purchase arms. But throughout the 1920s and 1930s no effort was made by the United States to overthrow the Mexican government, despite the urging of US Catholics during the twenties when the Church was being persecuted, and of oil companies and others when the companies were expropriated during the 1930s. In fact the Mexican Revolution was much more threatening to actual United States security and economic interests than anything that has happened since in Central America. Substantial American oil holdings were expropriated, as were American landowners. Churches were burned, and priests and nuns were killed. Not far south of my own home in New Mexico, American citizens were killed on American soil.

Yet the governments of revolutionary Mexico have survived to become co-operative neighbours and major trading partners, their presidents ritually exchanging *abrazos* with US presidents amid the pomp of Washington or the dust of some border town. This was the result of a policy of forbearance and restraint on the part of the United States, a policy that appreciated that in the normal course of events a government of any complexion situated in the American sphere of influence will find sooner or later that its best interests lie in its coming to terms with its North American neighbour, and that a minimum of sympathy and courteous treatment will eventually lead to the establishment and maintenance of co-operative relations with the United States. Why would anyone in his right mind prefer a Nicaragua that went in the direction of Cuba or Guatemala rather than in the direction of Mexico?

SUMMARY AND CONCLUSION

The United States' government would, of course, prefer to have a Central American situation in which it did not feel a necessity for creating and overtly maintaining exile counter-revolutionary forces. Under the classic model of indirect US rule in Central America, parameters are implicitly established – the 'open door' to US investment and loyal espousal of the US line in world politics – the violation of which bring sanctions in the form of the denial of markets and credit. To ensure the parameters are understood and respected, firstly, the attempt is made, by cultivating rising leaders and sometimes by influencing elections, to assure that right-thinking people come to power; and, secondly, strong relations of dependency are created between Central American armed forces and the US defence establishment, so that the military can be relied on to bring pressure on a leader who proves difficult, and, in the last analysis, remove him from power.

Normally, these mechanisms prove effective and the United States is able to avoid open involvement with military forces, either of exiles or, if all else fails, the US Marines; military adventures are costly and uncertain, and unpopular at home and abroad. In the Washington policymaking constellation, the State Department is normally a voice for moderation, restraint, and business as usual, arguing that pressures exercised behind the scenes by the normal diplomatic techniques will achieve satisfactory results. The traditional pattern for an American administration is for a president to take office with a distinctive perspective and constituency, to try to impress his own objectives on policy, and to staff key positions with his own people. Gradually, though, the established State Department position and way of doing things tends to grow up through the cracks and reimpose itself on the president's new direction, like the jungle relentlessly overgrowing the monuments of a vanished civilization. In recent years, at least, dissident centre–left policy initiatives have seemed less resistant to the remorseless forces of centrism, not being able to call on the resources of financial power and national chauvinism available to the right. Jimmy Carter's emphasis on human rights had run out of steam after eighteen months or so, while, with half of his second term over, Ronald Reagan has managed to maintain and implement many of his extreme positions against all attempts at co-optation by the State Department. One can speculate on the reasons for the extraordinary persistence of right-wing policies that are irrational and counterproductive even on their own terms, even if one overlooks the quantity of unnecessary suffering they cause. Reagan may even, in an extraordinary demonstration of what is meant by a self-fulfilling prophecy, manage to convert Nicaragua into an armed Soviet satellite.

Why has the return to centrism failed to occur in this case? Perhaps because Reagan himself is unusually ideological for a US president; that is, he refuses to accept the existence of facts that are not predicted by his *Weltanschauung*, rather than modifying his views in the light of such facts. Moreover, many people appear to find him persuasive, so that the feedback from public opinion to the Congress tends to reinforce his position rather than undermine it. The most cynical view is that Reagan is not particularly interested in what actually happens in Central America, but only in the public relations effects of his policies in the United States – that is, his policies have expressive rather than instrumental functions – either because their real purpose is simply to keep happy his primary reference group of wealthy right-wingers from California and Texas, or even because the President's former profession did not prepare him to distinguish between reality and wish-fulfilment.

Fantastically enough, the real purpose of the policy may be precisely to permit the survival of the right-wing world-view. David MacMichael, the former CIA analyst who testified for Nicaragua in its World Court case against the United States, reported that the contra army was organized to force the Sandinistas to become repressive, thus losing popularity.[3] That is, its purpose was not to overthrow the Sandinistas, but to create conditions that would enable right-wing fanatics to maintain that left-wing revolutionary regimes are necessarily unpopular, economically incompetent, and dependent on the Soviet Union. Reality becomes a tool for the maintenance of fantasy.

It remains at this point unclear whether the phenomenon of the fact

Martin C. Needler

that the Reagan presidency existed at all can be ascribed to purely
accidental factors, such as the unusually self-destructive character of the
Carter Administration and campaign, in which case US policy in the future
might be expected to retreat to the *marais* that is the normal habitat of the
State Department, where it would become more rational if not altogether
benign. Or was Reagan's election a response to some fearsome mutation in
the DNA that guides the regeneration of the American body-politic, with
all the unpredictable consequences that implies?

NOTES

1. Helio Jaguaribe, *Political Development: A General Theory and a Latin American Case Study*
(New York: Harper and Row, 1971).
2. Cited in Robert J. Alexander, *Prophets of the Revolution* (New York: Macmillan, 1962),
p. 138.
3. 'Hague Court Judges Listen to Latin Arms Testimony', *New York Times*, 17 September
1985.

Part III: Solutions

9   The militarization of the Commonwealth Caribbean

Tony Thorndike

I was the first political leader in the Caribbean to call for intervention in Grenada. I did so because I was horrified at having a brutal military rule established right beside the islands I represent in Parliament. I am just as appalled at having my country militarized. The Americans arming these islands are making the same historical mistake the Grenadian revolutionaries made. The armies you set up to deter others always end up pointing their guns at the government and people. Who, I want to know, will guard the guards? That is the unfortunate stage now being set in the Caribbean. What we need is technology and jobs, not guns.[1]

This cry from the heart by James 'Son' Mitchell, the then newly elected Prime Minister of St Vincent and the Grenadines in July 1984, expressed the dilemma facing the independent states of the Commonwealth Caribbean. With few exceptions, all are small with populations between 40,000 and 200,000; with even fewer exceptions, all are poor. All share the security problems that confront any state and a few others specific to their relative diminutiveness. Furthermore, they have to co-exist with a superpower neighbour in a region which resembles an arena of international competition for power and influence, with the Cuban ideological challenge undimmed. Their policies must be constrained not so much by being in the United States' primary sphere of influence or the 'backyard', as by the fact that the United States is in their front gardens.

As a sub-region of the Caribbean Basin, a geopolitical concept defined by United States' security interests, the Commonwealth Caribbean states share many of the problems of the region as a whole, such as dependency, underdevelopment, open economies and drug-related gangsterism (see Chapter 2). They are also beginning to share another problem, that of militarization. It is a side-effect of the matrix of international relationships which distinguishes the Basin.[2] The reality of stunted growth, economic dependency and popular demands and expectations led several to identify readily with the North–South dimension in international relations. Super-imposed upon that from about 1978 was the new Cold War, the East–West dimension, whereby they in common with their neighbours became unwilling objects of superpower confrontation.

The pressures associated with this dimension were late in coming, considering that the United States had concluded a treaty with Great Britain in 1940 permitting the construction and lease of air and other bases between the Bahamas and British Guiana (later Guyana) in return for fifty old destroyers. They had been gradually vacated after the Second World War except for a remaining facility in Antigua, Washington regarding the security of the Commonwealth Caribbean territories as being primarily a British concern. Colonial division and policy had effectively divided them from their Spanish-, French- and Dutch-speaking neighbours to the extent that the Cuban revolution of 1959 barely caused a ripple except in British Guiana: in any case, US influence was effective in other ways, through tourism, investment and migration. Their awakening to a consciousness of a wider world was due to the world depression from the mid-1970s which coincided with effective British withdrawal from the region. It led several of their leaders – Michael Manley in Jamaica and Forbes Burnham in Guyana in particular – and opposition groups and intellectuals both to examine the Cuban experiment and come to political terms with it, and to attempt to diversify trade towards socialist bloc markets, in spite of US preferences and disquiet. As the sub-region struggled to survive, familiar political patterns appeared undermined as hitherto alien racial and political ideologies surfaced. The Grenadian revolution was a clear indication of disquiet with the old order, but it was countered by an insistence by the United States and much of the Commonwealth Caribbean elites that the new order that it purported to represent could not be tolerated.

The dramatic implosion of the revolutionary government in Grenada in October 1983 was as much due to these tensions as to internal differences.[3] But although the US-led invasion that followed resolved the immediate internal crisis in that unfortunate island, the emerging contradictions were deepened particularly as US arms and US-trained forces were deployed in most of the sub-region of the Caribbean Basin. Political expressions of economic expectations and demands for reform sit uneasily with all-embracing notions of security identified, at least in spirit, with anti-socialism and very wide interpretations of what constitutes Marxism–Leninism. But the first requirement of a sovereign state is to provide for the security of its population. For very small states with limited resources and open economies, the problem is a real one. As a Commonwealth Consultative Group observed,

it is evident that, compared to other nations, most small states possess only a minimal deterrent capacity. They thus require substantial assistance not just initially to acquire vital self-help techniques but semi-permanent support provided both on a bilateral basis and multilaterally through institutions such as the United Nations and the Commonwealth.[4]

The impossibility in practice of the multilateral option leaves only the bilateral with all the threats to autonomy involved for 'small states located close to a great/superpower are especially vulnerable'. In the Caribbean, 'the concept and practice of spheres of influence has been entrenched for centuries. The fact that its dominant great power has become a superpower has created a special dynamic which has distinctly shaped regional foreign relations and increased the political and economic pressures.'[5] It is therefore a valid conclusion that 'the most obvious fact about small powers is that their security policy is governed by the policy of others. It follows that the student of small power policy, even more than the student of great power policy, must concentrate on the environment in which his subject exists.'[6]

This, then, is the wider context of the dilemma posed by Mitchell. The search for security by the small Eastern Caribbean states in particular threatens individual and political freedoms and deepens dependency. What is at risk are the values, tenets and institutions of the Westminster model, which security policy is aimed to protect. Bequeathed and deeply ingrained through up to three centuries of British colonialism on scattered societies the indigenous cultures of which were brutally smashed by the experience of slavery and the plantation, the central concept is that of a loyal opposition within a context of adversarial party politics. It also emphasizes non-partisan bureaucracy and military, freedom of expression, press and assembly and a supremacy of constitutionalism and of an independent judiciary over arbitrary power of governments, particularly when perceptions of natural justice are put to the challenge. In short, a cluster of vague, but firmly liberal, bourgeois presumptions and assumptions: no wonder it is an easy target for authoritarians, whether of the left, the right or of the bureaucratic–military variant.

It is clear that whatever the imprint of the Westminster model, authoritarianism is not new in the Commonwealth Caribbean. After all, colonialism itself was in its very nature authoritarian, however benign in expression. Furthermore, most of the territories have experienced personalist-type rule since universal suffrage was granted between 1944 and 1951, and some continue to do so. Normally associated with very small polities, it is by no means a phenomenon exclusive to them, as the experience of Guyana illustrates. Although the example of Sir Eric Gairy in Grenada and the intimidation, gangsterism and corruption associated with his regime was the most blatant, other leaders exhibited many of the traits of his style of 'maximum leadership', if not his tactics. What emerged in many of the societies were relationships between ruler and the ruled with a distinct patrimonial flavour, although the political and administrative systems remained formally constructed upon rational–legal lines. State control was, and is, a prize to be protected and as the state represents by far the strongest source of political power, government of the state, by the state and for the state is imperative. For any small state, public administration is proportionally a far more important employer than what would be the case in a larger entity. Public expenditure has an equally proportionally higher importance. For a small and poor state, both therefore are critical; consequently the power of patronage and budgetary allocation not only enhances the leader's position but also significantly affects the political and bureaucratic process. Opposition groupings and popular movements, particularly if they express what are considered non-orthodox philosophies or radical demands, may be met with force.

Small states do not differ significantly from larger Third World countries in the core social, political and economic demands of their populations ... Faced with such demands and often unable to meet them, states have been known, in their search for order, to increase the level of coercion with possible consequences for the weakening of democratic institutions. This, regrettably can happen more easily in very small states where government control is often far more pervasive than in larger entities ...[7]

Imperceptibly but surely, opposition movements become in turn more militant and radical, inviting a further turn of the government screw: national security forces are boosted above and beyond what is required and what the economy can sustain, leading to a reliance upon external military aid. Westminster parliamentary institutions in these situations no longer provide opportunities to redress wrongs, and bullets rather than ballots become the norm. When aberrations of socialism are added to the recipe for justification, armed forces rapidly expand 'to protect the revolution'. And the world second-hand arms market is easily accessible to supplement, if need be, arms supplies from ideological mentors on either side of the ideological divide.

Although such a scenario has not been realized beyond Guyana and, to a certain extent, in revolutionary Grenada (1979–83), the Commonwealth Caribbean has experienced since 1982 a growing militarization, a new development that has disturbed many. Whereas the militarization of Guyana dates to the early 1970s as a function of authoritarian rule, that experienced by the remainder of the Commonwealth Caribbean substantially devolves from US security policy. The insurrection by the New Jewel Movement in Grenada against the Gairy regime on 13 March 1979 was the spark, as what followed was an assertion of a specific political ideology backed up by substantial stocks of North Korean, Cuban and Soviet weapons, which destabilized a hitherto politically uniform and tolerantly pluralistic region. It was the fear of another Grenada that energized latent and existing authoritarian tendencies among many of Grenada's Commonwealth Caribbean partners and which encouraged the acceptance of military aid. In this way, the tensions inherent in the matrix of international relations in which the sub-region now found itself combined with authoritarianism to create a very obvious military presence. It did not develop without protest, however: by 1986, St Vincent and Barbados joined Trinidad and Tobago in refusing to participate in the largely US-inspired design for sub-regional defence and security.

Militarization has been succinctly defined as a condition whereby increasingly large sections of the population of a society become progressively influenced and dominated by, or inducted in one way or another into military and para-military institutions. It is a condition in which military type institutions become viewed by a ruling elite as an organisational panacea for the 'problematics' of external defence, social instability, indiscipline and the problems of . . . national mobilization within a society. It is a social condition in which regimentation is seen as a way of life. Individuals are either involved in or perpetually controlled by military institutions . . . Militarization in an ex-colonial society represents a particularly effective method of displacing an 'old' indigenous elite and replacing them with a 'new' and different type of elite.[8]

But while, as suggested above, this may apply to Guyana and – arguably – to revolutionary Grenada, these characteristics are more associated with Latin America than with the Commonwealth Caribbean. In contrast to the Latin American experience, militarization has not resulted in military regimes except in the instance of the very short-lived (six days) period of rule by the Revolutionary Military Council in Grenada immediately prior to the US-led invasion of 25 October 1983. In addition, there is neither a historical tradition which accords status and legitimacy to the military as a political institution nor an acceptance that the military is a medium of social mobility and a significant source of educational opportunity to the highest levels. The reason is two-fold: the presence until the 1960s of British military contingents as and when appropriate for security purposes, and the heritage of the Westminster model. But that does not mean that there are no threats to security.

Several key questions have therefore to be addressed. First and foremost, what are the security threats, whether perceived or real, facing these territories; second, how are they being met; and third, what are the political consequences of security policy? Wrapped up in these questions is another: how far, and in what circumstances, is militarization in the Commonwealth Caribbean a function of domestic authoritarianism, external pressure or a congruence of United States' and local foreign and security policy concerns?

There are four identifiable security requirements demanded by all states, and the Commonwealth Caribbean is no exception. They are the need to counter economic subversion, to provide external defence, to ensure internal control and to guard against revolutionary takeover.

The first, however, cannot be met by military action. The economic susceptibility of the small islands in particular to carpet-bagger entrepreneurs is remarkable. By a mixture of blandishments, deceit and an ability to capitalize upon naiveté, extraordinary concessions are often granted. The Space Research Corporation scandal of 1978–9 in Antigua is a notable example, whereby South Africa was able to import badly needed 155 mm shells via false documents unknowingly issued by the Antiguan government. The near-sale of 45% of Dominica to a 'shell' corporation in Texas, in 1974, and to another in 1980 representing, again, South African interests, is in the same category. The spread of off-shore banking is another; St Vincent soon acquired a most unfortunate reputation in international banking circles and kept it until the US Treasury forced the Vincentian government to take remedial action. Off-shore finance is also associated with the international drug trade, the profits of which can be laundered by the myriad of institutions involved. In attempting to counter this, the US Internal Revenue Service has only been effective in the remaining British dependencies because they were included in an Anglo-American disclosure treaty of 1961. To strengthen and clarify its terms, new treaties were signed with each, starting with the Cayman Islands in July 1986.[9] But similar action was impossible in the worst offender, the independent Bahamas. However, intense pressure by the US government, coupled with a domestic scandal regarding drug-trafficking and finance which led to resignations of Cabinet Ministers and a Royal Commission of Inquiry into the affairs of Prime Minister Lynden Pindling himself, prompted some reforms.[10] The interest of the United States in the Bahamas centred as much on the outer islands ('Cays') of the archipelago by drug-smugglers as the financial laundering facilities. However, by mid-1986 the Bahamian government finally agreed to joint action with the United States. Through the Drug Enforcement Agency (DEA) and the US coastguard, enormous seizures were made. Even the lethargic British government was finally forced to act in the Turks and Caicos Islands by sending police advisers and permitting DEA agents to operate on British territory. But that was insufficient: in March 1985 the Islands' Chief Minister and others were arrested by the US authorities for drug-smuggling and subsequently convicted and imprisoned, while in August 1986 the whole government was removed and the constitution suspended following a British investigation into corruption in the territory.[11]

The second security need, that of external defence, is the most orthodox and one for which armed forces are normally provided. Ironically, both Commonwealth Caribbean continental enclaves have unresolved border disputes. Belize's dispute with Guatemala has obliged Britain to break its rule of withdrawing militarily from any colony following independence,[12] and 1,600 troops and a RAF squadron of Harriers and helicopters guard the borders. While a Belize Defence Force is being built up, it must be admitted that a population of 140,000 can neither financially nor in terms of manpower support a credible force. Also, as Britain has refused to state what exactly its troops would do in the event of an invasion except act as a 'tripwire', there have been defence talks with the United States. Since the Belizian government is most anxious to keep the country out of the continuing Central American crisis, strict limitations have been placed on the type and scale of US military aid. Notwithstanding that, Guatemala is a close ally of Washington and it is difficult to see US forces mounting a counter-offensive should parts of Belize be effectively occupied by Guatemalan troops.

As for Guyana, the Venezuelan claim was the original justification for the development of its armed forces. In 1964, the British Guiana military totalled 2,135, or one to every 300 citizens. In that year the ruling People's National Congress (PNC), led by Forbes Burnham, assumed power with the covert aid of the CIA from the Marxist People's Progressive Party (PPP) administration. The military increased rapidly, accelerating after independence in 1966. By 1984, it reached 15,373 personnel, representing an increase of 673% and commandeering over 10% of recurrent expenditure on published figures.[13] Although there is an external security need, only 4,500 personnel are actually military pure and simple. The Guyana Defence Force is a minority, being supplemented by the para-military police force (4,208), National Service (4,500), People's Militia

(2,500) and National Guard Service (2,000). Not only does the total amount to an enormous burden in terms of opportunity cost given Guyana's destitute economy, but the bulk of the armed forces are clearly for internal control purposes.

This third need, that of ensuring internal control, is more insidious. Guyana is perhaps an extreme case, with a ruling party which declared its 'paramountcy' in 1974 and a government which has both delayed elections and falsified the results, and faces opposition on ethnic and ideological fronts. The armed forces are regularly used to control demonstrations and do not hesitate to use armed undercover agents ('the Death Squadron') when necessary, as most dramatically shown by the assassination of the radical intellectual Walter Rodney in 1980. In the latter days of President Burnham's regime, private armies funded by fugitives from US justice were occasionally called upon as a *quid pro quo* for Burnham's protection. That of 'Rabbi Washington' (David Hill) of the self-styled House of Israel was especially prominent, his forces being particularly effective in violently suppressing demonstrations organized by Catholic clergy, with fatal results.[14] Fortunately, Burnham's death in November 1985 led to the suppression of such forces by President Hoyte. However, although there have been reforms, falsification of election results and general repression continue, as much to contain popular dissatisfaction with national bankruptcy as to ensure the continuance of PNC paramountcy.

It is not entirely fanciful to suggest that Jamaica may follow at least part of the same path. Its forces are comparable in size – 9,700 in the Jamaica Defence Force and 6,000 police – and they are being increasingly used in the political service of the Jamaica Labour Party government of Edward Seaga to curb growing unrest. Political turmoil has considerably increased, fuelled by economic distress and deep-seated political frustration at the 'fraudulent' election of December 1983 – which resulted in a one-party Parliament after an opposition boycott on the grounds that outdated voters' lists were used – and the centralization of political power with the virtual emasculation of local government. Because the political alternative, Michael Manley's People's National Party, is viewed suspiciously by Washington, United States' military aid to Jamaica continues. It was considerably boosted to help pay for Jamaica's enthusiastic involvement in the Grenada invasion, from $1.1 million to $44.2 million in 1983–4. The 1985 budget was for $45.25 million, with a reduced sum for 1986. It should be recalled, however, that Manley also used armed forces to control demonstrations; but whereas Seaga does not advance justifications except law and order laced with some 'anti-communism', Manley explicitly justified force in clear ideological terms. It was necessary 'to combat imperialist-inspired terrorism and imperialism's local agents, and to defend socialism'.[15]

The Grenadian revolutionaries used approximately the same apology for the People's Revolutionary Army. With a population of only 90,000, it is astonishing to discover that a Grenadian army of 11,000 was planned by 1986, with motorized armour.[16] As the only militarily credible enemy both able and willing to use military action was the United States, even a force that size would be ineffective. The obsession with 'armed revolution' according to the Soviet–Cuban lexicon was both ridiculous and, as events were to unfold so tragically, sinister. Ironically, it was to prevent a repetition of what the embryonic PRA had done in toppling the Gairy dictatorship in the insurrection that led to its subsequent growth.

It is the fourth need, that of preventing revolutionary takeover, which is the most politically contentious, and one which has involved the United States deeply in the Eastern Caribbean in particular. The Grenada insurrection of March 1979, which involved only forty armed men, mainly youths, dramatically forced the issue onto the regional political agenda. But the issue was already a pressing one since there has been widespread realization that a serious security problem already existed in the area, bequeathed by the withdrawal of Britain and its economic parsimony.[17] The ability of most of the small islands to resist sudden takeover was nonexistent; Deputy Prime Minister Hudson Tannis of St Vincent complained that there was sufficient ammunition in the police armoury on independence only for three of the ten Second World War vintage Lee-Enfield rifles![18]

The first incident was in November 1976 in Barbados. Prime Minister Adams announced that a mercenary-led conspiracy had been foiled: John Banks, of Zaire fame, and a Barbadian exile, former opposition Democratic Labour Party (DLP) activist Sidney Burnett-Alleyne, were allegedly involved. Adams had been elected only two months previously, the DLP having been defeated. His Barbados Labour Party manifesto had eschewed any military force:

The party will not commit our country to any foreign defence pacts. Internally, the defence forces will be limited to such as are adequate to maintain law and order. There will be no need to maintain any standing army.[19]

But prudence dictated a modest arms purchase in London.

Another and far more bizarre plot involving Burnett-Alleyne emerged in late 1978. He persuaded Prime Minister Patrick John of newly indepen-

143

dent Dominica to allow him to use Dominica as a base to invade Barbados. John would then be named Prime Minister of both islands. Full of hope, the naive John travelled to Barbados under a false name and in disguise to await the invasion and 'call to the Palace'. Unfortunately, both the British and French intelligence services had intercepted Burnett-Alleyne. Deposed soon afterwards Patrick John was declared a prohibited immigrant into Barbados. Not surprisingly, these episodes led Adams to include in the 1981 BLP Manifesto a promise:

Events within Barbados, the Caribbean and elsewhere, have proved the need for Barbados to have a limited Defence Force with a capacity to withstand the immediate assault of potential marauders, terrorists and mercenaries.[20]

The events in 'the Caribbean' referred to the extraordinary sequence of events in nearby Dominica in 1981. There were three armed *coup* attempts against Prime Minister Eugenia Charles and her government, two involving pro-Patrick John members of the Dominica Defence Force and the third, Ku Klux Klan mercenaries from the southern United States. They and their mysterious backers wanted to secure a large part of Dominica for illegal commercial and financial operations. Charles disbanded the Defence Force but only after clandestine help was given by French troops from neighbouring Martinique. In the third and most serious crisis they were secretly flown in to restore order. Patrick John was subsequently imprisoned for his part in the raid. There was also the minor insurrection by a few armed rastafarians on Union Island in December 1979. The St Vincent government was unable to restore its authority and Barbados police flew in. The leader, 'Bomba' Charles, fled to nearby Carriacou whereupon the Grenadian People's Revolutionary Government (PRG) jailed and later deported him to St Vincent and Kingstown prison.

Notwithstanding that action by the PRG, fears grew in the region about the spread of leftist groups whose admiration of Cuba and its model and record of development was loudly proclaimed. Concern centred, for instance, on the 'Declaration of St George's' in late 1979, when representatives of the newly elected left-of-centre St Lucia Labour Party government and of the left-leaning Dominica Labour Party met with the PRG to declare common radical principles and positions. Their convictions were bolstered by a public demonstration which among other causes proclaimed 'St Vincent next'.[21] This unhappily coincided with a sharp about-turn in United States' foreign policy under President Carter. From advocating liberal positions on human rights and non-intervention, domestic political pressures dictated a far more *realpolitik* position. On the pretext of a stated 2,600-strong Soviet brigade in Cuba, a new Caribbean Joint Task Force was established, headquartered in Key West, Florida. Impressive naval manoeuvres were mounted and military advisers despatched to the Caribbean region as a whole. The Administration found much to encourage, especially on-going talks on a possible regional security arrangement.

The regional security concept grew out of talks began by Eastern Caribbean neighbours of newly proclaimed revolutionary Grenada with Britain during April and May 1979. Prime Minister John Compton of St Lucia had demanded that Britain intervene in Grenada to remove the illegal government, notwithstanding Grenada's sovereignty, but one by one most regional leaders came to terms with the situation.[22] As a consolation, Britain granted $10 million worth of coastguard equipment to Barbados. Backed up by Royal Naval technical assistance, it was earmarked for use on a multinational basis. By contrast, a request for arms by the People's Revolutionary Government was refused. Adams was reported 'delighted' at the designation of Barbados as the effective centre of operations and strongly urged the formalization of an agreement.[23] The eventual result was a Memorandum of Understanding Relating to Security and Military Co-operation, signed on 29 October 1982 by the Prime Ministers of Antigua, Barbados, Dominica, St Lucia and St Vincent. St Kitts–Nevis acceded upon independence in September 1983.

The objective was three-fold: to co-ordinate each signatory's security policies; to prepare plans for the use of police and defence forces on a regional basis; and to create an operational headquarters which could direct such national forces as might be required following a request by a signatory government. In short, it rested upon the stated principle that 'the interests of one participating country are the interests of the others'. Article 2 of the Memorandum named the 'areas of co-operation'.

The parties hereto agree to prepare contingency plans and assist one another on request in 'national emergencies', prevention of smuggling, search and rescue, immigration control, fishery protection, customs and excise control, maritime policing duties, protection of off-shore installations, pollution control, natural and other disasters and 'threats to national security'.

Part of this was a provision that the forces of each participant shall have the right of 'hot pursuit' within each other's territorial waters. A Central Fund was established, 49% ($734,039) of which would be met by Barbados and the remainder by the other signatories. This was to meet the cost of the Central Liaison Officer (a senior Barbadian officer) and his staff, located in Barbados, and the expenses involved in co-ordination and the maintenance of a spares and documentation facility at the Barbados coastguard base. About 1,000 troops and police would be earmarked for regional use by the signatories.[24]

The Regional Security System (RSS) was thus born. Despite North American and Western European attention centred upon the perceived threat of further Grenada-style takeovers, the signatories of the Memorandum were more concerned in daily operational terms with coastguard and associated duties aimed at smugglers and mercenaries, together with relief work in the event of natural disasters such as hurricanes. It was inevitable, however, that the vaguely worded provision to combat 'threats to national security' would attract interest. Antiguan Prime Minister Vere Bird took no time to express his enthusiasm.

The whole idea behind the Defence Force is that if so called revolutionaries get through today on your own island, don't forget there will be forces in all the other islands and you will have to answer for them. In this region, we cannot afford another Cuba or another Grenada. If this was ever to happen, our people will never be able to live in peace.[25]

In fact there was another route to possible regional action but one which had been largely overlooked: the Charter of the Organization of Eastern Caribbean States (OECS), signed in 1981 by Antigua, Dominica, Grenada, Montserrat, St Kitts–Nevis, St Lucia and St Vincent. Article 8 established a Defence and Security Committee charged to 'advise the Authority (of Heads of Government) on matters relating to external defence and on arrangements for collective security against external aggression, including mercenary aggression, with or without the support of internal or national elements'. The Committee was also charged with the task of co-ordinating the collective defence and security efforts of the OECS members and developing close ties among them in these matters.

The main reasons why the provisions of the OECS relating to security were overlooked were, first, that the Organization was primarily seen as a vehicle for co-ordinating economic and foreign policies on a sub-regional basis to help promote a more united voice by the smaller islands in regional and international fora and in international relations generally. Second was the fact of Grenadian membership which permitted the PRG to add the OECS to its defensive armour against the United States. Third was the reservation imposed by Britain upon any involvement by Montserrat in matters of security by virtue of Montserrat's continued colonial status. Despite these factors, the OECS was to play a prominent role in the US decision to invade Grenada.

Whereas Grenada's Eastern Caribbean neighbours were more worried about the lack of constitutional legitimacy and various human rights abuses by the PRG, United States' concern centred upon the PRG's close ties with Cuba in particular. Not surprisingly, therefore, US interest in the Memorandum was soon to be translated into involvement through training facilities and equipment. Soon after its signature, a small security team was installed at the US Embassy in Barbados and, when the new Embassy was opened in Antigua, a branch office was included. Again Vere Bird had no reservations: 'We, the little birds of the Caribbean', he announced, 'need a big eagle to protect us.'[26] His sentiments were echoed by Eugenia Charles upon her installation as OECS chairperson. By February 1983, thirty US military advisers were stationed in the Commonwealth Eastern Caribbean, plus another twenty-one in Belize.

In fact little was done in terms of regional organization as such: what was needed was a stimulus. The stimulus was the killing of the Grenadian Prime Minister Maurice Bishop and up to sixty others on 19 October 1983 and the subsequent assumption to power of the Revolutionary Military Council. The Authority of the OECS met two days later, at which all members but Grenada were represented. It determined to use force to remove the military government.[27] In so doing it acted in contravention of its Charter in that decisions were subject to an unanimity rule – but Grenada was absent. The decision was also legally dubious as there was no specific authorization for military action by the Organization against one of its members.[28] In the event, it was under the auspices of the 1982 Memorandum and the Regional Security System rather than the OECS that a Caribbean Peacekeeping Force entered Grenada once the US armed forces had secured the island.

The Grenada crisis not only made the Regional Security System much more of a reality but also ensured a much higher US profile. US training teams were attached to the Caribbean contingents in Grenada, both army and police, and additionally to the various home bases. Teams of eight were sent to the five small islands (Antigua, Dominica, St Kitts–Nevis, St Lucia and St Vincent), twenty-five to Barbados and twelve to Jamaica.[29] In a different theatre, fifty-two were despatched to Belize. These were quite apart from the 6,500 US combat troops involved in the invasion, which were soon reduced to 250 by January 1984 and finally withdrawn in June 1985 despite loud protests by the post-revolutionary and strongly pro-US government of Prime Minister Herbert Blaize.[30]

What kind of training and aid was given? Equipment and uniforms only were distributed to Belize, US army trainers working with their British counterparts in the Belize Defence Force using British NATO standard arms. Military training, arms and equipment were allocated to Jamaica

Tony Thorndike

and Barbados, reinforced by joint manoeuvres of US and Jamaican troops in the United States. In the small Eastern Caribbean islands, however, it took the form of police paramilitary training and the creation of paramilitary units within the national police forces dubbed Special Support Units (SSUs). However, a constitutional problem had to be overcome with this particular programme.

The difficulty was that for the United States, section 90 of the Foreign Assistance Act passed by the US Congress in 1974 specifically wound up the US Agency for International Development's Public Security Assistance Program. In other words, the training of foreign police forces was forbidden. This was overcome by a creative interpretation of 'police'; police trained in US Special Weapons and Training (SWAT) methods alongside the US National Guard were classified as neither wholly military nor a police force but rather as a 'militia'. Accordingly, militia rather than police courses incorporating SWAT had commenced secretly in early 1982 at the Caribbean Police Academy in the Roosevelt Roads US naval base in Puerto Rico. Billed as providing training in 'interrogation techniques and data storage and retrieval', Jamaican and Trinidadian forces predominated. Previous to that, police forces from the Dominican Republic, Jamaica, Barbados and Dominica received 'civil disobedience' combat training at the Puerto Rico National Guard camp at Salinas from early 1981: this was a logical outcome of the island's National Guard's acquisition of a regional training role from 1979 onwards.[31] The training of the SSUs commenced in November 1983, their size ranging from forty (St Kitts–Nevis) to eighty (Grenada). 'Normal' police training was provided by Britain, through the UK-financed regional police facility in Barbados. Opposition to their formation was swiftly suppressed: the Superintendent of Police in Dominica was forced to resign.

The finance for such work and equipment (including rocket launchers, machine guns, M-16 carbines, telecommunications and armoured vehicles) came from two sources, the Military Assistance Program and the International Military Education and Training budget. Costing only $1.2 million in 1982, it rose sharply to $7.2 million in 1984, rising to an estimated $8.5 million in 1985, including three coastguard vessels at $1.4 million each.[32] The training and equipping of the Caribbean Peacekeeping Force in Grenada cost a further $15 million. By contrast, the Belize programme cost a mere $1 million per year. Indeed, 'the smell of cordite hardly had time to dissipate in Grenada when special forces training teams from Fort Bragg, North Carolina, began landing on neighbouring islands with new weaponry'.[33]

148

The training and equipping of the SSUs and defence forces was paralleled by a series of manoeuvres involving them and US troops airlifted from the United States. Not only did this make clear America's ability to move substantial numbers at very short notice but also its willingness to do so if asked, a point firmly made by the US Ambassador on a farewell visit to Dominica in May 1984.[34] Moreover, the manoeuvres had a thinly disguised political message. The first, codenamed 'Exotic Palm', took place in September 1985 and involved a sea and air action against St Lucia utilizing US and British forces and all the SSUs bar that of St Vincent. The scenario was of a small island, 'Linus', the government of which had been toppled by fifty insurgents supported by 'Carumba' and 'Niggaro' and which had requested RSS and US assistance.[35] A similar scenario was enacted in part of the much bigger 'Ocean Venture' manoeuvres of April–May 1986, an annual exercise specifically for US forces dating from 1981. Although the bulk of the exercise was conducted around Puerto Rico, the Eastern Caribbean segment concentrated upon Grenada and involved over 1,000 soldiers and police from the US, Jamaica, Antigua, Dominica, Grenada, St Kitts–Nevis and St Lucia, directed by the RSS staff in Barbados. Controversy was made all the sharper by the fact that it coincided with the opening of the trial of the 18 accused of the killing of Bishop and others.

But controversy was not limited to that incident. The manoeuvres and training programmes glossed over differences in policy between the parties involved, a lack of full support and a developing disquiet concerning the use of the Special Support Units in particular.

Once the Grenada operation was over, Prime Ministers Adams and Compton in particular argued forcefully for a multinational force-based Regional Security System. They pressed for the up to 1,000-strong force, earmarked for regional use under the auspices of the 1982 Memorandum arrangements, to be a permanent contingent and multinational in composition and leadership. It should either be located in Barbados or split between up to three bases and, they stressed, be able to strike when necessary and to call upon local troops and police for additional assistance as circumstances demanded. One factor was the threat posed to governments in small islands by their own security forces, a reference to the unloved period of military rule in Grenada, a point made clear by Adams in a speech to the Barbados Labour Party in January 1984.

A study is now underway to determine whether we can establish a full regional defence force, thus extending the protection available against mercenary adventurers, other external aggression, domestic revolution and other violent episodes. My feeling is that one regional army rather than a number of national armies would give us an additional safeguard, namely the protection of small governments against their own armed forces.[36]

The United States did not favour the proposal, dubbed 'a Caribbean NATO'.[37] It pointed out that there was no agreement, nor could there be in advance, on the exact circumstances of the use and deployment of such a force. The United States was also mindful of the doleful history of co-operation between the Commonwealth Caribbean territories and foresaw arguments as to bases and appointments, particularly if Jamaica, by far the largest country, was a participant. There was also the implicit assumption that it would have to provide most of the funding, at least in the first instance. A further problem was the exclusion of Trinidad and Tobago. Prime Minister Chambers had stood aloof from the Grenada operation and refused point blank to permit the inclusion of the oil-rich twin-island Republic in any regional defence arrangements which appeared to serve US political and economic interests as much as the strategic. In the event, Vere Bird and Blaize were lukewarm: both preferred bilateral agreements with Washington. The last straw was a U-turn by Eugenia Charles on the issue. Admittedly, Vere Bird's son, Deputy Prime Minister Lester Bird, eventually endorsed the multilateral scheme but only in reaction to his father's virtual total support for the United States.

In March 1984, it was announced that the Eastern Caribbean islands would be given extra coastguard equipment in a joint programme with Britain and Canada and that no formal bilateral agreements would be negotiated, bearing in mind expected Congressional opposition and hemispheric political reaction. Instead, informal 'understandings' were to be reached with each island in turn, US resolve being shown by the regional manoeuvres. True to its word, 'understandings' were reached with each RSS signatory between May and September 1984. In addition, agreement was reached in November 1985 with the Antiguan government for the use by the United States of its naval base on the island for training regional defence forces and police.[38]

Rudely interrupting this process, however, was the surfacing of strong reservations about the exploitation of the RSS by the United States, the use of the island-based Special Support Units by their respective governments and the potential of the region as an arms producer for the United States. Within hours of his party's victory in the July 1984 St Vincent general election, Prime Minister Mitchell made it clear that he would neither permit Vincentian forces to participate in regional manoeuvres nor allow the Vincentian SSU to operate except under extreme circumstances. The newly trained paramilitary force had to return to barracks, remove their camouflaged fatigues and become unarmed policemen, as before. His attitude to both the RSS and SSU was doubtless influenced by the misuse of both by the outgoing defeated Prime Minister, Milton Cato. Faced with a hostile crowd demanding his resignation as the poll results became known, Cato radioed for Barbadian assistance – which was despatched in the form of an armed coastguard vessel and a small Defence Force contingent – and put the SSU on full alert. Mitchell was informed and Adams readily agreed to the force's withdrawal once the facts were known. Prime Minister Blaize also misused the Grenadian SSU: in July 1985 it was mobilized with full equipment to arrest the operator of a private radio station and to close it on its first day of operation despite the fact that the operator had a licence.[39] Mitchell's obduracy was later reinforced by the electoral victory of the Democratic Labour Party in Barbados in May 1986. Prime Minister Errol Barrow made his position clear.

We have to watch this regional security scheme very carefully because it was contrived in Washington and I have reservations about anybody in Washington sitting down and telling us what we should have in the Eastern Caribbean. We opposed militarisation when we were in opposition, and we will oppose it now.[40]

He went on to suggest that the Barbados Defence Force should be reduced from over 1,000 to between 180 and 350, the surplus personnel directed to the under-staffed police force. As if this was not enough to alarm his more conservative neighbours, he went on to remark that Seaga and Eugenia Charles 'think the solution to their country's problems is to get President Reagan to play Santa Claus'.

Although an angry Eugenia Charles retorted that the RSS was a Caribbean creation, its close identification with US interest was becoming an embarrassment. Even Compton, an ardent supporter of the system and of the SSUs, privately expressed fears that the US Department of Defence and senior US military officers 'may have misunderstood the region's interest' in establishing such forces.[41]

The controversy was rekindled by a firm denial by Barrow of a statement from a Dominican official in late August 1986 that Barbados had agreed to the upgrading of the 1982 Memorandum to the status of an international treaty with binding provisions in relation to the regional deployment of national forces and SSUs. Barrow reaffirmed, however, Barbados' obligations under the Memorandum with regard to coastguard duties and limited forms of training. Although Eugenia Charles admitted that there had been no such agreement, a RSS staff paper stressed not only 'the likelihood' of its conversion to a treaty but also the necessity for more arms and resources to prevent 'internal security problems in a member state'.[42] An exasperated Barrow warned all other RSS participants that his government

has firm reservations over the use of our resources for militaristic purposes or for the unjustifiable usurpation of the sovereignty of our country by alien influences. Consequently, the government of Barbados is not prepared to elevate or upgrade the Memorandum to the status of a treaty and does not support the proposal that this should be done.[43]

Almost in the same breath, he supported a call by the Caribbean Conference of Churches at its 1986 conference for a 'peace zone' in the region. Before the conference was a report alleging that the United States was encouraging the establishment of plants for the manufacture of military equipment in the area through the auspices of the 1984 US trade access agreement, the Caribbean Basin Initiative.[44]

Barrow's reaction was well received, an indication that the political implications of the RSS were beginning to be appreciated. The Commonwealth Caribbean style of militarization had frozen the status quo and contributed to the lack of direction which has become such a marked feature of this segment of the Caribbean Basin since October 1983. The English-speaking territories are caught between US perceptions of the Basin as a geopolitical unity and, moreover, one under a constant Soviet–Cuban threat, and the need to permit dissent within the general framework of the Westminster model. Indications of hysteria, such as the willing response to Blaize's call in November 1986 for assistance under the Regional Security System when death sentences were imposed upon fourteen of those convicted of involvement in the murder of his predecessor, Maurice Bishop, have done little to inspire confidence. Given the clear necessity for security, the need for an acceptable balance with freedom is clear. The newly independent Commonwealth Caribbean states are slowly coming of age in their attempt to resolve the conundrum. But the attempt will fall short if it is not accompanied by a deepened sense of national pride and a belief that, after centuries of colonialism, it is time for their peoples generally to develop values and institutions suited to their own circumstances and which respect the central importance of political and constitutional legitimacy and democratic practice. This respect distinguishes the Commonwealth Caribbean states from their Hispanic neighbours as well as from the Third World generally, and its loss in the name of security would be irreparable.

NOTES

1. *Caribbean Insight* (London), August 1984.
2. A. J. Payne, *The International Crisis of the Caribbean* (London: Croom Helm, 1984), p. 156.
3. Tony Thorndike, *Grenada: Politics, Economics and Society* (London: Frances Pinter, 1985), pp. 176–91.
4. Report of a Commonwealth Consultative Group, *Vulnerability: Small States in the Global Society* (London: Commonwealth Secretariat, 1985), p. 38.
5. *Ibid.*, p. 28.
6. J. E. Spence quoted in Michael Handel, *Weak States in the International System* (London: Frank Cass, 1981), p. 4.
7. Commonwealth Consultative Group, *Vulnerability*, p. 36.
8. G. K. Danns, *Domination and Power in Guyana* (New Brunswick, NJ: Transaction Books, 1982), pp. 143–4.
9. *Caribbean Insight*, August 1986.
10. *The Economist*, 12 October 1985.
11. *Turks and Caicos Commission of Inquiry 1986*, by Louis Blom-Cooper QC (London: HMSO, Cmnd 21, December 1986).
12. Apart from Cyprus, the only other exception to the author's knowledge was the Anglo-Nigerian Military Agreement which, however, only lasted for a year after independence in 1960.
13. A more realistic estimate is nearer 15%. Figures from G. K. Danns, 'The Role of the Military in the National Security of Guyana', unpublished paper presented to Caribbean Studies Association Conference, June 1984.
14. *Caribbean Contact* (Barbados), June 1982.
15. Address to PNP National Congress, November 1978.
16. Thorndike, *Grenada*, p. 121.
17. R. Sim and J. Anderson, *The Caribbean Strategic Vacuum* (London: Institute for the Study of Conflict, Conflict Studies no. 121, August 1980).
18. *House of Assembly Debates, St Vincent*, 30 October 1983, p. 16.
19. *Barbados Labour Party Manifesto*, 1976, p. 15.
20. *Barbados Labour Party Manifesto*, 1981, p. 13.
21. *The Guardian*, 19 November 1979.
22. *Latin American Political Report* (London: Latin American Newsletters), 23 March 1979.
23. *Barbados Advocate*, 5 September 1982.
24. *Bulletin of Eastern Caribbean Affairs*, vol. IX, no. 1, February/March 1983, pp. 15–21.
25. *Caribbean Insight*, April 1983.
26. *Caribbean Contact*, March 1983.
27. Statement by the Secretariat of the Organization of Eastern Caribbean States, UN Security Council Doc. S16070, 25 October 1983.
28. W. Gilmore, 'Legal and Institutional Aspects of the Organization of Eastern Caribbean States', *Review of International Studies*, vol. XI, no. 4, October 1985, p. 132.
29. *Nation* (Barbados), 30 January 1984.
30. *Caribbean Insight*, July 1985.
31. Information from interviews with US personnel, Grenada and Barbados, January–July 1984.
32. *Miami Herald*, 1 March 1984.
33. Bernard Diederich, 'The End of West Indian Innocence: Arming the Police', *Caribbean Review*, vol. XIII, no. 2, spring 1984, p. 11.
34. *Miami Herald*, 22 May 1984.
35. *Caribbean Contact*, October 1985.
36. *Nation*, 23 January 1984 (the speech was delivered on 21 January 1984).
37. *The Observer*, 22 February 1984.
38. *Caribbean Insight*, December 1985.
39. *Caribbean Insight*, August 1985.
40. *Latin American Newsletters: Caribbean Report*, no. RC-86-05, 13 June 1986.
41. *Caribbean Insight*, June 1985.

42. *Nation*, 10 September 1986.
43. *Latin American Newsletters: Caribbean Report*, no. RC-86-08, 2 October 1986.
44. *Boots, Boots, Boots* (San Juan, PR: Caribbean Project for Justice and Peace, September 1986).

10 Pacification, security and democracy: Contadora's role in Central America

Esperanza Durán

Since January 1983 the Contadora group, formed by Mexico, Panama, Colombia and Venezuela, has tried to mediate between the Central American countries and to find a negotiated solution to the conflicts in the region which threatened regional (or even global) peace and security. And yet, after more than four years of negotiations the Contadora group is still far from achieving its main objective. However, during this time the Contadora process has occupied a central role in attempts at mediation and compromise among hostile neighbours. It has kept the dialogue between the Central American countries going and has provided the forum for negotiations.[1] In fact, this is probably the most valuable contribution Contadora has rendered the Central American countries: continued communication among themselves and, with it, the self-assurance that differences could be resolved by negotiations.

The peacemaking process started by Contadora, however, seems to have been overtaken by events and situations which, ironically, Contadora itself helped to create. The Central American countries acting in parallel or independently of Contadora, began playing a much more active role in launching initiatives aimed at the same objectives as Contadora: the easing of regional tensions through dialogue and negotiation.

The purpose of this chapter is to examine the evolution of the Contadora process, focusing particularly on the ways it tried to resolve political and security problems. The obstacles to achieving consensus around Contadora stalled the process and led the Central Americans to take more assertive actions. Thus the second part will focus on the relations between the Central American countries and the background to and the prospects of the peace initiatives proposed by them. The third part will concentrate on the major actor in the region, the United States, how it perceives the Central American situation affecting its national interests and what have

155

Esperanza Durán

been its responses both to the Contadora process and, in policy terms, its actions against Nicaragua. Finally, a concluding section will reflect on two of the issues which have proved more contentious in the Contadora negotiations and on which so far the parties involved in the Central American conflict have been unable to find accommodation and compromise: security and democracy.

THE CONTADORA PROCESS UNFOLDS

The task Contadora set for itself during its first year of existence was to establish a process of mediation which would help to ease the tensions in Central America, at a time when a minor incident could threaten armed confrontation. It was thought that the best way to achieve this objective was to find a formula which would incorporate the security concerns of all the actors involved: Nicaragua's as well as those of the other Central American countries and by implication those of the United States, although being an independent Latin American effort, in some ways consciously in opposition to the US, American security concerns were not stated explicitly.

Contadora's diagnosis was that the roots of the region's instability were more related to worsening economic and social conditions than the East–West confrontation. But the pacification of the area would need to tackle security questions as well as an all-encompassing programme for economic recovery and political and social reforms. The all-encompassing scope of Contadora first emerged with the publication in September 1983 of the 21-point statement of objectives which covered five broad areas: relations between the states; matters concerning internal stability and peace; national security questions; problems of refugees; and inter-state co-operation for social and economic development.

But the most important questions the document dealt with from the point of view of changing the status quo were those referring to security. It called for a freeze on arms levels and size of armies, a reduction in the number of foreign military advisers, and a non-aggression pact banning the use of national territories as sites for launching attacks against other countries.

The follow-up of the 21-point statement of objectives was the 'norms of implementation', issued following a meeting of the Central American and Contadora foreign ministers in Panama City in January 1984. It was decided that in order to carry out the objectives proposed it would be necessary to establish three commissions the task of which would be to develop a series of recommendations on security, political and socio-economic matters.

The basic goals and the actions needed to resolve security, political and social and economic matters were incorporated later into the Act of Contadora on Peace and Co-operation in Central America, a document presented to the Central American countries for comments in June 1984. It was drafted in the form of a peace treaty which would be binding on the five Central American countries. But the Act included an additional protocol aimed at other countries which were interested in the same objectives as Contadora and would agree to abide by the Act's rules by adhering to it.

A brief description of some of the Act's main provisions seems necessary in order to assess its possible reach as well as its limitations. The Act sought to harmonize the various proposals that had been put forward in the past by various countries, trying to accommodate the differing interests of the Central American countries to create some sort of convergence between them. The spirit of the Act was conciliatory, it stressed the need for detente in Central America and the importance of adopting confidence-building measures (CBMs).[2]

On questions relating to security, considered central for defusing tensions and allaying mutual suspicions, the Act of Contadora included, among other, commitments to freeze arms imports and limit the size of the regional armies, a ban on both the conduct of military exercises and the establishment of foreign military bases, a reduction of foreign military advisers and an end to the military build-up and support for 'irregular forces'.

In order to dissipate fears about lack of compliance by one or another country, the Act proposed the setting-up of mechanisms of control and verification. A commission would be formed to monitor compliance with the signatories' undertakings. The commission would consist of five persons 'representing four States of recognised impartiality' (presumably from the Contadora group) proposed by the Contadora countries and accepted by the signatories. The importance of the verification process for the eventual success of Contadora's mediation efforts could not be under-estimated. Verification was to become a major stumbling bloc in the signature of the Act. Some argued that the Contadora Act offered only weak guarantees that the treaty's commitments would be respected at all because the verification system would not be able to detect violations. And even if it did, to what higher authority would the Commission report it? Which bodies would be able to implement possible sanctions? All these questions which were left unanswered raised doubts about the feasibility of effective control and verification.

Another question which was to hinder consensus around the principles laid down by the Act referred to the political aspects of the document. The Act upheld the principles of pluralism and democracy and called for measures conducive to national reconciliation and dialogue, including amnesty for political opponents and guarantees for its beneficiaries. A political commission would be created to receive and assess information about the implementation of political, electoral and human rights' obligations undertaken by the parties to the agreement. Just as was the case with verification, several political aspects of the Act were to prove contentious and to slow down the process of agreement. Chapter II of the Act, which referred to commitments on political matters, called for the adoption 'of measures for the establishment or, as the case may be, the further development of representative and pluralistic democratic systems'. The Act was vague about the state of democratic development in Central America. It did not go as far as specifying in which cases it advocated the 'establishment' and in which others it recommended the 'further development' of democratic systems.[3] This ambiguity called in question the resoluteness of its commitment.

Regarding irregular forces, the Contadora Act called for a ban on political, military, financial or any other kind of support to unconventional forces involved in the destabilization of other governments. It also demanded the prevention of the use of territory to organize attacks on another state. The Act urged the signatories to maintain a strict control of their borders to prevent their territories from being used to organize attacks in another state, as well as to disarm and remove from border zones irregular forces responsible for attacks against neighbouring states.

The draft of the Act was presented to the Central American countries for comments and a revised Act was presented to them in September 1984, with 15 October as the deadline for signature. Negotiations had gone relatively smoothly until then, but the easy ride was over. In September, before the deadline was reached, Nicaragua announced its decision to sign the revised Act without modification, and urged the US to sign the additional protocol.

Taken by surprise by Nicaragua's resolution, three of the Central American countries, Honduras, El Salvador and Costa Rica, responded by voicing reservations to several of the Act's provisions. The foreign ministers of these countries met in Tegucigalpa after the October deadline to discuss their objections to the revised Act and to propose modifications.

These were contained in a document which became known as the Act of Tegucigalpa. Guatemala was also present at the meeting but maintained a low profile. It was widely believed that the US had a major influence on these countries' decision to revise the Act of Contadora once again before signature. It was also believed that the modifications to the Act proposed by the Tegucigalpa group (as it became known) were either dictated by or drafted in close collaboration with the US.[4]

The modifications proposed by the Tegucigalpa group concerned security questions: the timing of the negotiations on disarmament, the question of international military exercises and the control and verification procedures. The Tegucigalpa draft sought simultaneity between the signing of the treaty and enforcement of arms freeze and arms and troops limits. It called for the latter to be negotiated prior to signature and not afterwards as the Contadora Act stipulated. On the question of international military exercises, the Tegucigalpa group called for regulation rather than prohibition. It also proposed that the commitments undertaken under the treaty should enter into force after ratification by the five Central American countries rather than after signature. On control and verification, the Tegucigalpa version modified the provision requiring any decision of the five Central American foreign ministers on charges of non-compliance and disputes regarding the security provisions or political and economic issues to be unanimous. Instead such decisions could be by consensus and appeals should be referred to the nine foreign ministers instead of only the Contadora four. This was obviously intended to neutralize Nicaragua in case of any disagreement.

In its role of mediator, Contadora sought to accommodate the suggestions of the Tegucigalpa group. Managua's reaction to this action was rejection, insisting that it would only abide by the Act of Contadora as originally presented, without further modifications. The Sandinista government also insisted that any regional peace treaty would only be effective if it was supported by a formal and binding assurance from the US. In fact, Nicaragua made its acceptance of the Act conditional on the US adherence to the protocol.

The Contadora process continued after this major predicament with varying degrees of success in the negotiations, and a couple of temporary suspensions. One of them was due to a bilateral dispute between Nicaragua and Costa Rica in December 1984 over Costa Rican claims that Nicaragua had violated its right to grant political asylum.[5] But the incident was resolved on Managua's initiative in February of the following year, with the group resuming negotiations in March. Between mid-May and

September 1985, Contadora concentrated its agenda on negotiations aimed at reconciling the conflicting interests of the would-be signatories on security matters, such as military exercises, foreign military bases and advisers, reductions in arms and troop levels, arms trafficking, etc. But compromises were proving hard to achieve.

A major boost for the Contadora process' flagging efforts occurred during the summer of 1985, when on the occasion of the inauguration of Peru's new President Alan Garcia in July 1985, the Contadora process received the formal support of four Latin American democracies: Argentina, Brazil, Peru and Uruguay.[6] At this time, when the Contadora process was in bad need of a new breath of life, the Latin American endorsement boosted the process by giving it a formal regional legitimacy. What had moved these countries to espouse the Contadora cause? The countries of the 'support', or Lima group, as it became known, did not have any direct interest in Central America. However, there were powerful reasons which led them to join in the effort of promoting negotiations and an eventual peaceful solution to the problems plaguing Central America. Two of these countries, Argentina and Uruguay, had faced the destabilizing effects of guerrilla activities and one, Peru, was still waging a war against them. All of the countries in the recent past had undergone military dictatorship, but all had managed to make the transition to pluralistic societies and democratic governments. Thus they had a vested interest in promoting political stability through dialogue with rebel groups and in working for the preservation of democratic values in Latin America. Regional (i.e. hemispheric) unity on such important goals was considered an imperative.

But in concrete terms, as regards results, the support group did not make any significant difference in pulling the process out of its impasse. A new draft was presented to the Central American countries in September 1985 with some important changes and additions, of which the most imaginative one was the establishment of an international corps of inspectors to monitor arms levels and military activities. At this point the Contadora negotiators announced that their group would be wound up if this draft still proved to be unacceptable to the would-be signatories. However, Contadora was spared taking such drastic action. At the request of Nicaragua, the group suspended all negotiations for a period of five months, this time on the grounds that new governments were to take office in the following months (Guatemala and Honduras in January and Costa Rica in April) and the changes in administrations could have a major impact on future negotiations.

As it turned out, the installation of new governments in these countries did not have any immediate impact on facilitating compromises and agreements, and negotiations continued to drag on. But the peaceful political transitions seems to have helped to instill in the new leaders a greater degree of self-assertion and a greater commitment to contribute to the resolution of Central America's problems.

The occasion of the inauguration of President Vinicio Cerezo of Guatemala provided a favourable climate for relaunching the regional peace effort, this time with the help of Cerezo himself. The inauguration provided the opportunity for all the Central American Presidents to meet, as well as the foreign ministers of the Contadora and Lima groups. Cerezo expressed his full support for the Contadora process, but he added an original idea he had expressed since he was campaigning for the presidency: the creation of a Central American parliament to be elected by universal suffrage which would act as a permanent forum for discussions of the region's problems. The idea itself was not only original and in line with the democratization process that had taken place throughout the region, but it pointed to a possible 'in-house' alternative to the 'external' mediating efforts such as those of Contadora, by focusing on the need for consultation with and among Central Americans proper.

But in parallel to this Central American initiative, the Contadora process continued in its own right. One of the attempts to revive it and give it a new impetus occurred almost immediately after the 'summit' in Guatemala City. In mid-January 1986, the foreign ministers of the Contadora and Support groups met at the Venezuelan resort of Caraballeda. The result of this meeting was a document entitled 'The Caraballeda Basis for the Achievement of a Permanent Peace in Central America', which put in capsule form the objectives set out in the Act of Contadora. It stressed that Latin American problems should have a Latin American solution, which was the only way to guarantee that the region would not become involved in the East–West strategic confrontation. According to the Caraballeda document the other requisites for the establishment of a permanent peace included self-determination, non-intervention in the internal affairs of other states, territorial integrity, pluralist democracy, renouncement of arms or military bases which would endanger peace and security in the region, to bar the presence of foreign military troops or advisers as well as the political or military support for subversion or destabilization of the constitutional order in the region, respect for human rights.

In order to achieve these requisites for peace, the Caraballeda declaration stressed the re-launching and finalization of the Contadora negotiations, and actions aimed at halting the support for irregular and insurrectional groups in the region (though the difference between them was not specified), an arms freeze, phasing out foreign military advisers and installations, etc. Doubtless the objectives and plan of action of the Caraballeda declaration were laudable aims to strive for and, as such, support and praise for it were almost universal. And yet, the document lacked a measure of realism, as became evident from the subsequent failures to move anybody towards these worthwhile objectives.

The test-case for the new Contadora spirit came to a deplorable end during the following meeting of the Group of Thirteen (the representatives of the Central American and Contadora countries plus those of the Support group) which took place in Panama City in April 1986. The meeting was a stormy one. The difference between the Tegucigalpa group and Nicaragua had become exacerbated. These disagreements, which had persisted since the first Contadora draft, centred on the security provisions. While the Tegucigalpa group wanted to regulate foreign military exercises, Nicaragua wanted them abolished altogether. On the scaling down of military installations and armaments, Nicaragua refused to agree unless the US became a party to the agreement. Nicaragua also made clear that it would not sign any document until the US ceased support for the contras. In short the meeting resulted in failure. The vice-president of El Salvador declared after the meeting 'Nicaragua rejected everything that was presented to it ... there was nothing left to talk about.'[7] The Salvadorean foreign minister was equally pessimistic: 'Nicaragua is not going to sign anything', he said.[8] A final deadline was set for 6 June, but illusions about a possible success of the Contadora process, with a final version being signed by the five Central American countries, had already faded. And as Colombian Foreign Minister Augusto Ramírez Ocampo stated after the meeting, the Contadora process 'had put an end to its mediation' in the Central American conflict.

It was evident by now that Contadora had an uncertain future. However, the Contadora countries did not give up yet. In July 1986 the Mexican Foreign Minister travelled to Europe to try to enlist the support of several European countries. In August there was a meeting in Colombia of the Contadora and support group, and an announcement was made that a new strategy would be developed to get the Central American countries back to the negotiating table. In December the two groups met again, this time in Rio de Janeiro, motivated by two main concerns: the need to renew the stalled Contadora peace process, and to 'preserve and deepen' their political leadership.[9] On the first question, the revival of Contadora, the 'group of Rio' as it became known, obtained the support of the United Nations (UN) and the Organization of American States (OAS). An announcement was made at this meeting that the two groups were planning a tour of the Central American capitals to be held in January 1987 and would be joined by the general secretaries of the UN and the OAS, who had also attended the Rio meeting.

The Rio meeting marked the end of an era for Contadora. It had set in motion the bases for a more permanent and institutionalized form of regional consultation and co-operation on a variety of important regional problems which could be resolved by a gradual economic and political integration (the main theme of the meeting). Then the problem of Central America was touched upon, but in a different light than heretofore. The enlistment of the general secretaries of the UN and OAS marked a completely different approach to the one followed by Contadora until then. Contadora had made clear that its peace efforts were to be carried out *independently* of both multilateral organizations, particularly of the OAS, where the US had an overwhelming voice. In fact, the OAS Secretary General, João Baena Soares, was questioned by American officials on the legal grounds for his participation in the Rio initiative, since he should have obtained permission from the OAS member states before endorsing the Rio Group's actions.

But the Rio meeting, although doubtless a significant advance in the cause of Latin American unity, failed to inject new life into Contadora. This became clear in the third of a series of meetings which had taken place between foreign ministers of the countries of the European Community (EC) and those of the Group of Thirteen. The purpose of these meetings had been to strengthen European links with Central America through increased economic aid and technical assistance. But they had had a more lasting effect as a symbol of European concern about a troubled region than as an effective economic instrument. They enabled Europe to demonstrate its disapproval of US policy, bent on military pressure, and to express support for Contadora. The first one took place in San José in September 1984, the second one in Luxembourg in November 1985 and the third in Guatemala City in February 1987.

The final document which emerged from the meeting in Guatemala reflected that the Europeans had become more receptive to frequent charges levied against Nicaragua's lack of political pluralism and democracy. The document made constant reference to the need for democracy as a requisite for peace, keeping in line with the spirit of Contadora. The statement repeated its support for the Contadora process pointing out that it was 'currently the only viable forum for reaching a peaceful and negotiated solution'. But as the *Christian Science Monitor* reported 'While

Contadora diplomats stressed the word "only", Costa Rica's foreign minister Rodrigo Madrigal Nieto, stressed "currently".[10] The door was open for Central America to fill in the vacuum left by Contadora, and ultimately to the acceptance of the Arias Plan in August 1987.

CENTRAL AMERICA COMES OF AGE

It has been argued above that perhaps the most significant effect that the years of dialogue under Contadora may have created is a sense of Central American awareness and identity. This has been particularly true at any rate amongst the four Central American countries other than Nicaragua, whose strongest political bond has increasingly become one between themselves directly, as opposed to their identity as US allies in the region. No doubt this interpretation may be somewhat of an overstatement and could be open to disagreement. However, there certainly seems to exist an increased level of intra-regional consultations in Central America, not excluding Nicaragua. The increased degree of Central American self-assertion has given rise to some important Central American initiatives aimed at defusing regional tensions and creating permanent mechanisms to discuss common problems. Nicaragua, too, has not escaped this increasing sense of self-identity in relation to its neighbours. Indeed, Nicaragua has been part and parcel of most of the newest regional initiatives (Guatemala, Esquipulas) not to mention the meetings with the EC, and maintains its long-standing participation in the still-alive Central American Common Market (CACM).

These closer ties have been created no doubt under the aegis of Contadora, but there is a crucial underlying development that has fuelled the sense of historic empathy amongst the countries concerned: the vigorous process towards democracy in the region.[11] Of course Costa Rica has had a long-standing democratic tradition. But whereas in the past it stood alone in Central America as a unique case among either military or civilian dictatorships, at present it shares with other states in the region the features of democratic rule. Indeed, although the countries in the region may be far from resembling ideal liberal democratic regimes, their political evolution from persistent authoritarian patterns is certainly a step forward.

The most striking and recent case is Guatemala, now governed by a democratically elected civilian president for the first time in at least sixteen years. In fact, since the overthrow of Jacobo Arbenz by a US-staged *coup* in 1954, Guatemala had lived through a succession of military governments (with some civilian interludes), fraudulent elections and *coups* and the 1966 elections could not be described as free with great confidence. Yet Guatemala at least returned to a constitutional regime with the elections to a constituent assembly in July 1984 and presidential elections in November 1985. No doubt Guatemala's military are still a powerful force in Guatemalan politics (the gradual evolution towards democracy was promoted by General Oscar Humberto Mejía Victores, the then self-appointed President). But so far it seems that it is the civilians under Cerezo's leadership who are at the helm.

In El Salvador, where the army ruled virtually without interruption since 1931 and a civil war has been going on with varying intensity since 1979, the process of reform and democratization under President José Napoleón Duarte has received a substantial measure of domestic support. This became clear from the 1985 municipal and legislative elections, when Duarte's party became the undisputed victor. Also, internationally, Duarte has received recognition as the leader who is likely to stabilize the political situation in El Salvador. Though the military and the extreme right are still a threat that cannot be underestimated, conditions in El Salvador as far as political stability and human rights are concerned have improved substantially by comparison with the situation in the early 1980s.

In Honduras, the presidential elections of November 1985 were peaceful and the transition to power for the new President José Azcona was without major complications. In the case of Honduras, with the country's growing dependence on US economic aid and increased military presence, this democratic transition was all the more laudable. It is evident that in this country which has become a US strategic base for any actions against Nicaragua, the prospects of civilian rule independent from military power, or even of sovereign decisions may be considered slim. However, despite the odds, Honduras has been able to keep the military at bay.

Nicaragua also held elections in 1984, much to the surprise of those observers who thought the Sandinista regime would do away with electoral legitimation. The Nicaraguan elections were reported to be peaceful and fair, though they were far from controversial.[12] It has been argued that since elections took place the Sandinista government has tightened its authoritarian grip, by keeping the state of emergency and expanding its control of civil society. The severe limitations to free political play and the silencing of the opposition press have been stressed by critics of the Sandinista regime as clear signs of the regime verging on totalitarianism. These measures have been justified by the government in Managua as an unavoidable consequence of the violent destabilization efforts of the

US through its proxies, the contras. But despite the fact that there are security reasons behind the state of emergency and the closer official control, Nicaragua's deviation from democratic principles caused alarm among its Central American neighbours and gradually lost for Nicaragua the international, almost unqualified support for the Nicaraguan revolution.[13]

Having examined the recent evolution of each country's internal regime, a brief overview of the relations between the Central American states is necessary, as these are the vital clue to the possibility of a negotiated solution to the region's conflicts. Intra-regional relations in Central America were not always easy. The extreme case of strained relations was the so-called 'Football War' between Honduras and El Salvador (1969). More recently, however, relations between Nicaragua and its neighbours turned sour soon after the Sandinistas came to power in 1979. It is worth remembering that one of Nicaragua's immediate neighbours, Costa Rica, had taken active steps to aid the Sandinistas in their fight against Anastasio Somoza Debayle. The main element of concern among the Central Americans was the perceived threat Nicaragua posed to their own political stability: the self-reinforcing vicious circle of Nicaragua's military build-up and the US response of pouring military resources into Honduras and El Salvador and building up the direct military pressure on Nicaragua through the contras. But equally, the perceptions (justified or not) that Nicaragua was bent on exporting its revolution, the curtailment of civil liberties inside the country and what were regarded as increased ties with the Soviet Union and the Eastern bloc turned the Central American countries against Nicaragua.

It was Nicaragua's growing militarization which was used by Honduras, El Salvador and Guatemala to try to revive the 1965 military pact CONDECA (Central American Defence Council) in 1983, not long after the Contadora initiative was launched. This action was denounced as being done under the direct guidance of Washington and as an effort by the Reagan Administration to undermine the Contadora process.

Other early initiatives taken by the Central Americans geared towards finding 'peaceful' solutions to their problems were those proposed during 1982 and 1983 by them (in conjunction with the US). One was the Central American Democratic Community (CDC) formed in January 1982 by Costa Rica, Honduras and El Salvador and joined at a later date by Guatemala. The joint communiqué issued by its members expressed concern at the rise in subversion and terrorism in the area and supported proposals for disarmament, national reconciliation and supervision of the region by international inspectors. The government of Nicaragua was informed by CDC members that there was anxiety about its actions which threatened regional peace and stability through its 'disproportionate military build-up'.

The meeting of the CDC from which this communiqué was issued took place in July 1982, following a plan put forward by the Panamanian government. This plan proposed, among other things, treaties of non-aggression between Nicaragua and the other Central American countries and guarantees of territorial sovereignty for all Central American states to prevent hostile groups from finding sanctuary in neighbouring countries. Panama's proposal received the express backing of the Presidents of Colombia, Costa Rica, Honduras and Venezuela and also of an official spokesman of the Sandinista government. However, just as was to happen with the Contadora process, no progress was made towards the implementation of these proposals.

Another attempt to search for a regional peace was that of the Forum for Peace and Democracy (also known as the Enders' forum) formed by Colombia, Belize, Jamaica, Panama, Honduras, the Dominican Republic, Costa Rica, El Salvador and the US. The Forum issued a declaration in October 1982 condemning totalitarian forces of all trends in the region, particularly Marxism–Leninism, a veiled reference to Nicaragua, which explains why Nicaragua was excluded. It is interesting to note the comments on this declaration by a highly placed Mexican foreign ministry official: its 'discriminatory content was especially directed against Nicaragua. Its paragraphs first and ninth clearly hinted at a lack of democratically elected regime in that country and at the supposed actions of subversion carried on by the Sandinista government. It excluded from its origin the dialogue with Nicaragua, and with that, the alternatives for a permanent and trustworthy peace for all parties concerned.'[14] The exclusion of Nicaragua, was of course a major blunder in this frustrated initiative, as was later recognized by the then Costa Rican President Luis Alberto Monge.

In general, the essence of the peace initiatives described resembled the main tenets of Contadora: disarmament, confidence-building measures, national reconciliation, supervision by international inspectors. However, the launching of the Contadora initiative was to introduce two fundamental differences into all the peacemaking proposals put forward until then: it was going to be a regional initiative, independent of the US and it was going to include all the Central American countries in its negotiations. An advantage of the Contadora countries was that since they did not form part of the Central American region and were not directly involved in the conflicts therein, they could mediate impartially among the conflicting interests of the Central American countries. However, as was claimed by critics of Contadora later on, the 'impartiality' of some of the Contadora members could not always be guaranteed.

It has often been argued that the Contadora countries were influenced during the negotiations by their allegiance and sympathy with one or another of the Central American countries. For instance, it is generally believed that Colombia and Venezuela were frequently closer to the position of the Tegucigalpa group and were hostile to Nicaragua. The reasons which could be adduced range from their sharing similar democratic political systems to Colombia's territorial dispute with Nicaragua over the islands of Providencia and San Andrés or the alleged support of the Sandinistas for the M-19 guerrilla movement in Colombia. Equally, for political reasons it was believed that Mexico, because of its own political structure, did not mind the authoritarian style of the Sandinistas, and supported them wholeheartedly. Criticisms were levied against Mexico's 'rigid and obstinate defence of Sandinism'[15] and its lack of decisive support for making democracy a crucial topic in the Contadora agenda.

From this review of the Central American side of peacemaking it appears that two basic features characterized the Central American countries in the early 1980s: their unease and concern about the militarization and increasing authoritarianism of the Sandinista government and the fact that the possible solutions they searched for centred on the approval and active participation or support of the US. Although the first characteristic mistrust of Nicaragua, remains strong, the second one is less visible than before. The US seems to have been pushed into the background by its allies in the region. In this respect it is Contadora that has left its mark, by creating a feeling of regional identity and self-confidence. The relations between Nicaragua and its neighbours may not have improved in bilateral terms, but a dialogue among them has been possible and the armed confrontation which was feared by all, has not taken place. Ironically, Contadora's greatest achievement, increased communication between the Central American countries and the creation of a feeling of self-reliance among them, may be the cause of its final demise. The Central American countries may have outgrown the era when 'fraternal tutelage' was not only possible but desirable, and have started to take into their own hands the attempts to find solutions to their problems. The first sign of this trend was the meeting at Esquipulas and the decision to create a Central American parliament. But there have been other attempts.

The most recent one and the one which could have greater chances of success is the Plan proposed by President Oscar Arias of Costa Rica. President Arias invited his counterparts of El Salvador, Honduras and Guatemala to meet in San José in February 1987 to discuss the ways to put an end to the conflicts in the region, particularly the war in Nicaragua. Arias' initiative consisted of four main points: a cease-fire; an amnesty for the rebels or contras; a dialogue between the Sandinista government and the internal political opposition; and a timetable for the implementation of genuine democracy within Nicaragua, including the holding of free elections.

Arias presented a preliminary version of his Plan during his visit to Washington in December 1986, when he expressed a realistic view of the situation and stressed to American officials that the contras would never be able to oust the Sandinista government. The US seemed to welcome a non-Contadora peace initiative, but Arias' Plan was not altogether congenial. A spokesperson from the State Department declared that a democratic outcome in Nicaragua would necessarily have to be achieved through direct talks with the contras. However, Arias was firm on this point. Ever since he campaigned for the presidency he stressed that his administration would defend Costa Rica's tradition of neutrality which had become threatened by the escalation of the conflict in Central America and by the contras using Costa Rican territory. After coming to power Arias' dislike for the contras turned into active opposition and he took severe measures against them, including arresting several contra rebels. Arias made clear that his government would be inflexible with individuals who violated Costa Rica's neutrality.

But the basic thrust of Arias' Plan was the belief that the first and foremost condition for solving the region's problems was the establishment of democracy. In contrast with the Contadora proposals, which mentioned this objective in the abstract, Arias stated that if democracy was not implanted in Nicaragua there would be no end to the armed struggle.

As could be expected, the Sandinista government rejected Arias' first proposal and denounced it as a pro-US plot. However, it would be simplistic to ignore the fact that the Costa Rican peace initiative was not fabricated in the US (as some other initiatives had been in the past). In fact the peace plan, by seeking to eliminate the contras from any negotiations with the Sandinistas and restricting the definition of legal opposition to the 'internal political adversaries', was undermining one of the pillars of US policy: pressure on Nicaragua through the contras and the demand that they be included in any democratization process which would take place in Nicaragua. Arias, however, left the possibility open for the contras to become incorporated into the domestic legal opposition under an eventual amnesty.

Arias' perceptions differed widely from those of the policymakers in the US. He believed that putting military pressure on the Sandinistas through the contras was not the only way to change the Nicaraguan system and make it more open. Rather, US policy had the reverse effect, he believed: it gave the Sandinistas an excuse not to democratize.

The peacemaking efforts pursued by President Arias were a clear indication that the Central American countries were drifting away from old patterns, in which efforts to solve their conflicts peacefully were directed from above by the US or equally were directed by external peers such as those of the Contadora group.

A basic difference between Arias' proposal and the Contadora blueprint was that whereas the latter laid a heavy emphasis on the security aspects and demanded a Central American commitment to reduce arms and troop levels, the former concentrated on the political aspect, on which Contadora was imprecise, stressing the need for democratization.

Although the first reaction on the part of Nicaragua was to state that the Arias Plan was made in Washington, the Sandinista leadership reversed its position as was noticed at Daniel Ortega's opening speech of the 1987 legislative session. Ortega stated that he supported in principle the establishment of this Central American dialogue. In line with this, officials from the Nicaraguan foreign ministry agreed to meet with their counterparts from other Central American countries to debate the details of the plan, with a view to discussing it in a summit due to take place in May 1987, and in August 1987 it was accepted by all the Central American states at their summit in Guatemala.

It is too early to assess the long-term success of Central American efforts at peacemaking. The Guatemalan plan to establish a Central American parliament and the Costa Rican proposal for a cease-fire, non-support for the contras and concrete steps towards the democratization of Nicaragua give some hope for a more realistic approach being taken in the future towards the problems of the region. Although Contadora identified the issue it did not go as far as clearly stating who was committed to do what. While Contadora stressed military aspects, the Guatemalan and Costa Rican initiatives focused on the political front. As the Costa Rican foreign minister stated: 'Peace is not just weapons but democratic environment.'[16]

THE US AND CONTADORA

US policy toward Central America cannot be said to have been formulated in one piece. A variety of actors have participated in its conception and implementation, more often than not in an unco-ordinated way. At first it seemed that the division was between an American President obsessed with the security risks posed by a Marxist–Leninist regime with close ties with Moscow right next door, and a Legislature which sought to moderate the impulses of the Executive branch. But as the Iran–contra scandal has clearly shown divisions were greater than that. Within the White House and the National Security Council (NSC) individuals were formulating independent foreign policies, of which Congress and even the State Department were not informed.[17]

Leaving those divisions aside, the objectives of US policy towards Nicaragua have been clear: to change the nature and structure of the Sandinista regime. What has remained less clear is the means to carry out this objective. When the Contadora process was first launched, it received a mild endorsement by the US. President Reagan welcomed the adoption of the twenty-one-point document of objectives and several officials in the administration stated their 'willingness to support its comprehensive and verifiable implementation'.[18]

It was hoped that the US would eventually become party to the agreement through its signing the protocol to the Contadora Act. Indeed, during Contadora's first year the Contadora process was finding widespread support within the US Congress. In early 1984 meetings took place between US officials and leaders from the Contadora group. At some point President Reagan offered help with the verification process and to provide financial aid to carry out the economic objectives. It was during this period that President de la Madrid from Mexico suggested to President Reagan the advisability of holding bilateral talks with Nicaraguan officials.

These talks started taking place in 1984, mainly in the Mexican resort of Manzanillo. However, after nine sessions the talks were suspended by the US in January 1985. American negotiator Harry Shlaudeman stated that the Manzanillo talks had not produced any results and had been stopped because the Nicaraguans were seeking a bilateral treaty with the US on security matters rather than a multilateral comprehensive agreement. According to the US, this attitude proved that Nicaragua was not serious in making commitments and sticking to them, since Nicaragua's position during the talks, they argued, was not consistent with its earlier position that it was willing to sign the September 1984 Act of Contadora provided no changes were made to it. On his part, the Nicaraguan negotiator, Vice-Minister Victor Hugo Tinoco argued that the reason Nicaragua wanted a bilateral treaty with the US was to make sure the US would abide by the Contadora commitments. It was equally argued that what the US was demanding was the eradication of Nicaragua's revolutionary programme and a diminution of its national sovereignty.

However much verbal support the US Administration may have given Contadora, it was repeatedly pointed out by external observers as well as by members of the US Congress, that Reagan's policy was seeking to undermine the Contadora process, mainly through its support for the contras and the continued and growing US military presence in Honduras. The US position was made clear in the Report of the Bipartisan Commission on Central America (also known as the Kissinger Report), which stated that in view of the fact that the 'interests and attitudes' of the Contadora countries were not identical, since these four countries lacked experience in working together and the process they had started had not been tested in designing specific policies to provide for regional security 'the United States cannot use the Contadora process as a substitute for its own policies'.

The US considered the first Contadora Act insufficient for guaranteeing US security interests, and viewed it as helping to achieve two major Sandinista objectives: the elimination of US support and safe havens for the contras in Central America and the prohibition of international manoeuvres in Central America. In addition there were other points of uncertainty. On the 'establishment or improvement' of pluralist democratic regimes in the region Contadora was not specific on deadlines for compliance. On the question of arms and troop levels, there were no guidelines; these were left to be negotiated later. Equally, the US regarded the process of control and verification as ineffectual. These objections were taken partially into consideration by the amendments of the Act proposed by the Tegucigalpa group. Probably at this time the US had not altogether rejected the Contadora initiative. Although it was argued at the time that by putting pressure on the Tegucigalpa group to change the Contadora draft the US was in effect undermining the process, a more convincing interpretation is that the reason why the US administration was interested in having some of the elements of the Act modified was that it supported the continuation of the process in some form[19]

When no progress was made on the Contadora front, the US was then able to rely on its own policy which rested on continued support for the contras, and increasing the pressure on Nicaragua on all fronts, economic, diplomatic and military. A boost to this policy came during the summer of 1986 when Congress approved $100 million for the contras. A crucial factor which determined to a large extent the approval of these funds was the failure of Contadora to come up with a signed Act after its last deadline of 6 June.

However, internal, rather than external forces may now augur a bleak future for continued US support for the contras. The Iran–contra scandal discredited an already debatable policy alternative. Congress has not as yet approved new funds for the contras and may start working on other options. Indeed, the peace plan presented by President Arias may now be the most viable alternative for the US.

CONCLUSIONS ON SECURITY AND DEMOCRACY IN CENTRAL AMERICA

It is clear that the efforts to deal with the Central American conflict and to achieve a negotiated solution have concentrated on two inter-related concepts: political objectives (with democracy and respect for human rights in the forefront); and security concerns, mostly centred around those of the major actor in the region, the US, and by implication those of its Central American allies.

The justification offered by the US for putting direct and indirect pressure on the Sandinista government in Nicaragua is two-fold: the protection of democracy and human rights, and its defence of its national security interests. Close examination of the first part of the argument does not seem to hold. Although there is a general frustration in democratic countries (not only in Mexico, Central and South America, but also in Europe) with the limitations on free political activities found in Nicaragua, these do not warrant the kind and scale of measures the Reagan Administration has advocated since it took office.

The argument that the existence of the Sandinista regime is a threat to US security may be more convincing. It touches on both the regional and the extra-regional (East–West) dimensions. On the regional side, the Reagan Administration persuaded Congress to support its strategy of destabilization of the Sandinista government presenting the contras as the best means to put pressure on Managua to halt the arms supply to the Salvadorean guerrillas and thus the 'export of revolution' by the Sandinistas. But the security concerns went further, and the US placed the conflicts in Central America as part of the East–West confrontation, given Nicaragua's increasing links with the Soviet bloc.

Esperanza Durán

The Reagan Administration contended that Nicaragua represented a genuine threat to its security because the close military relation between Managua and the Eastern bloc would open the possibility of the establishment by the rival superpower of new bases in the Western hemisphere.[20] Also, Nicaragua's objective of exporting its revolution to neighbouring countries would pose for the US the danger of 'additional platforms for regional subversion and communist expansion, north to Mexico and south towards Panama', not to mention the complications for defence planning of keeping open the sea lanes in the Caribbean through which trade, petroleum supplies and eventual reinforcements for NATO would have to go.[21]

Observers, both from the US and elsewhere, have disputed the veracity of the argument that Nicaragua can be a security risk for the US. They contend that it is not altogether clear why the Soviet Union would wish to establish new bases apart from those it already has in Cuba, given the enormous costs of maintenance and defence of them (at a time when the Soviets are having pressing economic problems of their own) which would far exceed the US cost in neutralizing them in case of an open conflict between the superpowers. Thus, those supporting this position would endorse the view that Nicaragua's threat to US security is more a political than a military argument.[22]

A more balanced position would lie somewhere between these two extreme arguments. Provision by Nicaragua of an outlet for the Soviet Union to the Pacific Ocean in the Western Hemisphere would be a significant addition to Soviet strategic interests. But it is doubtful whether to obtain it the Soviets would risk provoking the US into direct military intervention in the area. This would not be in their interest. However arming the Nicaraguans at a relatively low cost and orchestrating a certain amount of military destabilization in the region would form a natural objective for increasing the Soviet Union's strategic power in the Third World, particularly in those parts of it close to the US. At any rate having two military allies in the region would render the Soviet position more flexible. Although at present Central America may have a low strategic value for the Soviet Union, much greater stakes would be placed in terms of East–West strategy on the future stability of Mexico and Panama. But at present, providing Nicaragua with arms, mostly defensive and not high-performance equipment does not turn Nicaragua into a major security risk for its neighbours or the US.

A greater concern for the US and one which has been more difficult to tackle because it is somewhat more abstract is the strictly ideological dimension: the US inability to live with a Marxist regime so close to home. Contadora attempted to remove this obstacle to peaceful co-existence in an imprecise way. It is now being specifically dealt with by the Central American initiatives. Democracy as a pre-condition to peace could prove the way out of the impasse.

Let us consider two possible scenarios, one focusing on the security aspects, the other on the question of democracy and political pluralism. The Sandinistas pledge not to export revolution, to reduce their arms and troop levels and to sever their ties with Moscow. Would that satisfy the US policymakers and induce them to pursue a hands-off policy? From the political perspective President Arias' proposal becomes feasible, a cease-fire is declared, the support for the contras comes to an end, and US pressures cease. Would the Sandinistas allow a pluralist democracy to flourish in Nicaragua? The answer to these questions seems to be the key to the future of any negotiations aimed at bringing about a peaceful settlement of the Central American conflicts and preventing a military solution from coming to the fore. That, in the last instance, would be no solution at all.

NOTES

1. There is a large and growing body of literature on the Contadora process, from both the Latin American and the US perspectives: René Herrera Zuñiga and Manuel Chavarria, 'México en Contadora: una busqueda de limites a su compromiso en Centroamérica', *Foro Internacional*, vol. xxiv no. 4, April–June 1984, pp. 458–83; Esperanza Durán, 'The Contadora Approach to Peace in Central America', *The World Today*, vol. xL, nos. 8–9, August–September 1984, pp. 347–54; Fernando Cepeda Ulloa and Rodrigo Pardo Garcia Peña, *Contadora: Desafío a la diplomacia tradicional* (Bogotá: Editorial La Oveja Negra, 1985); Apolinar Diaz-Callejas, *Contadora: Desafío al imperio* (Bogotá: Editorial La Oveja Negra, 1985); Tom Farer, 'Contadora', *Foreign Affairs*, vol. LXIV, no. 1, autumn 1985, pp. 59–72; Ricardo Valero, 'Contadora: La busqueda de la pacificación en Centroamérica', *Foro Internacional*, vol. xxvi, no. 2, October–December 1985.
2. Confidence-building measures were originally associated with high intensity conflict situations between the superpowers. However, it has been argued that CBM principles could be applied to low-level conflict situations such as the inter-state tensions in Central America and the regional insurgencies; that in fact CBMs formed the bases of the Contadora proposals. See for instance Falk Bomsdorf, 'Confidence Building Measures outside Europe', in Jack Child (ed.), *Conflict in Central America: Approaches to Peace and Security* (New York: St Martin's Press for the International Peace Academy, 1986), pp. 88–112.
3. First clause in section 2 on 'Commitments with regard to national reconciliation'.
4. The *Washington Post* leaked a secret document from the National Security Council which recommended the search for support of US allies in the region to modify the Act in order for it to be more in accordance with the Central American goals of the Reagan Administration.
5. The incident was over a Nicaraguan draft dodger who took refuge in the Costa Rican embassy in Managua. According to Costa Rican officials Nicaraguan security forces had violated Costa Rican immunity. Nicaragua on its part claimed that the draft dodger had left the embassy before being arrested.

6. Ecuador initially figured within the group. However frictions between Ecuador and Nicaragua were exacerbated after some remarks by the President of Ecuador on the non-democratic nature of the Sandinista regime. Relations between them were severed in October 1985 and Ecuador left the group.

7. 'Contadora Talks Break Down', *International Herald Tribune*, 8 April 1986.

8. 'Central American Peace Talks Collapse; Contadora Sets Deadline', *The News* (Mexico City), 8 April 1986, p. 1.

9. 'Contadora Members Fear Spread of Conflict', *The News* (Mexico City), 12 December 1986, p. 1.

10. Peter Ford, 'Contadora is "Emperor Without Clothes", Europeans worry', *Christian Science Monitor*, 12 February 1987, p. 13.

11. Some would argue that these changes towards democracy have been skillfully imposed by the US on the countries in the region in order to reassert its pre-eminence there and to establish its *Pax Americana*; e.g. George Irvin, 'Central America: reshaping *Pax Americana*', *Third World Affairs 1987*.

12. The controversy on the Nicaraguan elections surfaced in the different coverage they received in the press. Reports in European newspapers tended to stress that the process itself was fair. See for instance: David Gardner, 'Sandinistas Seek National Consensus After Poll Victory', *Financial Times*, 7 November 1984; Jonathan Steele, 'The Revolution that Proved itself at the Poll', *The Guardian*, 7 November 1984. There were, however, other opinions both the US and Europe which saw the elections as a sham. For instance: 'A Charade in Nicaragua', *The Baltimore Sun*, reproduced in the *International Herald Tribune*, 7 November 1984; George Black, 'US Pressure, Sandinista Quarrels Make Nicaragua's Vote a Travesty', *International Herald Tribune*, 3–4 November 1984; Marcel Niedergang, 'Le Front est Partout', *Le Monde*, 3 November 1984.

13. The Sandinista government's imposition did not go down well among those sectors which had supported the FSLN's revolution. This and other repressive actions on the part of Managua, plus the changes in government in West Germany and France, for instance, produced a setback for the backing in political and economic aid the Sandinistas had been receiving.

14. Valero, 'Contadora: La busqueda de la pacificación en Centroamérica', p. 135.

15. Rene Herrera Zuñiga, 'Las relaciones entre Nicaragua y México', in Mario Ojeda (ed.), *Las relaciones de México con los paises de América Central* (Mexico: El Colegio de México, 1985), p. 150.

16. Quoted in Jim Morrell, 'Contadora Vows to Continue', *International Policy Report*, August 1986, p. 5.

17. See *The Tower Commission Report* (New York: Bantam Books/Times Books, 1987).

18. US Department of State, *The Contadora Resource Book* (Washington DC, January 1985), p. 1.

19. Nina María Serafino, 'Estados Unidos y la Iniciativa de Contadora', in Cepeda Ulloa and Pardo Garcia-Peña, *Contadora: Desafío a la diplomacia tradicional*, p. 133.

20. An illustration of the US concern about the threats posed by Nicaragua as the possible springboard of Soviet and Cuban penetration of Central America is a pamphlet published by the State Department: *The Soviet and Cuban Connection in Central America and the Caribbean* (Washington DC, March 1985).

21. For a detailed analysis of the possible implications of Nicaragua's military build-up for US security see Joseph Cirincione, 'Military Threats, Actual and Potential' in Robert S. Leiken (ed.), *Central America: Anatomy of a Conflict* (New York: Pergamon Press, 1984).

22. See for instance, Richard H. Ullman, 'At War with Nicaragua', *Foreign Affairs*, autumn 1983, p. 53.

11 Problems and policies: an agenda for the 1990s

Peter Calvert

'Where you stand depends on where you sit'[1] – and the view of where the challenges to security lie in Central America and the Caribbean varies as to whether they are viewed from Washington or Moscow, London or Kingston, Havana or Tegucigalpa. The purpose of this volume has been to develop a synthesis between these views, and, taking advantage of Europe's remoteness from the area, to try to establish a degree of detachment in handling them.

WHAT IS THE PROBLEM?

The main problem, as so often happens, is that there is no agreement on what is the problem. Washington sees its vital interests as threatened by Communist penetration of the area, masterminded from Moscow by way of Havana and Nicaragua. Havana has developed a siege mentality; in many years of resisting what it sees as American imperialism it has been prepared to forego much of its independence in order to secure the friendship of the only other superpower which exists at this time. Nicaragua is governed by men who also see the United States as an alien military power which has intervened in their country by force in the past and is doing so again now. The Contadora states all have interests in ensuring that armed conflict in Central America does not continue. They are not themselves afraid of US intervention, though they are strongly aware of its power and each sees itself as bidding for Washington's favour, whatever they may say to their electorates. They recognize that Communist activity in Central America does not pose any direct threat to them. But they fear an alliance between Havana and/or Nicaragua and an armed opposition in their own countries. The smaller island states watch what is going on on the mainland with concern, and occasionally find themselves drawn into the debate about it, as they are invited to use their votes for one side or another in the regional conflict.

THE PROBLEM AT THE INTERSTATE LEVEL

Beginning with the interstate level of analysis, the global context, two aspects are of particular interest to the student of Central America and the Caribbean area generally. These are the perception in Washington of the Cubans as mere surrogates for the ambitions of the Soviet Union and the continuing search for mutually agreed superpower codes of conduct which would in turn have a direct relevance to the current problems of Central America.

Given this tendency for both superpowers to conceive of the solutions to regional problems in terms of superpower relationships, curiosity focuses first on the problem of symmetrical superpower intervention. Since the outbreak of the Cold War it has not yet happened that both superpowers have intervened at the same time in the same part of the world, despite the persistent perceptions on both sides that the causes of conflict are to be found in the machinations of their opponents. If such perceptions were correct, both parties could be expected to wish to intervene simultaneously, but in practice they have established a consistent pattern of asymmetrical intervention. The reasons why this is the case are still not entirely clear, given that the establishment of a norm of avoiding direct superpower conflict, however rational, may conflict with other objectives in any given case. Despite heavy emphasis on the importance of Central America to the defence of the Western Hemisphere in general and the United States in particular, the Reagan Administration appears to share the views of its predecessors that the real danger to world peace is to be found not in Latin America but in the Middle East. Hence any study of Central America must at some stage take account of the overall defence posture of the United States and the position of the Caribbean within the general scheme of things.

Four features of US defence strategy in the eighties seem to be of particular relevance: the Strategic Defense Initiative (SDI – popularly known as 'Star Wars'); the naval build-up; the concept of 'horizontal escalation' enunciated by the then Defense Secretary Weinberger (which by arguing in favour of a policy of counter-attack in a region other than that where a crisis exists runs counter to previous assumptions about crisis management); and the so-called 'Reagan Doctrine' – support for counter-revolution, particularly but not exclusively in Angola, Afghanistan and Nicaragua.

The Administration's position is in some technical respects (e.g. SDI) novel, but in other respects (e.g. the emphasis on naval capability to project force globally – although elements of this maritime strategy are new) entirely consistent with previous American policy. It has sought and seeks to treat problems within a superpower framework, which it sees as the dominant paradigm for foreign policy in the nuclear age. It regards the world as a bipolar zero-sum system, in which any gain to one superpower results in a proportionate loss to the other. Hence it shares in the post-Vietnam revival of the 'domino theory', and sees the Cubans and the Sandinistas as proxies of Moscow in the calculated destabilization of the Caribbean area. The Soviet Union however appears to place a low priority on the area, which it regards as lying clearly within the US sphere of influence. Its policymakers are keenly interested in the United States itself but much less so in any other state in the region. Cuba is useful to them, and they have learned to tolerate its idiosyncrasies. A 'second Cuba' would be an asset of dubious value and could instead be a serious liability. Soviet urgency to conclude an INF Treaty confirms that the Soviet Union is concerned about what it sees as Washington's recklessness, and that this anxiety has been accentuated by the 'Rambo' phenomenon – the willingness to use force in Grenada to compensate for the loss of face sustained in the Iran hostage crisis. Secretary Weinberger has by no means been the most belligerent policymaker within the Administration, and, as the Irangate affair has since disclosed, the Soviets have been right to be concerned about the amount of power accorded within the American system to middle-ranking military officers.[2]

What is not known is whether the Soviet Union has in the past consistently been deliberate in avoiding symmetrical intervention in the Caribbean basin. Their tendency has certainly been to avoid risk-taking. US concern about possible shifts within the Politburo resulting in substantial changes of policy have, however, been reinforced by the fall of Boris Yeltsin and in any event deeply held suspicions will take a long time to ebb. It must always be remembered that for over a generation Americans have been able to luxuriate in anti-communism, but few Americans have ever consciously seen a communist except on television; the isolation of the USSR makes the same point even more true for them.

From 1933 onwards the United States established a norm of avoiding overt intervention in the Caribbean area. It maintained it into the Cold War period because the hegemony established at that time had been immensely strengthened by the Second World War and its aftermath, and this hegemony still exists. The Reagan Administration did not need to intervene with its own military forces in Nicaragua or Grenada in order to damage their economies disproportionately and render their governments harmless. Intervention in Grenada was a public relations exercise, demonstrating resolve without incurring risk. Intervention in Nicaragua, in the tradition established in Guatemala and Cuba, has been indirect, and from a political point of view successful. The Sandinistas in Nicaragua have in any case consistently had internal problems of command and control. The situation there is not at all and never has been like Cuba in the early 1960s. Only five of the commandantes of 1979 are now left in the top leadership. Following Grenada, any Cubans there are now far from conspicuous, in striking contrast to the 'Sandalistas' – the large number of overseas civilian sympathizers from the West.

The suggestion that the government might further consolidate its position following the July/August 1985 offensive has in practice proved to be only partly true. At that time the contra campaign was having an effect, and the strength of the regime to resist all out attack was limited, yet it seemed clear that any casualties at all among American troops would be too much for American public opinion. Since Irangate things have changed somewhat. Though the Nicaraguan government is still seen as unacceptable by American public opinion, it is unlikely that the contras would be acceptable either. Resistance has revived towards any deeper involvement in the region. However if, following the installation of the civilian government, President Ortega has made a strong effort to impart central direction, the Nicaraguan government still has a long way to go before it can relax in its efforts to rebuild the damage that has been done. Meanwhile Washington is well aware that the Cubans have told the Nicaraguans that they are 'on their own' in the event of a full-scale attack from the United States. If there is only room for one Cuba in the Americas, as the high cost of Soviet support has long suggested, then it is going to be Cuba and not Nicaragua.

THE PROBLEM AS A REGIONAL PROBLEM

At the regional level the first problem is to define the region. To some extent this is in itself a political decision, depending on what aim is intended. Definition of the Central American crisis as an issue for the OAS would place disproportionate influence in the hands of the US, and since 1982 that body has lost both power and influence as the result of the failure of the US to heed the views of the Latin American states on the Falklands/Malvinas question. No effective regional organization however exists for the Caribbean as such; indeed, by using the sub-regional OECS as a vehicle for intervention in Grenada the US effectively wasted one of its most useful assets; its ability to dominate any Caribbean organization through the sheer weight of its economic power and influence.

The latter is exercised not only directly but indirectly, though the United States' dominant role in regional trade and finance, directly and through the major international lending agencies. Jamaica's dealings with the IMF, discussed above in Chapter 7, form a case-study in the problems confronting the smaller countries of the regional system. It was not the IMF as much as American destabilization with which the Manley government had to contend. The continuity between the Carter and Reagan policies in this respect was in fact very marked. In 1980 the incoming Seaga government had received some $900 millions in three weeks. Seaga was the first foreign visitor to the White House after the Inauguration in 1981, and in return for favours received acted both as co-sponsor of the Caribbean Basin Initiative and promotor of the Grenadian invasion. But the economic costs of IMF approval may be as serious as those of disapproval. Pressure for the dismantling of import controls in April 1985 flooded Jamaica with Volvos and, with unemployment at some 35%, drove social stresses to the limits of acceptability. In this respect Jamaica is not necessarily typical of smaller states confronted with drastic economic readjustment, but it is a warning of how vulnerable these states are to regional political and economic changes.

If lenders wish to get their money back, as they might reasonably expect to do, they might do well to pay less attention to economic nostrums and more to the political context. Stable government can perhaps be better secured by having regard to the latter than to the former. Until 1982 there was a belief that – although uncomfortable – the IMF 'short back and sides' treatment worked and people were prepared to accept it even if they did not like it. Now the thesis has been openly challenged by both Peru and Brazil, there is a danger that the richer states may get favoured treatment and the full rigours of international financial probity fall on the smaller states.

The overall lesson is that the Caribbean remains such a complex and diverse area socially that parallels between one country and another – and in particular between the larger mainland and the smaller island states – should be accepted only with great caution. Given the relatively small resources required, there seems no reason why a substantial betterment of conditions in the smaller states should not be possible and the risk of future destabilization averted. A new Caribbean Basin Initiative is needed, with real funding, which does not simply make hopeful noises about funds being forthcoming from a private enterprise which cannot afford to invest for political rather than economic returns.

Apart from the US there are only two potential regional powers: Cuba and Mexico. Mexico, as we shall see below, has internal problems which have prevented it from assuming a regional role. But, as shown above by Alistair Hennessy in Chapter 7, Cuba, as a regional power, has been and certainly remains at the political, economic and diplomatic fulcrum of North–South security relations. It is not a puppet of the Soviet Union. Unlike many other Latin American states it can not, on the other hand, be seen in a purely regional context. Since the 1960s it has been acting at times independently and occasionally contrarily to the wishes of the Soviet Union, both inside and outside the Western Hemisphere.

Consequently Cuban foreign policy shows four clear phases:

1   1958–68 – the *via armada*. Belief in imminent regional revolution was terminated by the success of counter-insurgency, matched by the increasing dependence on the Soviet Union which led both to the unequivocal support for Soviet intervention in Czechoslovakia and the crisis of the economy (the 'Harvest of the Ten Millions',1970).

2   1968–75 – the 'new realism'. During this time new contacts were built up on the basis of the 1966 Tricontinental, ending in the break-up of the OAS embargo 1972–5.[3]

3   1975–9 – global involvement. This has precedents from the early 1960s: in 1963 Cuban combat troops were being sent to Algeria and Nkrumah later invited Cuban advisers to Ghana. Cubans were also present in Syria during the Yom Kippur war (1973), but did not take part. In Angola there was evidence that Cuba had acted on its own initiative and used its own transport – Bristol Britannias and a large proportion of its fishing fleet (Operación Carlota). In Ethiopia, however, relations had been difficult as Cuban troops had been unwilling to serve against Eritrean separatists. But in 1977–8 the 19,000 Cuban troops had served under integrated Soviet command against the Somalis and played a key role, which had had an important spin-off in African support for Castro's election to the Presidency of the Non-Aligned Movement for 1979–82. The Havana Conference of 1979 was marked by pressure for a tilt towards the Soviet Union, and

terminated by a Cuban orientated communiqué in which the objective of the NIEO was stated. But the Soviet intervention in Afghanistan undid much of the gains, and this time Cuba was careful not to support or condone the Soviet action.

4   Since 1979 – the radicalization of the Caribbean. This was initiated by the revolutions in Nicaragua and Grenada. The Soviet Union recognized that the US would not tolerate another Cuba (as Grenada was intended to show). Cuba has been constantly accused of supplying arms to El Salvador via Nicaragua, but European observers confirm Cubans in Nicaragua are civilians, and easily distinguishable from Nicaraguans.

Trends have been much harder to distinguish in the most recent developments. Castro's initiative towards the Church has been variously interpreted as a personal crisis or a reawakening of interest in its revolutionary potential. After Grenada a new conciliatory note has, however, been apparent in Cuban relations with the secular powers of the Caribbean also. With the acceptance of the Contadora group's offer to mediate in Central America the revolutionary initiative there seems to have been lost and it is unlikely to be revived as long as there is a serious prospect of a tolerable peace.

In the meanwhile the efforts of the United States to strengthen military forces in Central America have conspicuously failed to halt the outbreak of civil war and, by contributing to the growth of authoritarianism, have in fact helped erode confidence in the capacity of civilians to govern. The extension of similar programmes to the Eastern Caribbean, discussed in Chapter 9 above, is clearly intended to avert the possibility of another Grenada. But many of these states are so small that they are vulnerable even to the force capability of drug-smugglers and/or gangsters. Spreading military capability, therefore, may well, as in the larger states, come in time to have exactly the reverse effect to that intended.

Regional military alliances between a superpower and a number of small powers varying widely in size and population consolidate a hegemony to which insurgency in the past has been seen as the only counter. Formal structures have not been necessary to assure regional dominance, and the Central American alliance system, CONDECA, intended to co-ordinate regional strategy, has only served to strengthen the relationship between the Pentagon and the military governments of the client states.[4] This relationship has been maintained, even when, as under Carter, the formal policy of the United States was to distance itself from them, and revived when, as under Reagan, concern grew in Washington about the possible strategic threat of Soviet penetration in Central America. The United States must be particularly careful, as Martin C. Needler warns in Chapter 8, not to exaggerate the risks. The tendency to exaggerate stems at least in part from a very inadequate understanding of the major problems confronting individual state governments in the region. The US has shown a persistent tendency to ignore regional views when they do not suit its own purposes.

The military build-up in the Eastern Caribbean, as Tony Thorndike points out above (Chapter 9), had four main objectives:

1   To counter economic subversion – US influence in the region was seen as a way of serving notice to carpet-bagging entrepreneurs and shady business interests.

2   To counter external attack – ironically the two main 'hot spots' were internal to the region: Belize where the UK government steadfastly refused to say what it would do in the event of a Guatemalan invasion, and Guyana, much of whose territory had been claimed by Venezuela and whose army, only 2,000 strong in 1964, now numbers 4,500 with a further 11,500 armed reserves divided into no less than five paramilitary forces each keeping an eye on one another.

3   To maintain internal control – as in Guyana and Suriname, and, increasingly in Jamaica. The latter now has an army of 10,000 and police force of 8,000, and was the recipient of $5.25 million in aid in 1985 alone.

4   To guard against an internal takeover – it has to be remembered that the Grenadan Revolution was carried out by only forty men, only two of whom were over twenty-five years old. The exploits of Patrick John were perhaps more absurd than dangerous, but in 1981 Eugenia Charles of Dominica had to borrow French forces from neighbouring Martinique. In the revolt on Union Island in December 1979 St Vincent borrowed forces from Barbados. However, when the leader of the revolt fled to Carriacou he was put into jail by the then PRG of Grenada, and there can be no doubt that the 'trade union of rulers' is as strong in the region as elsewhere.

It was, of course, alarm at events in Grenada that stimulated the development of the concept of regional security in the Eastern Caribbean and it began not with President Reagan but with President Carter's belated conversion to *realpolitik*. Though Britain was reluctant to get involved, seeing the problem as a coastguard matter, some assistance with police training was given and this was supplemented from US sources despite the 1974 decision of Congress to end the training of foreign police forces. The Memorandum of Understanding of October 1982 (which St Kitts joined on independence) established training teams (SSUs) which were seen as having a primarily military rather than a police function (see Chapter 9). The US expected to carry most of the cost though Barbados did offer to pay 49% of its own. However this in itself illustrates the miltary weakness of the system. The exercise 'Exotic Palm', which was held in September 1985 in the middle of the hurricane season, went badly wrong, and the Barbadian forces were unable to arrive at all. The history of poor co-operation between the islands limits the possibilities of using forces outside their own home territory, and there was and is no agreement on the exact circumstances in which the informal alliance could be invoked.

In this context the role of the Caribbean Basin Initiative (CBI) of 1983 must be reassessed. How far was this a real attempt to undercut indigenous unrest by an effective programme of economic betterment? In fact, in economic terms the CBI has been generally unsuccessful, since it did not provide for the export of commodities to the United States but rather for tax concessions to US businessmen. Its major significance, however, was its value as 'cover' for military aid to Central America, and in the Caribbean in the wider sense, in order to prevent further Grenadas. It resulted in minor but very significant military aid to the island states. Creation of a Regional Defence Force in the Eastern Caribbean, urged by Barbados, was especially significant.

Even those who recognize that the US has legitimate security interests on its southern coast – one-fifth of the coastline of the continental United States abuts on the Caribbean – question how far these interests really extend and how far they are upheld by the policy of military aid to the 'microstates'. It is recognized that among policymakers in the US there are those who, rightly or wrongly, felt 'left in the lurch' by Britain's 'scuttle' away from the West Indies and have turned to the idea of direct US involvement only with some reluctance. But the question remains, how far are these states really a threat to other countries in the region, let alone to the United States? The threat of possible rocket emplacements is not a major concern to the US Administration; a re-run of the Cuban Missile Crisis is not seen as a serious possibility in the world conditions of today. The need to deny naval repair and in particular submarine base facilities to the Soviet Union, as in Cuba in 1970, is taken very seriously in Washington, but it is not necessary to arm the states to ensure that. The SDI, even if successful in its primary objective of providing protection against

Peter Calvert

Inter-Continental Ballistic Missiles (ICBMs), would have great difficulty dealing with depressed trajectory missiles from close range. With renewed emphasis on naval strength, even less probable scenarios seem to have taken on new life, and the doctrines of Admiral Mahan have been 'dusted off'. Given persisting nuclear stalemate, an extended conventional war is seen in US defence circles as requiring renewed protection both for the Caribbean sea lanes and for the Panama Canal. How far such a scenario is realistic is another question. It is worth noting that the Caribbean was in fact the first sea area controlled by an underwater sonar detection system (in 1968), and the establishment of such a system does not require the presence of any bases outside US territory at all.

THE PROBLEM AT THE STATE LEVEL

The problem at the state level lies not merely in idiosyncratic features of the four states which here are made the subject of case studies, but in common features which many of these states share. The two most obvious ones are the dominance of the armed forces and the weakness of the independent state in face of world pressures. A third, an historical uncertainty about what the state actually comprises, is peculiar to mainland Central America. However in the late 1980s it can be assumed that the existing states will remain in their present form, and that the aspirations for Central American reunification, which bedevilled regional politics into the 1960s, have finally diminished to the point of irrelevance.

The role of the armed forces is obviously central to questions of security. The armed forces in Latin America generally and Central America in particular have, however, been the subject of many independent works, and hence it has not been thought necessary to include a specific chapter on this aspect here.[5] However a few words are needed to set the problem in context.

The military in Latin America are no longer seen as a reflection of civil society. Through their highly corporatist ethic, and their monopoly of the effective use of force, they show a considerable ability to deal with short-run crises, largely independent of the outside world. US training and support have undoubtedly contributed to maintaining their ascendancy. However that ascendancy was established before the United States rose to world dominance, and, as in Guatemala, has been able to persist even when US support has been removed.[6] Only in El Salvador has the influx of US power been decisive, and even there it has not succeeded in eliminating the insurgents.

186

The military, however, are a dangerous ally for a democratic government. Though strong on conflict suppression, they are weak on conflict resolution; their heavy-handed use of repression has created martyrs and sustained lost causes far beyond their intrinsic capabilities. The classic dictators have almost all vanished from Latin America as a result of changes in the international environment, and their 'crony militarism' has proved highly vulnerable to internal unrest in Haiti and the Philippines. There remain, as there have since the 1490s, foreign garrison forces in the Caribbean. Cuba, the key to the Caribbean, is an anomaly, the only country in the world that officially has forces of both superpowers on its soil. There has been, however, great uncertainty as to who or what would fill the power vacuum: neither in El Salvador – a client state – nor in Guatemala – formerly virtually a pariah state – have the military been able to stop the fighting.

It is impossible to overstate the significance of faction within military regimes. Factions succeed one another, but the corporate strength of the military remains. The nationalist/liberal dichotomy is unreal; all military regimes are nationalist. Apart from faction only inter-service rivalry divides them, and in Central America the traditional dominance of the Army and unification of National Guard forces makes this of little account. Beyond this there are serious difficulties: the military cannot be understood properly without a greater understanding of the key unit of loyalty, the regiment or mess, of which outsiders can know little. Certainly the specialist corps are however of great significance: the cavalry in Argentina, the intelligence branch in Peru and the artillery in Spain have each been recognized as having a dominant role. Detailed analysis is still badly needed of military forces in Central America and the Caribbean, where specialist counter-insurgency units have undoubtedly played a significant political role recently and may be expected to do so in the future.

The dictatorial tradition presents not only problems of analysis but problems of comprehension. It is clear that complex repressive regimes can and do misread the information coming to them. As the Argentine army misunderstood the Cordobazo of 1969, so the National Guard in Nicaragua failed to interpret aright the meaning of the rising of 1978.[7] The return to civilian rule, moreover, is not seen in the region as owing much to the United States, though President Reagan took credit for it, rather unwisely, in 1984. It is virtually a certainty that some government in the region will fall to force before 1995; if this did not happen it would mark a significant breach with past trends. The most likely trouble spot from the point of view of military politics in the region in the immediate future is generally agreed to be Haiti. There, following the flight of the younger Duvalier, there has been a power vacuum moderated only by the control on exiles returning home. This situation remains extremely unstable in 1988, both despite and because of the move towards civilian rule.

What would undoubtedly have a serious impact on the region would be any widespread move in adjoining states back towards military dictatorship. A recrudescence of military rule in South America still seems unlikely. However, there can be no doubt that there is now growing disenchantment with civilian rule, and that this must necessarily in turn affect the future of the Caribbean region if it is not checked. Special strategic importance also attaches to the situation in two lesser known countries. In Suriname, under a military government, Paramaribo has displaced Georgetown as a major listening post for the USSR. In Panama, where General Noriega has defied all attempts to shift him, the military also remain active in politics, and in strategic terms the country remains much more significant than its current low profile suggests. If the Panama Canal is to be extended, its strategic value is enhanced; if replaced, the alternative inter-oceanic route, through Nicaragua, may again be very significant.

Of greatest interest in the current context is the much less well-known situation of the armed forces in the smaller Caribbean states, mentioned above. There are, as will be seen, precedents for the present situation, e.g. the 1940 Destroyer Bases deal, but US involvement in the region has in the past always been incomplete, with the European colonial powers remaining responsible for public order in their own dependencies. The circle of the US Caribbean basin defence system was completed only in 1982 when the Eastern Caribbean islands were incorporated in the US security system. Some anomalies remain, for example US military aid to Jamaica remains in some ways a 'one-off' relationship owing to its particular sensitivity because of its proximity to Cuba. Despite left-wing criticisms, moreover, it can be shown that the security pattern is apparently largely independent of US economic involvement: the movement of the multinationals out of the area has in recent years been much more marked that the move in. One apparent exception, the Coca-Cola Corporation's purchase of some 20% of Belize, had a very clear commercial motive: to escape the Florida frosts.

The military involvement of the US has had important political consequences, however. It has introduced an alien tone to West Indian politics, previously only found in Guyana and Suriname, and this has been resented. There are certainly signs that the US is to some degree sensitive to the concerns of its small allies – US notions of 'collective security' have in West Indian parlance been attenuated to 'understandings'. But there was and is still considerable nervousness in the Eastern Caribbean about the possibility of being drawn into something much larger than they are accustomed to. The Prime Minister of Antigua/Barbuda refused to attend President Reagan's conference in Grenada in early 1987, and Mr Mitchell, the Prime Minister of St Vincent, who represents the Grenadines in his island Parliament and had been the first to call for US intervention in Grenada, now feels that the US has made some mistakes.

If social problems are alternatively seen as the main danger to stability in the islands, other considerations have to be taken into account. Not all social unrest is capable of leading to revolutionary outcomes; some believe that drugs, for example, lower rather than raise political consciousness. But the drug traffic is regionally organized, linking the producer states in northern South America, via the smaller Caribbean islands, with the largest consumer state, the United States itself. At key points in this chain, social strains and regional sensitivities intersect. In particular, the politico-military situation in Colombia has unravelled badly since 1985, and there too social conditions are potentially destabilizing.

Lastly there is the question of colonial commitments. Britain's only remaining dependencies in the region, the British Virgin Islands and the Turks and Caicos Islands, remain at a very low level of development and have only a modest coastguard and customs presence. Britain, which has been helping to strengthen police forces in the Commonwealth Caribbean since 1974, has extended its involvement by supplying gunboats for the defence of the Eastern Caribbean. More conspicuously, it retains a commitment to defend Belize against a Guatemalan attack which for the present seems increasingly unlikely. Colonial unrest in the French overseas *départements* and in Puerto Rico, regarded as a colony not merely by Cuba but by many other nationalist Latin Americans, is however likely to recur more than once between now and the early 1990s.

Grenada showed that the US was prepared in certain circumstances to intervene if the former colonial power was unable or unwilling to do so. It is now known, however, that on official US Defense Department figures the US operation in Grenada was much less successful than was stated at the time. It was and is highly unlikely that the United States will find itself impelled to intervene simultaneously in two or more locations in the Caribbean, but it is far from certain that it could do so successfully. Moreover any intervention in the region, however minor, necessarily has implications for US responsibilities in other parts of the world. The area as a whole clearly still lacks a co-ordinated policy, either from the US or from Europe.

With the United States so heavily engaged in the region already, the potential of Mexico and Cuba as regional powers, particularly in relation to Central America, requires special consideration.

In the regional context a special importance attaches to Mexico,[8] where troops have for some time been active on the Southern border and have been reported to be heavily involved in the marijuana trade on the Northern one. There has been disagreement on the extent to which militarization was proceeding, but there is no doubt that the armed forces are at long last being modernized and strengthened. The Mexican crisis of 1982 is the key factor limiting Mexico's role in the region. The onset of the crisis was not as sudden as is often believed. It had its roots in the late 1960s and early 1970s, with the failure of the import substitution model, the fixed peso and rising government borrowing to meet the problems of population increase, 30% un- and under-employment and the decline in nutrition rates. The oil bonanza of the late 1970s postponed but also exacerbated the crisis. Typically the political effects were felt in both the far north and the south of the country. In the north the industrialists of the Monterrey group, under US influence, hedged their bets on the National Action Party (PAN); in the south, in the Isthmus and Yucatán, oil undercut the power of regional leaders without arresting centrifugal tendencies. The ruling Party of the Institutionalized Revolution (PRI) is no longer unified, and though up to now it has not faced a significant secession, there is a risk that individual sectors might lose important blocks of support.

Mexico is a civilian state, however, and can be expected to remain so into the 1990s. Inertia coupled with the skilled use of co-optation and coercion promise to maintain the regime intact for some time to come, and the scaremongers in the US who denounced the 'making' of the mid-term elections were actually welcomed by the Mexican government as they increased their already considerable negotiating power with the US government. There are several reasons for this. To begin with, coercion is an expensive policy; it can easily cost more to coerce than to buy off potential opponents, and the Mexican system offers great rewards for those who stay in line and very subtle pressures on those who do not. There is no great incentive to leave the ruling PRI, especially since, uniquely for Latin America, the only credible opposition, the PAN, is on the right and not the left. As for the workers, the only significant blocks which could harbour secessionist ambitions are the oil workers and the teaching unions, and with the state the only major direct employer of so many, rewards can still be directed to where they can bring most returns.

The anti-drug campaign and the civil war in Guatemala have indeed strengthened the power of the Mexican armed forces. But reports of the militarization of Mexico can be discounted. Operational strengthening has been limited. Security on off-shore oil wells has been stepped up, helicopters purchased and the flood of refugees from Central America relocated away from the border. The establishment by Echeverria of the University of the Military was part of a growing political rather than military strength of the armed forces. But Mexico is still less an actor in the Caribbean basin than a potential problem area. The North–South divide is nowhere more visible than on its northern frontier, even though US fears of a major social revolution there are to be discounted. Concern about Mexico arises not because of any real revolutionary potential but because of endemic corruption and the failure to admit a genuine political opposition. The present administration of Miguel de la Madrid has, like some of its predecessors, taken a number of initiatives and then drawn back. It is difficult however to see what the new administration of Carlos Salinas de Gortari, which is scheduled to hold power from 1988 to December 1994, can do in the short term to change matters significantly. The 'Texanization' of Mexico's northern states has accompanied a genuine shift of power northwards, but there was and is no real outlet for it except within the existing order. Privatization, the vogue solution of the day, has been very limited; the problem is finding takers for the many enterprises the government has offered to sell off. The attempt to diversify exports, made even more urgent by the collapse of oil prices, is certainly not being held up by high wage costs. Only a major influx of capital can make diversification effective, and then only if the debts can be met and the markets found. Alvin Toffler's suggestion for symbiotic co-operation between Japan and Mexico seems far-fetched at first sight, but it makes sense. It is, however, not likely to be implemented on either side.

The other potential regional power, Cuba, also faces economic problems which severely limit its freedom of action. The result is that Cuba, while urging default on others, has compounded with its creditors and has advised both Brazil and the Dominican Republic to do the same. The 1985 collapse in oil prices had a critical significance for Soviet–Cuban relations owing to Cuban dependence on the resale of Soviet oil. Cuban involvement in Africa continues – the South Africans continue to claim that the only thing that stops them from withdrawing from Namibia is the presence of approximately 9,000 Cubans in Angola. Hence these costs, too, will have

Peter Calvert

to be carried for the foreseeable future, at a time when a new economic realism increasingly dominates Soviet thought.

The fact is that Cuba's diplomatic position is not as good as it was before 1979. The Cuban exile community in the United States (especially but not exclusively in Miami) has become a major influence in internal US politics. Cuba has turned again to Europe in the elusive search for diversification, and the prominence in Havana of the Institute of West European Studies confirms the importance attached to this initiative. But the overwhelming power of the United States and its own political and economic weakness remain the dominant facts in Cuban policy.

Cuban policy towards Central America has, therefore, been marked above all by extreme caution and a determination to preserve the Cuban Revolution at all costs. Cuba has taken offence at not being invited to Cancún, but its support for any initiative in Central America has consistently played into the hands of right-wing critics in the US and so proved counter-productive. Deep divisions have been noted over many years between Cuba and the Soviet Union on how to achieve a viable road to power in the Americas. A consistent theme in Cuban policy, it has been suggested, has been 'unity' among 'progressive' forces. The Cubans sought repeatedly to exploit the potential of Haiti and tried to extend their influence in the West Indies in the later 1970s but were rebuffed; they repeatedly urged unity in El Salvador, but there the left – all splinters from the pro-Moscow party – disliked the USSR intensely and failed to heed the advice until it was too late. The Nicaraguans have from the outset emphasized their desire to emulate Cuban achievements while retaining their own distinctive national identity. They share with the Cubans principally a strong antipathy to the US and its influence. Above all, the collapse of the Revolution in Grenada in 1983 and the subsequent US intervention was a fiasco for Cuba and was followed in Havana by much genuine self-criticism.

Cuba has other social and economic problems, too. It has, in the Latin American tradition, been overproducing technicians and bureaucrats. Development of its own off-shore oil reserves was an important step in lessening its dependence on the Soviet Union, but it will take a long time for that dependence to decline. Co-optation of the Church could be seen as a move to pre-empt the emergence of a Polish-style Solidarity in Cuba. Meanwhile, despite the rhetoric on both sides, Cuban–US dialogue has been proceeding and it looks as if the US may yet, even under President Reagan, agree to accept a Marxist–Leninist Cuba in return for no further aid for Nicaragua. Again, however, it is hard-line influence on the United

States electorate, and the diminished long-term possibility of a future Democratic president that the increased Hispanic vote implies that, as Professor Hennessy cogently argues in Chapter 5, is the really significant factor. It should not be forgotten, moreover, that the Cubans have signed neither the NPT nor the Treaty of Tlatelolco, and the possibility should not be discounted of Soviet pressure on Cuba to come into line with its policies of rapprochement with the United States, either through the cutting off of arms supplies, or the reduction of sugar imports.

Finally, as Eduardo Crawley shows above in Chapter 6, Nicaragua too must be seen as a separate entity with its own internal history, social structure and problems. It is impossible now to tell what the course of the Nicaraguan Revolution might have been had it proceeded autonomously, since the fact that it emerged with the expectation of US intervention and has been subject to US pressure continuously since 1979 has necessarily shaped its external policies. Nicaraguan perceptions and misperceptions have, therefore, been a significant factor in shaping the search for solutions.

THE PROBLEM AT THE SUB-STATE LEVEL

A major weakness of the US administration throughout the 1980s has been its failure to recognize or acknowledge the indigenous causes of revolution in the Caribbean basin. There is no doubt that the conjuncture of events which led to the Nicaraguan revolution was unique and is unlikely to be repeated. But the very existence of the Caribbean Basin Initiative (CBI), in however inadequate a form, does seem to suggest that there remains in US policy circles some awareness of the social basis of political discontent, even if the interpretation of that basis might not be shared by its political opponents.

In Central America there can be no doubt of the profound importance of indigenous factors in the current unrest, nor that it has its roots not in the East–West ideological divide, but in North–South economic relations and national policies on the distribution of economic resources. The region has been and is seriously undercapitalized. Investment takes place almost invariably in capital-intensive technology, resulting in a generally low value for labour, and consequent failure to develop an adequate internal market. Indigenous elites do not invest in their own countries, preferring to hold wealth in large tracts of under-utilized land, or in securities abroad. The value placed on land leads to increasing quantities being devoted to the growth of cash crops for export, and the twin tendencies of the concentration of wealth in the hands of great landowners and the continuing subdivision of the lands of the poorer agrarian sectors increasingly threatens to erupt into civil war. In this respect what is needed to lay the foundations for the balanced growth that alone could engender the abolition of poverty is the repatriation of capital and control of capital-intensive investment. Sponsoring the informal sector or investing in agriculture, however desirable in themselves, cannot achieve this as they tend to benefit only some of the population.

Ideally the development of intermediate technology would both achieve the desired end and be compatible with a good rate of capital formation. In theory it does not require the co-operation of the developed nations nor the alteration of the existing terms of trade, though COMECON, for example, has offered favourable terms to Cuba and Vietnam. But in practice advanced technology, though late to reach the region compared with other parts of Latin America, is already well entrenched, and the Central American Common Market (CACM) would have been checked by the limitations of import substitution had it not been first disrupted by the national rivalries between El Salvador and Honduras that erupted in the 'Football War' (Guerra de Fútbol) of 1969. Export manufacturing does act to create demand in the exporting countries; the real problem is one of productivity. The poor may work long hours but they earn very little for their labours, because in effect they are undercapitalized.

As regards agriculture, control of food export crops, if internal politics permit it, would increase jobs and lead to more realistic food prices, while improved marketing was the key to many problems of diversified agriculture. This model is essentially that of India and Tanzania, where low pay and emiseration persist, and it has to be conceded that this is the result of structural factors that also apply in Latin America, e.g. Ecuador's determination to build its own steel plant. Hence there is a strong case, as already noted above, for a real Caribbean Basin Initiative which can transfuse substantial sums of capital into the region without expecting substantial economic returns. Left-wing critics can already show that the US gets far more out of the Caribbean in the form of profits than it is now putting in in the form of investment.

Social causes of unrest in the Caribbean islands differ both in causes and effects. Historically the area has been very fragmented by the rivalry between European powers. Outside powers are only now beginning to see the area as a whole. Economically the area is wholly dependent on specialized agricultural export products and lacks much of the mineral basis for successful industrialization. Neither efforts to encourage industry nor tourism have altered this. Socially, race and class interact. Politically the dominant form is autocracy tempered by popular protest, e.g. in the Commonwealth Caribbean in the 1930s or in Cuba in the 1950s. Culturally the area is divided both from Central America and within itself; the island territories remain linked with their respective metropoles by emulation and emigration. Hence social stresses are effectively contained by the existing order. During the development decade of the CACM the Caribbean woke up – and is now going back to sleep.

During these years, the major new development has been the impact of the international drug traffic. So important is this development that it is not merely facetious to ask if the Caribbean countries are going back to sleep because they are stoned out of their minds. If so, some think, it is with large transistors and motorbikes rather than drugs, though the drug culture has always been part of the sense of West Indian identity. What is clear is that the growth of large drug-running syndicates in the region has had two very marked effects, and that while the attention of the US and Europe has been focused on the problems of producer states such as Colombia, both there and in the smaller island states where drug interests find convenient immunity, the drug question is seen as being primarily a problem for the states that provide the market. And if in general the actual consumption of drugs is not seen as a problem, in Jamaica the situation is much more serious than in the other island states. There social changes have brought a further increase in the number and use of handguns and a parallel reinforcement of the authoritarian tradition and the patron–client relationship.

Tourism is often seen from the United States and from Europe as the answer to problems of Caribbean development – after all the climate and facilities are ideal for the further development of large-scale tourist complexes. But tourists are easily frightened off by the slightest hint of internal unrest. Again, Jamaican unrest has been self-defeating. Furthermore, the actual value of tourism to the island states has been much overestimated – in the case of Antigua it has actually generated a net negative dollar balance owing to the need there as elsewhere to import goods and food for tourist consumption. Modern Cuba, which is now seeking to expand its tourist industry, could benefit hugely, as it does have the necessary indigenous resources. But pre-Revolution Cuba remains still a classic case of the undesirable political effects of tourism, in this case the mass post-war boom in visitors from the United States, which contributed so extensively to uhe anti-American feeling that underlay Castro's move towards Moscow. It is probable that such undesirable effects are not

Peter Calvert

universal, but stemmed from the sharpness of the contrast in incomes. In Uruguay, for example, tourism is a major industry, but is not seen as a destabilizing factor.

Other relevant social factors in the region include the future of youth, trade unions and the role of the Church. For youth, the chances of getting out are diminishing. The effect is felt in an increasing crime rate, but this is not politically directed and, except where it intersects with the drug traffic, poses no great problem for other states. Trade unions historically have been a stabilizing factor in the Commonwealth Caribbean; elsewhere they have been of little account, and in Central America they have been a major target for military repression. Church influence has been and is divided. The growth of fundamentalist movements has been encouraged by and contributed to the success of the Reaganites, yet they have reflected local needs, and church organizations are still the most promising non-governmental organizations (NGOs) for getting things done, at least in the former British and Dutch territories.

SOLUTIONS

The crisis in Central America has since 1979 been seen primarily in terms of crisis management techniques. If a solution is to be achieved, however, these techniques can only be a means to an end, the establishment of a crisis prevention regime for the area.

Irrespective of whether the crisis is seen as arising from local insurgency, Soviet or Cuban penetration or US intervention, it has been all too easy for all parties to define it as requiring no effort on their part. Hence the problem of crisis management calls first for diplomacy, mediation or arbitration. Bilateral diplomacy having failed to satisfy any of the relevant interests, and arbitration having no clear objective to decide, the next question has been who is to act as mediator? The Organization of American States (OAS) has failed to play an effective role in bringing peace to the region because the gap between US and Latin American interests revealed (though certainly not created) by the Falklands War has proved too wide to bridge. Its existence precludes effective intervention by the UN. The Contadora initiative, however, provided an effective framework for mediation which though not conclusive in itself, appears to have been adequate, as Esperanza Durán argues in Chapter 10, to enable the contending parties in Central America to find enough common ground in their regional identity to resolve their major differences.

In considering the effect of Contadora on security within the region, she argues it will be necessary to have regard both to the collective and to the individual. What in the United States has been seen primarily as an East–West conflict is believed in both Central America and elsewhere, e.g. Europe, to be primarily a North–South question. But regional and other powers in the region have their own concern for their own security, and see it as potentially threatened both by Nicaragua and by the United States. Their greatest danger, in fact, lies in conflict between the two which 'spills over' into their own territories and confronts them with unacceptable dilemmas of choice.

Three of the four Contadora powers faced significant domestic problems during the period of their diplomatic engagement in the search for a solution: Mexico the earthquake of 1985; Colombia the breakdown of the agreement with the M-19, the siege of the Palace of Justice and the eruption of Mt Nevado del Ruiz; and Panama continuing political instability which has since been overcome (if not resolved) by General Noriega consolidating his hold on the political system. The attempts to widen the circle of interested parties at San José and Luxembourg backfired: the entry of Ecuador into the peace process seemed designed to disrupt rather than to further it. On the other hand, even if the deadlines had continued to be extended and the Treaty had eventually been signed, the Contadora mediation would not necessarily have solved the situation that it was designed to meet. The US was not at any stage a party to the proposed Treaty, and those provisions designed to prevent territory being used for attacks on neighbouring states would therefore not necessarily have proved effective. It was the Irangate scandal, and not the work of the mediators, which had undercut the clandestine work of the US National Security Council staffers and brought the contras to the point of collapse.

On the other hand no outside mediation stood any chance of success in a region of such sensitivity to the United States. The United States Administration had all along believed that Europe did not understand US concern in the area, and in a divided and fragmented policymaking machine, those who were responsible for a 'forward' policy of 'rolling back the frontiers of communism' distrusted even the Christian Democrats as being tainted with leftism. And the real nature of European interests in the region was also questionable. The right were happy to have the Pentagon kept busy in Central America, the left admired plucky little Nicaragua and did not want to see it done down, and the Europeanists welcomed the opportunity to hammer out Community foreign policy. All, however, saw the conflict as endemic, a North–South question, and most, like Spain, recognized that it fell within the US sphere of interest. Hence it was unlikely to be amenable to a diplomatic solution. If it was an East–West question, the Russians might be prepared – at any summit that might emerge from Geneva or subsequently – to trade Nicaragua for Afghanistan, as had been publicly suggested in Washington. But if it was a North–South question merely diplomatic solutions were plainly inadequate.

A further problem throughout, therefore, has been the weakness and inconsistency of a United States' policy which has had no recognizable unifying force or centre. Mediation is only practicable where the contending parties each have a clear hierarchy of goals and a consistent bargaining strategy. The State Department lacked both the confidence of the President and clarity in their public statements on the Contadora negotiations. They were angling to bring the OAS into the question, while the Embassy in Managua talked boldly about the regime there being on the point of collapse. The underlying fear at the State Department was obvious, that what was seen as a 'bad' treaty would make matters worse. The one 'success' Contadora produced, in their eyes, was for Managua, in giving the government the chance to legitimize itself by elections. Elsewhere in Washington there were growing doubts about the political consequences of a contra victory. The Pentagon remained concerned about the emplacement of SAM missiles, both in Nicaragua and in El Salvador. Reagan and his West Coast business advisers continued to see things in East–West crisis terms, and ignored such arguments for patient negotiation as were advanced by the State Department.

Consistency was not a problem for the United States alone, however. Until 1985 Managua itself had disastrous public relations. Ortega's visit to Moscow could not have come at a worse time, and overt Congressional aid for the contras was the direct result of the provisional government's failure to realize the weakness of their position and the limited real assistance possible from the Soviet Union. Meanwhile the Cubans were effectively excluded from the Contadora process. In return they had been advising Latin American states to default on their debts to the West, while taking good care to meet their own targets.

As Eduardo Crawley shows above in Chapter 6, Nicaraguan security perceptions must be understood in their own terms if the shifting Sandinista attitudes towards Contadora are to be correctly interpreted. The Sandinistas saw the US as a threat since before they came to power; the first statement hostile to them had been made by Senator Edward Kennedy as early as July 1979. They responded before President Reagan came into office by putting their weight behind the so-called 'Final Offensive' of the FMLN in El Salvador in 1980. It was President Carter who first embarked on a strategy to preclude this, and by 1981 Nicaraguan aid to the FMLN had been scaled down to a trickle.[9] The Reagan Administration, disregarding the facts, saw the FMLN as mere proxies for Nicaragua. With presidential authorization, the CIA established the contras as a clandestine force, first acting through proxies, e.g. Argentina, until 1982, and then giving direct support through front organizations of various kinds.

Sandinista strategy meanwhile, as Crawley shows, had gone through four phases: (a) total mobilization, based on guerrilla tactics, and revised after observation of the failure of the FMLN and of the contras themselves; (b) defence of the cities against the uncertain threat of total US invasion, hence the relocation of the Miskito; (c) a big push in summer 1985, followed by the return of the contras in a mere four weeks, the calling of the Sandinista Assembly and the reorganization of government on more centralized lines under President Ortega and the Executive Committee; and, most recently, (d) acceptance of the Arias Plan and the acceptance of Cardinal Miguel Obando y Bravo as intermediary with the contras, who have conspicuously failed to oppose the opening of indirect negotiations.

Observing these moves, Washington has long been locked in a debate as to whether Sandinista behaviour was 'modifiable' or not. In Nicaragua the same question has been asked about the United States, for among the detailed reasons given for their rejection of Contadora, the most central was that it embodied no regular complaints procedure by which breaches of the Treaty (by the United States) could be monitored and redress sought. Although the draft Treaty was modified at the request of the United States to distinguish between technical and military advisers, the fact that US policy was neither public nor consistent did give the Nicaraguans justifiable grounds for suspicion that this was simply a manoeuvre to allow US intervention to continue under another name. The contras, after all, were believed to have some 10,000 men still in the field when the Irangate scandal broke, and even if they were being held, it was at a heavy cost to the increasingly dilapidated Nicaraguan economy.

There were, in the light of persistent belligerent statements from the US, reasonable grounds for fear in Nicaragua of a US 'surgical strike' on the cities, a possibility dismissed with scorn by US officials. Yet it is doubtful how far the cities (especially Managua) really matter from a purely strategic point of view. Support for the Sandinistas has remained strong and nowhere more so than in the countryside; as the outcome of the elections showed, if they are not universally popular, no other convincing force has demonstrated electoral strength. Above all significant efforts have been made to conciliate the Miskito, whose suspicion of the Sandinistas began as no more than the traditional doubt of the English-speaking inhabitants of the coast for the Spaniards. Hence it was clear even before Irangate that any direct engagement of US forces in Nicaragua could be incredibly costly in lives as well as in diplomatic credibility. Confidence building measures (CBMs) were therefore a necessary adjunct to successful mediation,[10] and the very existence of the Arias Plan is in itself a sign that a new confidence has been achieved, in the wake of Irangate, that the problem can now be settled within a Caribbean if not a Central American context.

Throughout the tortuous course of negotiations three major problems have concerned US policymakers, and these are in conflict with one another. They are: the growing refugee problem, the domino theory, and what was called the 'World War III naval reinforcement scenario'. In 1986 the Congress moved to legalize existing Hispanic immigrants to the United States, thus relegating this issue for the time being to a lower priority. The 'World War III naval reinforcement scenario' (discussed by Paul Sutton above in Chapter 2) seems less and less plausible in an age of superpower detente and possible nuclear disarmament, though the build-up of US naval forces in the Gulf cannot but reinforce concern in US naval command circles for their lines of communication. What then of the domino theory?

As noted above, the acceptance of the Arias Plan (however incomplete) shifts attention away from crisis management techniques, such as the mediation offered by Contadora and the CBMs of the Arias Plan itself, towards the ultimate goal, a satisfactory regime for Central America, which by now has come in effect to mean the entire Caribbean region. The obvious difficulty is securing any agreement which can bind the United States given the disparity between its power and that of all the other states in the region put together. Yet there are significant arguments that a policy of self-interested self-restraint will serve US interests better than any programme of intervention. Arms limitation in the region has broken down. As we saw earlier, the choice seems to lie between the free competition but crisis controlled zone which already exists and a self-regulating no-go zone. There are historical parallels for the United States treating the region as a self-regulating no-go zone, notably in the period 1857–98 and again under the 'Good Neighbor' Policy, 1933–54. During these periods, and indeed at all times in Central America, there has been a very clear tendency for the various states not, as predicted by the 'domino theory' to fall in one ideological direction, still less have any influence on Mexico or the larger regional states, but to shift their alliances to maintain a *de facto* balance of power – what can be termed the 'layer-cake model' of Central American politics, each layer being of a different colour from the one immediately above and below it. There is clear evidence that the Soviet Union attaches a very low priority to the region, and it is now well recognized that Khrushchev's 'adventurism' in supporting Cuba played a significant role in his downfall, so it should not be hard to obtain at least *de facto* agreement to leave the region alone. Soviet acceptance of US conditions for a summit on the INF Agreement suggests that this is now very much open for negotiation.

There will be a price; the US will have to tolerate a degree of ideological pluralism in the region, and insurrections may be expected to recur on a sub-national level which the states concerned will have to contain, if they can, from their own resources. For, as Laurence Whitehead notes, even if the Soviet Union can be excluded from the region, Cuba can not.[11] There can be no return, therefore, to the competition-free zone or 'sphere of influence' model of the Roosevelt Corollary. However, on the evidence of Irangate, it is far from clear that the US, for structural reasons, is wise to attempt to pursue any long-term strategy of close engagement when the framework for coherent organization and continuity in US foreign policy is so clearly lacking. To embark on any policy without the ability to carry it through is to invite disaster. The United States of all countries, therefore, should limit its long-term commitments. Disengagement is now very strongly in the interests of the United States, while, on the two hundredth anniversary of the US Constitution, it must be said that the North American precedents for allowing small states to form a self-regulating no-go zone appear to be quite compelling.

Given the disparity of interests within the region it is not so easy to see what form the institutional structure of such a zone might take. If it is to be self-regulating the US must be excluded, but must undertake, perhaps in conjunction with the Contadora group, to guarantee a treaty arrived at by the regional states themselves. This would have to allow for an efficient organ of consultation in which no one state could veto decisions and clearly recognize the primacy of the OAS and above it the United Nations as the only bodies permitted to authorize collective security measures within the region. Such a treaty would need explicitly to recognize the principle of ideological pluralism, which, in a world in which old ideologies seem to be dissolving and even older ones at times take their place, may in any case be inevitable. And if any significant inflow of development aid is to follow, Europe will now have to take part in raising it, for the United States' economy is plainly no longer able to take care of all the burdens for

Peter Calvert

the world without generating substantial imbalances which threaten the whole structure of world finance.

The Arias Plan offers the basic framework of such a new order for the region. The mere fact that it has been agreed is proof of a new determination of the leaders of the Central American states to assume responsibility for their own destinies. The Plan's hard provisions on arms limitation, verification and timetable mark it out among international agreements as being based on sharp realism. Its clauses on democratization, the holding of free elections and a common programme of economic development,[12] easily dismissed as mere 'window-dressing', are in fact no less essential if the baleful legacy of the Kirkpatrick years is to be overcome and a lasting peace achieved. Its call for the Central American parliament to resume its functions acknowledges the necessity for appropriate international institutions to carry on the work begun in Guatemala City. It is a dangerous mistake to believe that the security of states should be gained at the expense of the security of the individual, as the President of Guatemala, Vinicio Cerezo Arévalo, who has survived three assassination attempts, can testify. He is a black belt at judo, travels with 'a small arsenal of weapons' and subscribes to Soldier of Fortune; his view is that 'democrats cannot afford to be naive'.[13] Many of his unfortunate fellow citizens have not lived to see civilian government return to their country. Only through proper attention to the needs of individuals can a satisfactory long-term basis be achieved for security at state, regional or international level.

NOTES

1. Graham T. Allison, *Essence of Decision: Explaining the Cuban Missile Crisis* (Boston, Mass.: Little Brown, 1971), p. 176, quoting Don K. Price.
2. Oliver L. North, *Taking the Stand: The Testimony of Lieutenant Colonel Oliver L. North*, intro. Daniel Schorr (New York: Pocket Books, 1987).
3. The first regional breach in the embargo occurred under the Frei Administration in Chile with the signing of a trade agreement by which Cuba agreed to import Chilean vegetables.
4. Don L. Etchison, *The United States and Militarism in Central America* (New York: Praeger, 1975), pp. 64–8.
5. See *inter alia* R. A. Humphreys, 'Latin America, the Caudillo Tradition', in Michael Howard (ed.), *Soldiers and Governments: nine studies in civil–military relations* (London: Eyre and Spottiswoode, 1957); Samuel E. Finer, *The Man on Horseback* (London: Pall Mall, 1962); Edwin A. Lieuwen, *Arms and Politics in Latin America* (London: Praeger, 1963); John J. Johnson, *The military and society in Latin America* (Stanford, Cal.: Stanford University Press, 1964); Martin C. Needler, 'Military Motivations and the Seizure of Power', *Latin American Research Review*, x, no. 3, autumn 1975, pp. 63–79; George Philip, *The Military in South American Politics* (London: Croom Helm, 1985); Peter Calvert and Susan Milbank, *The Ebb and Flow of Military Government in Latin America* (London: The Centre for Security and Conflict Studies, 1987, Conflict Study no. 198).
6. *The Guardian*, 20 February 1984.

202

7. See Eduardo Crawley, *Dictators never Die: A Portrait of Nicaragua and the Somozas.* (London: C. Hurst, 1979; updated as *Nicaragua in Perspective* (New York, 1984)).
8. I am particularly grateful to David Stansfield's contribution in leading the discussion upon which this section is based.
9. See Robert A. Pastor, *Condemned to Repetition: The United States and Nicaragua* (Princeton, NJ: Princeton University Press, 1987), for a detailed analysis of the Carter Administration's policies.
10. On the role of CBMs in inter-American peacekeeping, see also Victor Millán, 'Regional Confidence-Building in the Military Field: The Case of Latin America', in Michael A. Morris and Victor Millán (eds.), *Controlling Latin American Conflicts: Ten Approaches* (Boulder, Colo.: Westview Press, 1983).
11. Laurence Whitehead, 'The Prospects for a Political Settlement: Most Options Have Been Foreclosed' in Giuseppe DiPalma and Laurence Whitehead (eds.), *The Central American Impasse* (London: Croom Helm in association with the Friedrich Naumann Foundation, 1986), p. 240.
12. 26 I.L.M. 1164 (1987).
13. James Painter, *Guatemala: False Hope, False Freedom* (London: Catholic Institute for International Relations and Latin American Bureau, 1987), p. 74.

INDEX

Index

Index